I Am a Memory Come Alive

I AM A MEMORY COME ALIVE

Autobiographical Writings
by
FRANZ KAFKA

Edited by Nahum N. Glatzer

SCHOCKEN BOOKS · NEW YORK

Library of Congress Cataloging in Publication Data

Kafka, Franz, 1883–1924.
 I am a memory come alive.

 1. Kafka, Franz, 1883-1924—Biography. I. Glatzer, Nahum Norbert, 1903- ed.
II. Title.
PT2621.A26Z5   833′.9′12 [B]   74–8781

Manufactured in the United States of America

I Am a Memory Come Alive

INTRODUCTION

In the final period of his life, F.K. (let us use these initials) tersely defined one of the central woes of his existence: "Without forebears, without marriage, without heirs, with a fierce longing for forebears, marriage, and heirs. They all of them stretch out their hands to me: forebears, marriage, and heirs, but too far away from me" *(Diaries* II, 207). Yet, interestingly, some ten years earlier, F.K., not without a certain pride, recalled his mother's ancestry. He bore the Hebrew name (Amschel) of his mother's maternal grandfather, whom the mother remembered "as a very pious and learned man with a long, white beard . . . [and] many books which lined the walls." His grandmother died of typhus at an early age, whereupon her mother "became melancholy, refused to eat, spoke with no one; once, a year after the death of her daughter, she went for a walk and did not return; her body was found in the Elbe." "An even more learned man than her grandfather was my mother's great-grandfather; Christians and Jews held him in equal honor; during a fire a miracle took place on account of his piety; the flames jumped over and spared his house while the houses around it burned down. He had four sons, one converted to Christianity and became a doctor. All but my mother's grandfather died young. He had one son, whom my mother knew as crazy Uncle Nathan, and one daughter, my mother's mother" *(ibid.,* I, 197–98).

Forebears—four generations into the past, lives remembered for their fate and fortunes: piety, learning, the miraculous, a mother's mourning, suicide, madness. But seemingly, considered from a different vantage point, these forebears lost their significance; and so did the fact that F.K. bore a forebear's name. What life offered now were substitutes, "an artificial, miserable substitute . . . for forebears, marriage, and heirs. Feverishly you contrive these substitutes, and if the fever has not already destroyed you, the hopelessness of the substitutes will" *(ibid.,* II, 207).

In about 1920, young Gustav Janouch asked F.K. whether he still remembered the old Jewish quarter in Prague, which, unknown to Janouch, no longer existed. F.K. answered: "In us all it still lives—the dark corners, the secret alleys, shuttered windows. . . . Our heart knows nothing of the slum clearance which has been achieved. The murky old Jewish town within us is far more real than the new hygienic town around us" *(Conversations with Kafka,* 47): And again to Janouch: "I am bound to my family and my race. They outlive the individual" *(ibid.,* 61). Yet, seven years earlier, he spoke of Franz Grillparzer, Dostoevski, Kleist, and Flaubert as his "true blood-relations" *(Letters to Felice,* 315–16).

It would be futile to search for consistency in F.K.'s life, for lines of development. Affirmation and rejection overlap, yes and no join and separate and join again, the opposites coincide. "The clocks are not in unison" *(Diaries* II, 202), and no man should attempt—through "interpretation"—to correct the discrepancies.

Life, he thought, is by no means hopeless, but where is hope? While the prisoner is being transferred from one cell to another there is some hope, "a vestige of faith that during the change the Master may chance to walk along the corridor, contemplate the prisoner, and say: 'You must not lock up this one again. He is to come to me' " *(The Great Wall of China,* 164). There is even a chance of happiness: "to believe in the indestructible element in oneself," though striving toward it would destroy that chance *(ibid.,* 175). "As I am alive, I also have life's love of self," he confesses in 1916 *(Diaries* II, 161). But life may become unbearable and suicide suggest itself as a convenient exit. The writer, deeply upset about being coerced to take an active part in a family-owned factory, "stood at the window a long time . . . and more than once felt like frightening the toll collector on the bridge" by his fall, he states, not without a dose of wry humor. What swung the decision to stay alive was the consideration that the latter would interrupt his writing less than would death (letter to Max Brod, *Briefe,* 109).

Though ambivalent about life itself, he is rarely ambivalent about that life's reflection in his writing. He speaks of "a great yearning to write all my anxiety entirely out of me, write it into the depth of the paper just as it comes out of the depth of me" *(Diaries* I, 173). "Tomorrow I shall start to write again," he writes to Felice in December 1912; "I want to delve into it with all my strength; when not writing I feel myself being pushed out of life by unyielding hands" *(Letters to Felice,* 116). And, a few days later, he speaks of "an urge, an urge, a screaming urge to write" *(ibid.,* 132). After a few more days: "The novel is me, my stories are me . . . ; it is through my writing that I keep a hold on life" *(ibid.,* 138)—a position the practical Felice could hardly appreciate. Felice's father, Carl Bauer, is given to understand F.K.'s preoccupation with writing: "My whole being is directed toward literature . . . and the moment I abandon it I cease to exist" *(ibid.,* 313).

Writing was an abysmally difficult pursuit. It was not only the zealous striving for excellence that created the obstacles. Rather, it was a deep feeling of insufficiency, of literary impotence. To Grete Bloch, Felice's and his friend, he writes in April 1914: "I have no control over my capacity of writing. It comes and goes like a phantom" *(ibid., 390)*. Nevertheless, he sees writing as a means of survival. On July 31, 1914: "I will write in spite of everything, absolutely; it is my struggle for self-preservation" *(Diaries II, 75)*. "If I can't take refuge in some work, I am lost" *(ibid., 68)*. He speaks of "the strange, mysterious, perhaps dangerous, perhaps saving comfort that there is in writing" *(ibid., 212)*. The imperative of writing prevails. In July 1922, he writes in a long letter to Max Brod: "My writing preserves me"; not writing is "quite intolerable in fact and must end in madness." "All I can do is write." "A writer's life actually does depend on his desk; if he is to avoid going mad, really he should never leave his desk, he must cling to it like grim death" *(Briefe, 384 ff.)*. It is difficult, even "impossible" to write, but it is equally (if not more) impossible not to write. "God does not want me to write, but I—I must write" to set free the "tremendous world" he has in his head (letter to his friend Oskar Pollak, *Briefe*, 21, and *Diaries* I, 288). Beyond all doubts, anguish, and relief, F.K. came to see "writing as a form of prayer" *(Dearest Father, 312)*.

F.K. had a special fondness for his diary. It permitted him to deposit there—in addition to the customary entries—ideas for stories, fragments of tales, reports of scenes, real and imaginary. Of course, recording events, reflecting on them, remained the chief purpose of this writing. "I won't give up the diary again. I must hold on here, it is the only place I can," he writes on December 16, 1910, the year he started to keep a diary *(Diaries* I, 33). And a year later: "One advantage in keeping a diary is that you become aware with reassuring clarity of the changes which you constantly suffer" *(ibid., 187 f.)*. On February 25, 1912, he admonishes himself again: "Hold fast to the diary from today on! Write regularly! Don't surrender" *(ibid., 233)*. When during a certain period he failed to make entries, he wrote to Felice: "No matter how little happens, how pointless it may be, how great my indifference to it all, I miss not keeping a diary" *(Letters to Felice, 221)*. However, at times, F.K.'s letters to Felice took the place of diary notations. But eventually he would return to the beloved diary: "It has become very necessary to keep a diary again. The uncertainty of my thoughts, F[elice], the ruin in the office, the physical impossibility of writing and the inner need for it" *(Diaries* I, 284 f.).

Actually, F.K.'s diaries can be thought of as preliminary sketches to an autobiography, a project he mentioned at the end of 1911. "The writing of the autobiography would be a great joy because it would move along as easily as the writing down of dreams" *(ibid., 181)*. In a letter to Max Brod, he notes a plan of "tracing the outline of my life with complete decisiveness" and hopes that "the next step would be that I would hold myself together, not fritter myself away in meaningless speculation, keep a clear vision" (Brod, *Franz Kafka*, 17). The "Fragments" contain a reference to a "plan for autobiographical investigations": "detection of the smallest possible component parts" out of which he wanted to "construct" himself. He uses the simile of a new house built out of the material of the old, unsafe one. But he feared that in the midst of this activity his strength would give out and he would end up with one house half-destroyed and one half-finished, "that is to say, nothing" *(Dearest Father, 350)*.

The autobiographical element is unusually strong in F.K.'s work. Autobiographical, for instance, is the *Letter to His Father* (1919) which, by giving a detailed account of the son's feelings, tries to bring "order" into the complex relationship between an autocratic father and a hypersensitive son. Autobiographical, too, is the background of *The Trial, The Castle,* and some of the short stories, including, of course, "The Judgment" and "Investigations of a Dog."

F.K. did not write an autobiography after all. However, he viewed his life biographically and often referred to his age or connected his age with that of the story's hero. The twenty-eight-year-old F.K. dwelled in his diary on the theme of how "dreadful" it seemed to be a bachelor *(Diaries* I, 150, November 14, 1911), and used this material in "Bachelor's Ill Luck," included in *Meditation,* published in 1913. Heinz Politzer observed that "it was at this same age that his father, who was setting the standards of his life, had begotten him as his firstborn son" *(Franz Kafka: Parable and Paradox* [Ithaca, N.Y., 1962], 31). Equally significant is the fact that Joseph K. in *The Trial* is thirty years old. F.K. notes, too, that Milena was born when he was thirteen, and the thirteenth birthday is "a special occasion" *(Letters to Milena,* 171). In the diary he speaks of "this inescapable duty to observe oneself" *(Diaries* II, 200).

The reader, too, may wish "to observe" this life as it takes its course, day by day, in a manner of speaking, and year by year, choosing for this pursuit F.K.'s own words and occasionally the words of his friends. It is the aim of the present volume to suggest such a reading and, possibly, to facilitate it. The following section is a very brief biographical sketch that may serve as background to the first period in F.K.'s life.

Franz Kafka was born in Prague on July 3, 1883; his father was Hermann Kafka, a businessman (1852–1931), his mother Julie, née Löwy (1856–1934). From 1889 to 1893 F.K. was a pupil in the elementary school at Fleischmarkt. The years 1889, 1890, and 1892, respectively, saw the birth of his sisters Gabriele (Elli), Valerie (Valli), and Ottilte (Ottla); two younger brothers died in infancy. During 1893-1901 he studied at the Prague German gymnasium. His friends at the time were his schoolmates Oskar Pollak, Hugo Bergmann, and Ewald Felix Přibram. In Bergmann's "album" F.K. entered the following couplet (November 20, 1897) which, apparently, is the earliest preserved Kafka fragment:

There is a coming and a going,
A parting and oft—no returning.

(It was published, in German, in *Orot* [September 1969], 75).

Additional friendships developed: with the later novelist, dramatist, and F.K.'s editor Max Brod, the philosopher Felix Weltsch, and the blind writer Oskar Baum.

The years 1901-6 were ones of university study: first of German literature, then of law at the German University, Prague, and partly in Munich. After receiving the degree of doctor juris at the German University, Prague (June 1906), he entered a one year's internship at the law courts. In October 1907 he took a position with "Assicurazioni Generali," an Italian insurance company; in July 1908 he accepted employment by the semigovernmental Workers' Accident Insurance Institute in Prague. Office hours were 8 A.M. to 2 P.M. He lived at his parents' home. He wrote "On Mandatory Insurance in the Construction Industry" for the Institute.

He read Spinoza, Darwin, Nietzsche, Goethe, Kleist, and A. Stifter. Of special interest to him were diaries, memoirs, letters: those of Byron, Grillparzer, Goethe, Hebbel, Eckermann, Macaulay, Flaubert, Stendhal, and Thomas Mann, as well as of Marcus Aurelius and Meister Eckhart. He was fascinated by the biographies of Schopenhauer and Dostoevski.

The summers of 1905 and 1906 were spent in Zuckmantel, Silesia. We hear of a love affair with an unnamed woman. In August 1907 he visited his uncle Dr. Siegfried Löwy (the "country doctor," whom he had also visited in 1902) in Triesch, Moravia. Here he met Hedwig W. and a correspondence developed.

F.K.'s early writings have not survived. In 1903 he was working on a novel of which only the name is known: *The Child and the City*. In 1904-5 he wrote "Description of a Struggle." In 1907-8 he wrote "Wedding Preparations in the Country," fragments of a novel. In 1908 he published eight prose pieces (*Betrachtung* [*Meditation*]) in *Hyperion;* in 1910, five more pieces (*Betrachtungen* [*Meditations*]) appeared in *Bohemia*. A vacation in the fall of 1909 at Riva and Brescia with Max

Brod and Brod's brother Otto occasioned his writing of "The Aero-planes at Brescia," published in *Bohemia*, 1909; this was the first de-scription of airplanes in German literature.

The text of the present volume is composed of selected auto-biographical portions of the diaries, edited by Max Brod (vol. I trans-lated by Joseph Kresh; vol. II by Martin Greenberg and Hannah Arendt), supplemented by passages from the collection of F.K.'s letters *(Briefe,* New York, 1958), translated by Gerald Onn (and partly by R. C. Ockenden) especially for this volume; from *Letters to Milena,* trans-lated by Tania and James Stern (New York, 1953); *Letters to Felice* (New York, 1973), translated by James Stern and E. Duckworth, edited by Erich Heller and Jürgen Born; aphorisms (published in *The Great Wall of China,* translated by Willa and Edwin Muir [New York, 1946], and *Dearest Father,* translated by Ernst Kaiser and Eithne Wilkins [New York, 1954]), reports on talks with Kafka by Gustav Janouch *(Conver-sations with Kafka,* translated by Goronwy Rees [New York, 1953]; only the first edition was considered) and by Max Brod (in his *Franz Kafka: A Biography,* translated by G. Humphreys Roberts). Included are some relevant letters from Max Brod and Milena Jesenská, the memoir by Dora Dymant, and letters from Robert Klopstock and an attending physician from F.K.'s last days. "Fragments" of an autobio-graphical nature (in *Dearest Father),* not dated in the original, were placed where they seemed to fit best, a procedure followed also in the case of Janouch's reports. A selection from the (undated) letters to Milena is placed after June 1920. The editorial notes, often in square brackets within the text, are confined to brief references to relevant facts and identifications. In these and in matters of chronology, the editor was aided by the works of Max Brod, Malcolm Pasley, Klaus Wagenbach, Ludwig Dietz, Erich Heller, and Jürgen Born. In a number of places the translation was revised. The gracious and skillful assist-ance of Beverly Colman is gratefully acknowledged.

The arrangement of the volume is chronological, starting with 1910, the year the diaries begin. This is preceded by a chapter on F.K.'s "Early Years" for which material was culled from letters and from reminiscences later recorded in the diaries and in the *Letter to His Father.* The nature of this chapter required using a method of reference to the sources different from that used in the chapters that follow. Each chapter is prefaced by a quotation from an F.K. narrative written (or published) in that particular year. Omissions are indicated by three dots in square brackets. Editorial notes and material not by Kafka are in italics.

It is known that F.K. occasionally discarded or destroyed his writings or had others do this for him. Of his earliest writings, nothing is extant. In December 1912 he "burned many old disgusting papers" *(Diaries* I, 250). On October 15, 1921, he notes that he has given all his diaries to Milena *(ibid.,* II, 193). In January 1922 he mentions having thrown a whole pile of letters into the fire *(Briefe,* 369). Dora Dymant burned some twenty notebooks while F.K. watched from his bed (Brod to Martin Buber, January 25, 1927; Martin Buber, *Briefwechsel* II [Heidelberg, 1973], 278). F.K.'s letters to her are lost. Yet, despite the lacunae, especially in the diaries (e.g., there are no entries from October 1912 to May 2, 1913, with three exceptions; from May 27 to September 13, 1915; from November 10, 1917, to June 27, 1919; from January 9, 1920, to September 15, 1921), and despite the fragmentary nature of much of the other material, it is possible to follow this "dreamlike inner life" *(Diaries* II, 77) and its manifestation in a strange, uncanny world through the author's own writings.

No attempt was made to alert the reader wherever F.K. pictured events in his life as if he were writing a story. In the *Letter to His Father* he reports in all seriousness that he feared he would fail in the first class at elementary school, and, when he finished successfully, that he would not pass the entrance exam for the gymnasium. Again he succeeded, but once more expected to fail at the next step. He calls himself most incapable, most ignorant, an outrageous case *(Letter to His Father,* 93). Yet from all available evidence we know that he was an exemplary student and that there was no cause "to live with such fantasies" *(ibid.)* To a high degree, fact and fiction appear intertwined: legend generated life, life begot legend, both enacting "reality's dark dream" (Coleridge), recording "a memory come alive" *(Diaries* II, 193).

NAHUM N. GLATZER

Boston University
January 1974

Editions and Key to Abbreviations

B   Max Brod, *Franz Kafka: A Biography*. Trans. by G. Humphreys Rob-
           erts and Richard Winston. Second ed. New York: Schocken Books,
           1963.
Br   Franz Kafka, *Briefe: 1902–1924*. Ed. by Max Brod. New York: Schocken
           Books, 1958. Selections translated by Gerald Onn.
DF   Franz Kafka, *Dearest Father: Stories and Other Writings*. Trans. by
           Ernst Kaiser and Eithne Wilkins. New York: Schocken Books, 1954.
DI   Franz Kafka, *Diaries: 1910–1913*. Ed. by Max Brod. Trans. by Joseph
           Kresh. New York: Schocken Books, 1948.
DII   Franz Kafka, *Diaries: 1914–1923*. Ed. by Max Brod. Trans. by Martin
           Greenberg and Hannah Arendt. New York: Schocken Books, 1949.
F   Franz Kafka, *Letters to Felice*. Ed. by Erich Heller and Jürgen Born.
           Trans. by James Stern and Elisabeth Duckworth. New York: Schocken
           Books, 1973.
GW   Franz Kafka, *The Great Wall of China: Stories and Reflections*. Trans.
           by Willa and Edwin Muir. New York: Schocken Books, 1970.
J   Gustav Janouch, *Conversations with Kafka*. Introduction by Max
           Brod. Trans. by Goronwy Rees. New York: Frederick A. Praeger, 1953.
           Reprinted by permission of New Directions Publishing Company,
           publishers of Gustav Janouch. *Conversations with Kafka*.
           Copyright © 1968, 1971 by Fischer Verlag GmbH, Frankfurt-am-Main.
LF   Franz Kafka, *Letter to His Father*. Trans. by Ernst Kaiser and Eithne
           Wilkins. New York: Schocken Books, 1966.
M   Franz Kafka, *Letters to Milena*. Ed. by Willi Haas. Trans. by Tania and
           James Stern. New York: Schocken Books, 1965.

The following editions have also been used:

Jürgen Born, Ludwig Dietz, Malcolm Pasley, Paul Raabe, and Klaus Wagenbach,
eds., *Kafka-Symposion*. Berlin: Verlag Klaus Wagenbach, 1965.

Martin Buber, *Briefwechsel aus sieben Jahrzehnten*. Ed. by Grete Schaeder.
Vol. I. Heidelberg: Verlag Lambert Schneider, 1972.

Franz Kafka, *Amerika*. Trans. by Willa and Edwin Muir. New York: Schocken Books, 1962.

Franz Kafka, *The Castle*. Trans. by Willa and Edwin Muir, with additional materials translated by Ernst Kaiser and Eithne Wilkins. New York: Schocken Books, 1974.

Franz Kafka, *Description of a Struggle*. Translated by Tania and James Stern. New York: Schocken Books, 1958.

Franz Kafka, *The Penal Colony: Stories and Short Pieces*. Trans. by Willa and Edwin Muir. New York: Schocken Books, 1948.

Franz Kafka, *The Trial*. Trans. by Willa and Edwin Muir; revised, and with additional materials translated by E. M. Butler. New York: Schocken Books, 1968.

EARLY YEARS

The Trees

For we are like tree trunks in the snow. In appearance they lie
sleekly and a little push should be enough to set them rolling. No,
it can't be done, for they are firmly wedded to the ground. But see,
even that is only appearance.   *The Penal Colony, pp. 39 f.*

My resemblance to Uncle Rudolf, however, is [. . .] disconcerting: both
of us quiet (I less so), both dependent on our parents (I more so), at odds
with our fathers, loved by our mothers (he in addition condemned to
the horror of living with his father, though of course his father was
likewise condemned to live with him), both of us shy, excessively
modest (he more so), both regarded as noble, good men—there is nothing of these qualities in me and, so far as I know, very little in him
(shyness, modesty, timidity are accounted noble and good because they
offer little resistance to other people's aggressive impulses)—both hy-
pochondriacal at first, then really ill, both, for do-nothings, kept fairly
well by the world (he, because he was less of a do-nothing, kept much
more poorly, so far as it is possible to make a comparison now), both
officials (he a better one), both living the most unvarying lives, with no
trace of any development, young to the end of our days ("well preserved" is a better expression), both on the verge of insanity; he, far
away from Jews, with tremendous courage, with tremendous vitality
(by which one can measure the degree of the danger of insanity), escaped into the church where, so far as one could tell, his tendencies to
madness were somewhat held in check, he himself had probably not
been able for years to hold himself in check. One difference in his
favor, or disfavor, was his having had less artistic talent than I, he
could therefore have chosen a better path in life for himself in his
youth, was not inwardly pulled apart, not even by ambition. Whether
he had had to contend (inwardly) with women I do not know, a story by
him that I read would indicate as much; when I was a child, moreover,
they spoke of something of the sort. I know much too little about him, I
don't dare ask about it. Besides, up to this point I have been writing
about him as irreverently as if he were alive. It isn't true that he was not

good, I never found a trace of niggardliness, envy, hate, or greed in him; he was probably too unimportant a person to be able to help others. He was infinitely more innocent than I, there is no comparison. In single details he was my caricature, in essentials I am his.   [DII, 207 f.]

I wasn't very strong even in my strong times, for instance in the first grade of elementary school. Our cook, a small dry thin person with a pointed nose and hollow cheeks, yellowish but firm, energetic and superior, led me every morning to school. We lived in the house that separates the Kleine Ring from the Grosse Ring. Thus we walked first across the Ring, then into Teingasse, then through a kind of archway in Fleischmarktgasse down to the Fleischmarkt. And now every morning for about a year the same thing was repeated. At the moment of leaving the house the cook said she would tell the teacher how naughty I'd been at home. As a matter of fact I probably wasn't very naughty, but rather stubborn, useless, sad, bad tempered, and out of all this probably something quite nice could have been fabricated for the teacher. I knew this, so didn't take the cook's threat too lightly.

All the same, since the road to school was enormously long I believed at first that anything might happen on the way (it's from such apparent childish light-heartedness that there gradually develops, just because the roads are not so enormously long, this anxiousness and dead-eyed seriousness). I was also very much in doubt, at least while still on the Altstädter Ring, as to whether the cook, though a person commanding respect if only in domestic quarters, would dare to talk to the world-respect-commanding person of the teacher. Perhaps I even mentioned something of this kind, whereupon the cook usually answered curtly with her thin merciless lips that I didn't have to believe it, but say it she would. Somewhere near the entrance to Fleischmarktgasse [. . .] the fear of the threat got the upper hand. School in itself was already enough of a nightmare, and now the cook was trying to make it even worse.

I began to plead, she shook her head, the more I pleaded the more precious appeared to me that for which I was pleading, the greater the danger; I stood still and begged for forgiveness, she dragged me along, I threatened her with retaliation from my parents, she laughed, here she was all-powerful, I held on to the shop doors, to the corner stones, I refused to go any farther until she had forgiven me, I pulled her back by the skirt (she didn't have it easy, either), but she kept dragging me along with the assurance that she would tell the teacher this, too; it grew late, the clock on the Jakobskirche struck 8, the school bells could be heard, other children began to run, I always had the greatest terror of being late, now we too had to run and all the time the thought: She'll tell, she

won't tell—well, she didn't tell, ever, but she always had the oppor⁼
tunity and even an apparently increasing opportunity (I didn't tell
yesterday, but I'll certainly tell today) and of this she never let go. [M, 65 f.]

Do you know that I never had any real feeling for flowers, and even
now can only appreciate flowers provided they come from you, and
even then I appreciate them only indirectly through your love of them.
Ever since my childhood there have been times when I was almost
unhappy about my inability to appreciate flowers. This inability is
associated to some extent with my inability to appreciate music, at
least I have often sensed a connection. I am hardly able to see the
beauty of flowers; one rose is to me a thing of indifference, two become
too much alike, an arrangement of flowers always seems to me both
haphazard and ineffective. And, as is the way with deficiencies, I have
often tried to pretend to others that I had a special liking for flowers. As
with all conscious deficiencies, I succeeded in deceiving those people
who had but a vague liking for flowers, not otherwise apparent in any
aspect of their character. For example, my mother certainly thinks I am
a lover of flowers, because I like giving them to people and because
flowers on wire almost make me shudder. But the wire does not really
worry me on the flowers' account; I am thinking only of myself, and
that piece of metal twining itself into a living thing is abhorrent to me
for this very reason. I might not have become so much aware of being a
stranger among flowers, if toward the end of my schooldays and during
my time at the university I hadn't had a great friend (his first name was
Ewald [Přibram], almost a flower-name, don't you think?) who, without being especially sensitive to delicate impressions, even without
having any feeling for music, had such a passion for flowers that if, for
example, he happened to be looking at flowers, cutting them (he had a
beautiful garden), watering them, arranging them in a vase, carrying
them, or giving them to me (what am I going to do with them? I often
used to ask myself, and yet did not like to say so explicitly, although in
general terms I said so often enough, for after all he was not to be
deceived), he was literally transformed by his love, so much so that his
whole voice changed—I could almost say acquired a ringing tone, despite the slight impediment in his speech. We would often stand by the
flower beds, he gazing at the flowers, while I, in my boredom, gazed
beyond them. I wonder what he would say now if he could see me
lifting the flowers carefully out of their box, pressing them to my face,
and gazing at them for a long time!   [F (March 10-11, 1913), 218 f.]

I remember that when I was at the gymnasium I often—even if not very
thoroughly, I probably tired easily even then—argued the existence of

God with [Hugo] Bergmann in a talmudic style either my own or imitated from him. At the time I liked to begin with a theme I had found in a Christian magazine (I believe it was *Die christliche Welt)* in which a watch and the world and the watchmaker and God were compared to one another, and the existence of the watchmaker was supposed to prove that of God. In my opinion I was able to refute this very well as far as Bergmann was concerned, even though this refutation was not firmly grounded in me and I had to piece it together for myself like a jigsaw puzzle before using it. Such a refutation once took place while we were walking around the Rathaus tower. I remember this clearly because once, years ago, we reminded each other of it.

[DI (December 30, 1911), 205]

As a child I was anxious, and if not anxious then uneasy, when my father spoke—as he often did, since he was a businessman—of the last day of the month (called the "ultimo"). Since I wasn't curious, and since I wasn't able—even if I sometimes did ask about it—to digest the answer quickly enough with my slow thinking, and since a weakly stirring curiosity once risen to the surface is often already satisfied by a question and an answer without requiring that it understand as well, the expression "the last day of the month" remained a disquieting mystery for me, to be joined later (the result of having listened more attentively) by the expression "ultimo," even if the latter expression did not have the same great significance. It was bad too that the last day, dreaded so long in advance, could never be completely done away with. Sometimes, when it passed with no special sign, indeed with no special attention (I realized only much later that it always came after about thirty days), and when the first had happily arrived, one again began to speak of the last day, not with special dread, to be sure, but it was still something that I put without examination beside the rest of the incomprehensible.

[DI (December 24, 1911), 189]

My parents were playing cards; I sat apart, a perfect stranger; my father asked me to take a hand, or at least to look on; I made some sort of excuse. What is the meaning of these refusals, oft repeated since my childhood? Such invitations opened the door to social, even, to an extent, public life; everything required of me I should have done, if not well at least in middling fashion; even card-playing would probably not have bored me overmuch—yet I refused. Judging by this, I am wrong when I complain that I have never been caught up in the current of life, that I never made my escape from Prague, was never made to learn a sport or trade, and so forth—I would probably have refused every offer, just as I refused the invitation to play cards. I allowed only absurd things to claim my attention, my law studies, the job at the office, and later on such senseless additional occupations as a little gardening, carpentering, and the like; these later occupations are to be looked on as the actions of a man who throws a needy beggar out the door and then plays the benefactor by himself by passing alms from his right hand to his left.

I always refused, out of general weakness, probably, and in particular out of weakness of will—it was rather a long time before I understood as much. I used to consider this refusal a good sign (misled by the vague great hopes I cherished for myself); today only a remnant of this benevolent interpretation remains.

A few evenings later I did actually join in, to the extent of keeping score for my mother. But it begot no intimacy, or whatever trace there was of it was smothered under weariness, boredom, and regret for the wasted time. It would always have been thus. I have seldom, very seldom crossed this borderland between loneliness and fellowship, I have even been settled there longer than in loneliness itself. What a fine bustling place was Robinson Crusoe's island in comparison!

[DII (October 25–29, 1921), 197 f.]

As a boy I was as innocent of and uninterested in sexual matters (and would have long remained so, if they had not been forcibly thrust on me) as I am today in, say, the theory of relativity. Only trifling things (yet even these only after they were pointedly called to my attention) struck me, for example that it was just those women on the street who seemed to me most beautiful and best dressed who were supposed to be bad.   [DII (April 10, 1922), 227]

I remember the first night. We lived at that time in Zeltnergasse, opposite a dress shop, in the door of which a shop-girl used to stand, upstairs I, a little more than 20 years old, walked incessantly up and down the room, occupied with the nerve-racking cramming of, to me, senseless facts required for my first State examination. It was summer, very hot, quite unbearable, I stopped each time by the window, the disgusting Roman Law between my teeth, finally we came to an understanding by sign language. I was to fetch her at 8 P.M., but when I came down in the evening someone else was already there—well, this didn't make any difference, I was afraid of the whole world, thus of this man, too; even if he hadn't been there I would *also* have been afraid of him. Although the girl took his arm she nevertheless signed to me that I should follow them. Thus we arrived at Schützen Island where we drank beer, I at the next table, then we walked, I following slowly, to the girl's apartment, somewhere near the Fleischmarkt, there the man said goodbye, the girl ran into the house, I waited a while until she came out again, and then we went to a hotel on the Kleinseite. Even before we got to the hotel all this was charming, exciting, and horrible, in the hotel it wasn't different. And when, toward morning (it was still hot and beautiful), we walked home over the Karlsbrücke I was actually happy, but this happiness came from the fact that at last I had some peace from the ever-yearning body, and above all it came from the relief that the whole experience hadn't been more horrible, more obscene. I was with the girl once again (2 nights later, I believe), everything went as well as the first time, but as I then left immediately for the summer holidays where I played around a bit with another girl, I could no longer look at the shop-girl in Prague, not another word did I exchange with her, she had become (from my point of view) my bitter enemy, and yet she was a good-natured, friendly girl, she followed me all the time with her uncomprehending eyes. I won't say that the sole reason for my enmity was the fact (I'm sure it wasn't) that at the hotel the girl in all innocence had made a tiny repulsive gesture (not worthwhile mentioning), had uttered a trifling obscenity (not worthwhile mentioning), but the memory remained—I knew at that instant that I would never forget it and simultaneously I knew, or thought I knew, that this repulsiveness and smut, though outwardly not necessary, was inwardly however very necessarily connected with the whole thing, and that just this repulsiveness and obscenity (whose little symptom had only been her tiny gesture, her trifling word) had drawn me with such terrible power into this hotel, which otherwise I would have avoided with all my remaining strength.

And as it was then, so it has always remained. My body, sometimes quiet for years, would then again be shaken to the point of not being able to bear it by this desire for a small, a very specific abomination, for something slightly disgusting, embarrassing, obscene, even in the best that existed for me there was something of it, some small nasty smell, some sulfur, some hell. This urge had in it something of the eternal Jew, being senselessly drawn, wandering senselessly through a senselessly obscene world.   [M, 163 f.]

To Oskar Pollak, November 9, 1903:
For we are abandoned, like children lost in the wood. When you stand before me, and look at me, what do you know of the pains that are in me, and what do I know of yours? And if I were to prostrate myself before you, and weep and talk, would you know any more about me than you know about hell when someone tells you that it is hot and fearsome? For this reason alone we human beings should stand before one another with as much respect, as much sympathy, and as much

love as if we were standing before the gates of hell. [. . .] By the way, nothing has been written for some time now. The truth of the matter is that God does not want me to write while I, I have to write. And so there is a constant tug-of-war; in the end God proves the stronger, and this causes more distress than you can imagine. [Br, 19, 21]

To Oskar Pollak, December 21, 1903:
Yesterday evening this idea took hold of me. For it is only by summoning up all their strength and helping one another with loving care that human beings are able to maintain themselves at a tolerable height above the infernal abyss toward which they gravitate. They are joined together by ropes, and it is a bitter thing when the ropes around one of them slacken and he sinks a little lower than the others into the void, and it is quite horrible when the ropes around one of them break, and he then falls. That is why we should always hold on to other people. I incline to the belief that the girls sustain us because they are so light; that is why we have to love the girls and why they should love us.

[Br, 22 f.]

To Oskar Pollak, January 27, 1904:
I believe that we should read only those books that bite and sting us. If a book we are reading does not rouse us with a blow to the head, then why read it? Because it will make us happy, you tell me? My God, we would also be happy if we had no books, and the kind of books that make us happy we could, if necessary, write ourselves. What we need are books that affect us like some really grievous misfortune, like the death of one whom we loved more than ourselves, as if we were banished to distant forests, away from everybody, like a suicide; a book must be the ax for the frozen sea within us. That is what I believe.

[Br, 27 f.]

To Brod, August 28, 1904:
Another day, when I opened my eyes after a short siesta, still not quite sure of who or where I was, I heard my mother asking from the balcony in a perfectly natural tone of voice: "What are you doing?" A woman answered from the garden: "I am taking tea in the open air." I was amazed at the fortitude with which people take life. [Br, 29]

To Oskar Pollak:
Have you already noticed how the soil comes up to meet the cow as she is grazing, how intimately it comes up to meet her? Have you already noticed how heavy, rich, arable earth crumbles at the touch of fingers which are all too fine, how solemnly it crumbles? [B, 178]

From a letter to Oskar Pollak (between 1902 and 1904) on the early writings of F.K. that have not survived:

Of the few thousand lines I am giving you there might be perhaps ten that I could listen to patiently, the flourish of trumpets in my previous letter was unnecessary, instead of a revelation emerges childish scribbling. [...] The greatest part of it, I openly say, I find repulsive. "Morning," for example, and other bits, too—I find it impossible to read it all, and I am satisfied if you can stand odd samples. But you must remember I began at a time when one "created work," when one wrote high-flown stuff; there is no worse time to begin. And I was so mad about grand phrases. Among my papers there is a sheet on which are written all the uncommon and particularly impressive names I could find in the calendar. You see I needed two names for a novel, and chose finally two, underlined, Johannes and Beate.   [B. 58]

Once I projected a novel in which two brothers fought each other, one of whom went to America while the other remained in a European prison. I only now and then began to write a few lines, for it tired me at once. So once I wrote down something about my prison on a Sunday afternoon when we were visiting my grandparents and had eaten an especially soft kind of bread, spread with butter, that was customary there. It is of course possible that I did it mostly out of vanity, and by shifting the paper about on the tablecloth, tapping with my pencil, looking around under the lamp, wanted to tempt someone to take what I had written from me, look at it, and admire me. It was chiefly the corridor of the prison that was described in the few lines, above all its silence and coldness; a sympathetic word was also said about the brother who was left behind, because he was the good brother. Perhaps I had a momentary feeling of the worthlessness of my description, but before that afternoon I never paid much attention to such feelings when among relatives to whom I was accustomed (my timidity was so great that the accustomed was enough to make me halfway happy), I sat at the round table in the familiar room and could not forget that I was young and called to great things out of this present tranquility. An uncle who liked to make fun of people finally took the page that I was holding only weakly, looked at it briefly, handed it back to me, even without laughing, and only said to the others who were following him with their eyes, "The usual stuff," to me he said nothing. To be sure, I remained seated and bent as before over the now useless page of mine, but with one thrust I had in fact been banished from society, the judgment of my uncle repeated itself in me with what amounted almost to real significance and even within the feeling of belonging to a family I got an insight into the cold space of our world which I had to warm with a fire that first I wanted to seek out.   [DI (January 19, 1911), 43 f.]

Man's fundamental weakness lies by no means in the fact that he cannot achieve victory but in the fact that he cannot exploit his victory. Youth conquers everything, including the original deception, the concealed devilry, but there is no one there to catch hold of that victory and make it come alive, for by then youth is over. Old age is past daring to lay a finger on the victory, and the new generation of youth, tormented by the new attack that instantly begins, wants its own victory. So although the devil is constantly being overcome, he is never destroyed.   [DF, 284 f.]

F.K.'s Letter to His Father (written November 1919) contains a number of references to the early years.

I was an anxious child, but I was certainly obstinate, too, as children are. I am sure that Mother spoiled me, but I cannot believe I was particularly difficult to manage; I cannot believe that a kindly word, a quiet taking by the hand, a friendly glance could not have got me to do anything that was wanted of me. Now you are, after all, at bottom a kindly and softhearted person (what follows will not be in contradiction to this, I am speaking only of the impression you made on the child), but not every child has the endurance and fearlessness to go on searching until it comes to the kindliness that lies beneath the surface. You can only treat a child in the way you yourself are constituted, with vigor, noise, and temper, and in this case this seemed to you, into the bargain, extremely suitable, because you wanted to bring me up to be a strong brave boy. [. . .]

There is only one episode in the early years of which I have a direct memory. You may remember it, too. One night I kept on whimpering for water, not, I am certain, because I was thirsty, but probably partly to be annoying, partly to amuse myself. After several vigorous threats had failed to have any effect, you took me out of bed, carried me out onto the *pavlatche* [a balcony around the inner courtyard], and left me there alone for a while in my nightshirt, outside the shut door. I am not going to say that this was wrong—perhaps there was really no other way of getting peace and quiet that night—but I mention it as typical of your methods of bringing up a child and their effect on me. I dare say I was quite obedient afterwards at that period, but it did me inner harm. What was for me a matter of course, that senseless asking for water, and the extraordinary terror of being carried outside were two things that I, my nature being what it was, could never properly connect with each other. Even years afterwards I suffered from the tormenting fancy that the huge man, my father, the ultimate authority, would come almost for no reason at all and take me out of bed in the night and carry me out onto the *pavlatche,* and that meant I was a mere nothing for him.

That was only a small beginning, but this sense of nothingness that often dominates me (a feeling that is in another respect, admittedly, also a noble and fruitful one) comes largely from your influence. What I would have needed was a little encouragement, a little friendliness, a little keeping open of my road, instead of which you blocked it for me, though of course with the good intention of making me go another road. But I was not fit for that. You encouraged me, for instance, when I saluted and marched smartly, but I was no future soldier, or you encouraged me when I was able to eat heartily or even drink beer with my meals, or when I was able to repeat songs, singing what I had not understood, or prattle to you using your own favorite expressions, imitating you, but nothing of this had anything to do with my future.

[LF, 15 ff.]

At that time, and at that time in every way, I would have needed encouragement. I was, after all, weighed down by your mere physical presence. I remember, for instance, how we often undressed in the same bathing hut. There was I, skinny, weakly, slight; you strong, tall, broad. Even inside the hut I felt a miserable specimen, and, what's more, not only in your eyes but in the eyes of the whole world, for you were for me the measure of all things. But then when we stepped out of the bathing hut before the people, you holding me by my hand, a little skeleton, unsteady, barefoot on the boards, frightened of the water, incapable of copying your swimming strokes, which you, with the best of intentions, but actually to my profound humiliation, always kept on showing me, then I was frantic with desperation and at such moments all my bad experiences in all spheres fitted magnificently together. I felt best when you sometimes undressed first and I was able to stay behind in the hut alone and put off the disgrace of showing myself in public until at last you came to see what I was doing and drove me out of the hut. I was grateful to you for not seeming to notice my anguish, and besides, I was proud of my father's body.   [LF, 19 f.]

Now, when I was the subject you were actually astonishingly often right; which in conversation was not surprising, for there was hardly ever any conversation between us, but also in reality. Yet this was nothing particularly incomprehensible, either; in all my thinking I was, after all, under the heavy pressure of your personality, even in that part of it—and particularly in that—which was not in accord with yours. All these thoughts, seemingly independent of you, were from the beginning burdened with your belittling judgments; it was almost impossible to endure this and still work out a thought with any measure of completeness and permanence. I am not here speaking of any sublime thoughts, but of every little childhood enterprise. It was only necessary to be happy about something or other, to be filled with the thought of it, to come home and speak of it, and the answer was an ironical sigh, a shaking of the head, a tapping on the table with a finger: "Is that all you're so worked up about?" or "Such worries I'd like to have!" or "The things some people have time to think about!" or "Where is that going to get you?" or "What a song and dance about nothing!" Of course, you couldn't be expected to be enthusiastic about every childish triviality, when you were in a state of fret and worry. But that was not the point. Rather, by virtue of your antagonistic nature, you could not help but always and inevitably cause the child such disappointments; and further, this antagonism, accumulating material, was constantly intensified; eventually the pattern expressed itself even if, for once, you were of the same opinion as I; finally, these disappointments of the child were not the ordinary disappointments of life but, since they involved you, the all-important personage, they struck to the very core. Courage, resolution, confidence, delight in this and that, could not last when you were against it or even if your opposition was merely to be assumed; and it was to be assumed in almost everything I did.   [LF, 21 f.]

Your whole method of upbringing was like that. You have, I think, a gift for bringing up children; you could, I am sure, have been of help to a human being of your own kind with your methods; such a person would have seen the reasonableness of what you told him, would not have troubled about anything else, and would quietly have done things the way he was told. But for me as a child everything you called out at me was positively a heavenly commandment, I never forgot it, it remained for me the most important means of forming a judgment of the world, above all of forming a judgment of you yourself, and there you failed entirely. Since as a child I was with you chiefly during meals, your teaching was to a large extent the teaching of proper behavior at table. What was brought to the table had to be eaten, the quality of the food was not to be discussed—but you yourself often found the food inedible, called it "this swill," said "that beast" (the cook) had ruined it. Because in accordance with your strong appetite and your particular predilection you ate everything fast, hot, and in big mouthfuls, the child had to hurry; there was a somber silence at table, interrupted by admonitions: "Eat first, talk afterwards," or "faster, faster, faster," or "there you are, you see, I finished ages ago."   [LF, 25 f.]

The impossibility of getting on calmly together had one more result, actually a very natural one: I lost the capacity to talk. I dare say I would not have become a very eloquent person in any case, but I would, after all, have acquired the usual fluency of human language. But at a very early stage you forbade me to speak. Your threat "Not a word of contradiction!" and the raised hand that accompanied it have been with me ever since. What I got from you—and you are, whenever it is a matter of your own affairs, an excellent talker—was a hesitant, stammering mode of speech, and even that was still too much for you, and finally I kept silent, at first perhaps out of defiance, and then because I could neither think nor speak in your presence. And because you were the person who really brought me up, this has had its repercussions throughout my life.   [LF, 33]

You would say: "Not a word of contradiction!" thinking that that was a way of silencing the oppositional forces in me that were disagreeable to you, but the effect of it was too strong for me, I was too docile, I became completely dumb, cringed away from you, hid from you, and only dared to stir when I was so far away from you that your power could no longer reach me—at least not directly. But you were faced with all that, and it all seemed to you to be "agin," whereas it was only the inevitable consequence of your strength and my weakness.

Your extremely effective rhetorical methods in bringing me up, which never failed to work with me, were: abuse, threats, irony, spiteful laughter, and—oddly enough—self-pity.   [LF, 35]

You reinforced abusiveness with threats, and this applied to me too. How terrible for me was, for instance, that "I'll tear you apart like a fish," although I knew, of course, that nothing worse was to follow (admittedly, as a little child I didn't know that), but it was almost exactly in accord with my notions of your power, and I saw you as being capable of doing this too. It was also terrible when you ran around the table, shouting, grabbing at one, obviously not really trying to grab, yet pretending to, and Mother (in the end) had to rescue one, as it seemed. Once again one had, so it seemed to the child, remained alive through your mercy and bore one's life henceforth as an undeserved gift from you.   [LF, 35 f.]

You put special trust in bringing up children by means of irony, and this was most in keeping with your superiority over me. An admonition from you generally took this form: "Can't you do it in such-and-such a way? That's too hard for you, I suppose. You haven't the time, of course?" and so on. And each such question would be accompanied by malicious laughter and a malicious face. One was, so to speak, already punished before one even knew that one had done something bad. Maddening were also those rebukes in which one was treated as a third person, in other words, considered not worthy even to be spoken to angrily; that is to say, when you would speak ostensibly to Mother but actually to me, who was sitting right there. For instance: "Of course, that's too much to expect of our worthy son," and the like.   [LF, 37 f.]

Fortunately, there were exceptions to all this, mostly when you suffered in silence, and affection and kindliness by their own strength overcame all obstacles, and moved me immediately. Rare as this was, it was wonderful. For instance, in earlier years, in hot summers, when you were tired after lunch, I saw you having a nap at the shop, your elbow on the desk; or you joined us in the country, in the summer holidays, on Sundays, worn out from work; or the time Mother was gravely ill and you stood holding on to the bookcase, shaking with sobs; or when, during my last illness, you came softly to Ottla's room to see me, stopping in the doorway, craning your neck to see me, and out of consideration only waved to me with your hand. At such times one would lie down and weep for happiness, and one weeps again now, writing about it.   [LF, 41 f.]

It is true that Mother was illimitably good to me, but for me all that was in relation to you, that is to say, in no good relation. Mother unconsciously played the part of a beater during a hunt. Even if your method of upbringing might in some unlikely case have set me on my own feet by means of producing defiance, dislike, or even hate in me, Mother canceled that out again by kindness, by talking sensibly (in the maze and chaos of my childhood she was the very prototype of good sense and reasonableness), by pleading for me; and I was again driven back into your orbit, which I might perhaps otherwise have broken out of, to your advantage and to my own. Or it happened that no real reconciliation came about, that Mother merely shielded me from you in secret, secretly gave me something, or allowed me to do something, and then where you were concerned I was again the furtive creature, the cheat, the guilty one, who in his worthlessness could only pursue backstairs methods even to get the things he regarded as his right.

[LF, 45 f.]

It is also true that you hardly ever really gave me a whipping. But the shouting, the way your face got red, the hasty undoing of the braces and laying them ready over the back of the chair, all that was almost worse for me. It is as if someone is going to be hanged. If he really is hanged, then he is dead and it is all over. But if he has to go through all the preliminaries to being hanged and he learns of his reprieve only when the noose is dangling before his face, he may suffer from it all his life. Besides, from the many occasions on which I had, according to your clearly expressed opinion, deserved a whipping but was let off at the last moment by your grace, I again accumulated only a huge sense of guilt. On every side I was to blame, I was in your debt.   [LF, 47]

If I was to escape from you, I had to escape from the family as well, even from Mother. True, one could always get protection from her, but only in relation to you. She loved you too much and was too devoted and loyal to you to have been for long an independent spiritual force in the child's struggle. This was, incidentally, a correct instinct of the child, for with the passing of the years Mother became ever more closely allied to you; while, where she herself was concerned, she always kept her independence, within the narrowest limits, delicately and beautifully, and without ever essentially hurting you, still, with the passing of the years she did more and more completely, emotionally rather than intellectually, blindly adopt your judgments and your condemnations with regard to the children, particularly in the case— certainly a grave one—of Ottla. Of course, it must always be borne in mind how tormenting and utterly wearing Mother's position in the family was. She toiled in the business and in the house, and doubly suffered all the family illnesses, but the culmination of all this was what she suffered in her position between us and you. You were always affectionate and considerate toward her, but in this respect you spared her just as little as we spared her. We all hammered ruthlessly away at her, you from your side, we from ours. It was a diversion, nobody meant any harm, thinking of the battle that you were waging with us and that we were waging with you, and it was Mother on whom we relieved our wild feelings. [. . .] Of course, Mother could not have borne all this if she had not drawn the strength to bear it from her love for us all and her happiness in that love.   [LF, 59 f.]

Here, it is enough to remind you of early days. I had lost my self-confidence where you were concerned, and in its place had developed a boundless sense of guilt. (In recollection of this boundlessness I once wrote of someone, accurately: "It was as if the shame of it must outlive him.") I could not suddenly change when I was with other people; rather, I came to feel an even deeper sense of guilt with them, for, as I have already said, I had to make up to them for the wrongs you had done them in your business, wrongs in which I too had my share of responsibility. Besides, you always had some objection to make, frankly or covertly, about everyone I associated with, and for this too I had to atone. The mistrust that you tried to instill into me toward most people, at business and at home (name a single person who was of importance to me in my childhood whom you didn't at least once tear to shreds with your criticism), was, oddly enough, of no particular burden to you. [. . .] This mistrust (which was nowhere confirmed in the eyes of the little boy, since everywhere I saw only people excellent beyond any hope of emulation) turned in me to mistrust of myself and perpetual anxiety about everything else.   [LF, 73 f.]

I found as little escape from you in Judaism. Here some measure of escape would have been thinkable in principle, moreover, it would have been thinkable that we might both have found each other in Judaism or that we even might have begun from there in harmony. But what sort of Judaism was it that I got from you? In the course of the years, I have taken roughly three different attitudes to it.

As a child I reproached myself, in accord with you, for not going to the synagogue often enough, for not keeping the fasts, and so on. I thought that in this way I was doing a wrong not to myself but to you, and I was penetrated by a sense of guilt, which was, of course, always ready to hand.

Later, as a young man, I could not understand how, with the nothing of Judaism you yourself possessed, you could reproach me for not making an effort (for the sake of piety at least, as you put it) to cling to a similar nothing. It was indeed, so far as I could see, a mere nothing, a joke—not even a joke. Four days a year you went to the synagogue, where you were, to say the least, closer to the indifferent than to those who took it all seriously, patiently went through the prayers as a formality, sometimes amazed me by being able to show me in the prayer book the passage that was being said at the moment, and for the rest, so long as I was present in the synagogue (and this was the main thing) I was allowed to hang about wherever I liked. And so I yawned and dozed through the many hours (I don't think I was ever again so bored, except later at dancing lessons) and did my best to enjoy the few little bits of variety there were, as for instance when the Ark was opened, which always reminded me of the shooting galleries where a cupboard door would open in the same way whenever one hit a bull's eye; except that there something interesting always came out and here it was always just the same old dolls without heads. Incidentally, it was also very frightening for me there, not only, as goes without saying, because of all the people one came into close contact with, but also because you once mentioned casually that I too might be called to the Torah. That was something I dreaded for years. But otherwise I was not fundamentally disturbed in my boredom, unless it was by the *bar mitzvah*, but that demanded no more than some ridiculous memorizing, in other words, it led to nothing but some ridiculous passing of an examination; and, so far as you were concerned, by little, not very significant incidents, as when you were called to the Torah and passed, in what to my way of feeling was a purely social event; or when you stayed on in the synagogue for the Memorial Service, and I was sent away, which for a long time—obviously because of the being-sent-away and the lack of any deeper interest—aroused in me the more or less unconscious feeling that something indecent was about to take place.—That's how it was in the synagogue; at home it was, if possible, even more miserable, being confined to the first Seder night, which more and more developed into a farce, with fits of hysterical laughter, admittedly under the influence of the growing children. (Why did you have to give way to that influence? Because you had brought it about.) This was the religious material that was handed on to me, to which may be added at most the outstretched hand pointing to "the sons of the millionaire Fuchs," who attended the synagogue with their father on the high holy days. How one could do anything better with that material than get rid of it as fast as possible, I could not understand; precisely the getting rid of it seemed to me to be the devoutest action.

[LF, 75 ff.]

Jewish schoolboys in our country often tend to be odd; among them one finds the most unlikely things; but something like my cold indifference, scarcely disguised, indestructible, childishly helpless, approaching the ridiculous, and brutishly complacent, the indifference of a self-sufficient but coldly imaginative child, I have never found anywhere else; to be sure, it was the sole protection against destruction of my nerves by fear and by a sense of guilt. All that occupied my mind was worry about myself, and this in various ways. There was, for instance, the worry about my health; it began imperceptibly enough, with now and then a little anxiety about digestion, hair falling out, a spinal curvature, and so on; intensifying in innumerable gradations, it finally ended with a real illness. But since there was nothing at all I was certain of, since I needed to be provided at every instant with a new confirmation of my existence, since nothing was in my very own, undoubted, sole possession, determined unequivocally only by me—in sober truth a disinherited son—naturally I became unsure even of the thing nearest to me, my own body. I shot up, tall and lanky, without knowing what to do with my lankiness, the burden was too heavy, the back became bent; I scarcely dared to move, certainly not to exercise, I remained weakly; I was amazed by everything I could still command as by a miracle, for instance, my good digestion; that sufficed to lose it, and now the way was open to every sort of hypochondria; until finally under the strain of the superhuman effort of wanting to marry (of this I shall speak later), blood came from the lung, something in which the apartment in the Schönborn Palace—which, however, I needed only because I believed I needed it for my writing, so that even this belongs here under the same heading—may have had a fair share. So all this did not come from excessive work, as you always imagine. There were years in which, in perfectly good health, I lazed away more time on the sofa than you in all your life, including all your illnesses. When I rushed away from you, frightfully busy, it was generally in order to lie down in my room. My total achievement in work done, both at the office (where laziness is, of course, not particularly striking, and besides, mine was kept in bounds by my timidity) and at home, is minute; if you had any real idea of it, you would be aghast. Probably I am constitutionally not lazy at all, but there was nothing for me to do. In the place where I lived I was spurned, condemned, fought to a standstill; and to escape to some other place was an enormous exertion, but that was not work, for it was something impossible, something that was, with small exceptions, unattainable for me.   [LF, 89 f.]

There was actually no such thing for me as freedom to choose my career, for I knew: compared to the main thing everything would be exactly as much a matter of indifference to me as all the subjects taught at school, and so it was a matter of finding a profession that would let me indulge this indifference without injuring my vanity too much. Law was the obvious choice. Little contrary attempts on the part of vanity, of senseless hope, such as my fourteen days' study of chemistry, or six months' German studies, only reinforced that fundamental conviction. So I studied law. This meant that in the few months before the exams, and in a way that told severely on my nerves, intellectually I fed myself exclusively on sawdust, which had, moreover, already been chewed for me in thousands of other people's mouths.   [LF, 95]

I remember going for a walk one evening with you and Mother; it was on Josephsplatz near where the Länderbank is today; and I began talking about these interesting things, in a stupidly boastful, superior, proud, detached (that was spurious), cold (that was genuine), and stammering manner, as indeed I usually talked to you, reproaching the two of you with having left me uninstructed; with the fact that my schoolmates first had to take me in hand, that I had been close to great dangers (here I was brazenly lying, as was my way, in order to show myself brave, for as a consequence of my timidity I had, except for the usual sexual misdemeanors of city children, no very exact notion of these "great dangers"); but finally I hinted that now, fortunately, I knew everything, no longer needed any advice, and that everything was all right. I had begun talking about all this mainly because it gave me pleasure at least to talk about it, and also out of curiosity, and finally to avenge myself somehow on the two of you for something or other. In keeping with your nature you took it quite simply, only saying something to the effect that you could give me advice about how I could go in for these things without danger. Perhaps I did want to lure just such an answer out of you; it was in keeping with the pruriency of a child overfed with meat and all good things, physically inactive, everlastingly occupied with himself; but still, my outward sense of shame was so hurt by this—or I believed it ought to be so hurt—that against my will I could not go on talking to you about it and, with arrogant impudence, cut the conversation short.

It is not easy to judge the answer you gave me then; on the one hand, it had something staggeringly frank, sort of primeval, about it; on the other hand, as far as the lesson itself is concerned, it was uninhibited in a very modern way. I don't know how old I was at the time, certainly not much over sixteen. It was, nevertheless, a very remarkable answer for such a boy, and the distance between the two of us is also shown in the fact that it was actually the first direct instruction bearing on real life I ever received from you. Its real meaning, however, which sank into my mind even then, but which came partly to the surface of my consciousness only much later, was this: what you advised me to do was in your opinion, and, even more, in my opinion at that time, the filthiest thing possible. That you wanted to see to it that I should not bring any of the physical filth home with me was unimportant, for you were only protecting yourself, your house. The important thing was rather that you yourself remained outside your own advice, a married man, a pure man, above such things; this was probably intensified for me at the time by the fact that even marriage seemed to me shameless; and hence it was impossible for me to apply to my parents the general information I had picked up about marriage. Thus you became still purer, rose still higher. The thought that you might have given yourself similar advice before your marriage was to me utterly unthinkable. So there was hardly any smudge of earthly filth on you at all. And it was you who pushed me down into this filth—just as though I were pre-destined to it—with a few frank words. And so, if the world consisted only of me and you (a notion I was much inclined to have), then this purity of the world came to an end with you and, by virtue of your advice, the filth began with me. In itself it was, of course, incompre-hensible that you should thus condemn me; only old guilt, and pro-foundest contempt on your side, could explain it to me. And so again I was seized in my innermost being—and very hard indeed.   [LF, 101 ff.]

1910

The Wish to Be a Red Indian

If one were only an Indian, instantly alert, and on a racing horse, leaning against the wind, kept on quivering jerkily over the quivering ground, until one shed one's spurs, for there needed no spurs, threw away the reins, for there needed no reins, and hardly saw that the land before one was smoothly shorn heath when horse's neck and head would be already gone.   *The Penal Colony, p. 39*

May: Beginning of the diaries (thirteen quarto notebooks).

Before May 17. I write this very decidedly out of despair over my body and over a future with this body.

When despair shows itself so definitely, is so tied to its object, so pent up, as in a soldier who covers a retreat and thus lets himself be torn to pieces, then it is not true despair. True despair overreaches its goal immediately and always, (at this comma it became clear that only the first sentence was correct).

Do you despair?

Yes? You despair?

You run away? You want to hide?

I passed by the brothel as though past the house of a beloved.

Writers speak a stench.

Finally, after five months of my life during which I could write nothing that would have satisfied me, and for which no power will compensate me, though all were under obligation to do so, it occurs to me to talk to myself again. Whenever I really questioned myself, there was always a response forthcoming, there was always something in me to catch fire, in this heap of straw that I have been for five months and whose fate, it seems, is to be set afire during the summer and consumed more swiftly than the onlooker can blink his eyes. If only that would happen to me! And tenfold ought that to happen to me, for I do not even regret this unhappy time. My condition is not unhappiness, but it is also not happiness, not indifference, not weakness, not fatigue, not another

interest—so what is it then? That I do not know this is probably connected with my inability to write. And without knowing the reason for
it, I believe I understand the latter. All those things, that is to say, those
things which occur to me, occur to me not from the root up but rather
only from somewhere about their middle. Let someone then attempt to
seize them, let someone attempt to seize a blade of grass and hold fast
to it when it begins to grow only from the middle.

There are some people who can do this, probably, Japanese jugglers,
for example, who scramble up a ladder that does not rest on the ground
but on the raised soles of someone half lying on the ground, and which
does not lean against a wall but just goes up into the air. I cannot do
this—aside from the fact that my ladder does not even have those soles
at its disposal. This, naturally, isn't all, and it isn't such a question that
prompts me to speak. But every day at least one line should be trained
on me, as they now train telescopes on comets. And if then I should
appear before that sentence once, lured by that sentence, just as, for
instance, I was last Christmas, when I was so far gone that I was barely
able to control myself and when I seemed really on the last rung of my
ladder, which, however, rested quietly on the ground and against a
wall. But what ground, what a wall! And yet that ladder did not fall, so
strongly did my feet press it against the ground, so strongly did my feet
raise it against the wall.   [DI, 11 f.]

Night of comets, *May 17–18*.
Together with Blei,[1] his wife, and child, from time to time listened to
myself outside of myself, it sounded like the whimpering of a young cat.

How many days have again gone silently by; today is May 28. Have I
not even the resolution to take this penholder, this piece of wood, in my
hand every day? I really think I do not. I row, ride, swim, lie in the sun.
Therefore my calves are good, my thighs not bad, my belly will pass
muster, but my chest is very shabby and if my head set low between my
shoulders . . .

Sunday, *July 19*, slept, awoke, slept, awoke, miserable life.   [DI, 13 f.]

*October 8 to 17: Paris, with Max and Otto Brod. Beginning of
December: Berlin.*

December 15. I simply do not believe the conclusions I have drawn
from my present condition, which has already lasted almost a year, my
condition is too serious for that. Indeed, I do not even know whether I
can say that it is not a new condition. My real opinion, however, is that
this condition is new—I have had similar ones, but never one like this. It

is as if I were made of stone, as if I were my own tombstone, there is no
loophole for doubt or for faith, for love or repugnance, for courage or
anxiety, in particular or in general, only a vague hope lives on, but no
better than the inscriptions on tombstones. Almost every word I write
jars against the next, I hear the consonants rub leadenly against each
other and the vowels sing an accompaniment like Negroes in a minstrel
show. My doubts stand in a circle around every word, I see them before
I see the word, but what then! I do not see the word at all, I invent it. Of
course, that wouldn't be the greatest misfortune, only I ought to be able
to invent words capable of blowing the odor of corpses in a direction
other than straight into mine and the reader's face.   [DI, 32 f.]

December 16. I won't give up the diary again. I must hold on here, it is
the only place I can.

I would gladly explain the feeling of happiness which, like now, I
have within me from time to time. It is really something effervescent
that fills me completely with a light, pleasant quiver and that persuades
me of the existence of abilities of whose nonexistence I can convince
myself with complete certainty at any moment, even now.   [DI, 33]

To Brod, from Prague, December 15 and 17:
I scarcely ever quarrel with my parents, who are well and happy. Only,
when my father sees me sitting at my writing desk late in the evening,
he gets annoyed because he thinks I am overworking.

I cannot write; I have not produced a single line that I am able to
endorse, and I have effaced everything—it was not very much—that I
have written since I was in Paris [October 1910]. My whole body cries
out against every word; before allowing itself to be written down by
me, every word scans the horizon; the sentences literally crumble in my
hands, I see inside them and have to stop at once.   [Br, 85]

December 17. Zeno, pressed as to whether anything is at rest, replied:
Yes, the flying arrow rests.

That I have put aside and crossed out so much, indeed almost everything I wrote this year, that hinders me a great deal in writing. It is
indeed a mountain, it is five times as much as I have in general ever
written, and by its mass alone it draws everything that I write away
from under my pen to itself.   [DI, 34 f.]

December 18, 11:30 P.M. That I, so long as I am not freed of my office, am
simply lost, that is clearer to me than anything else, it is just a matter, as
long as it is possible, of holding my head so high that I do not drown.

How difficult that will be, what strength it will necessarily drain me of, can be seen already in the fact that today I did not adhere to my new time schedule, to be at my desk from 8 to 11 P.M., that at present I even consider this as not so very great a disaster, that I have only hastily written down these few lines in order to get into bed.   [DI, 35]

December 19. Read a little in Goethe's diaries. Distance already holds this life firm in tranquility, these diaries set fire to it. The clarity of all the events makes it mysterious, just as a park fence rests the eye when looking at broad tracts of turf, and yet inspires inadequate respect in us.   [DI, 36]

December 20. How do I excuse my not yet having written anything today? In no way. Especially as my disposition is not so bad. I have continually an invocation in my ear: "Were you to come, invisible judgment!"   [DI, 36]

December 22. Today I do not even dare to reproach myself. Shouted into this empty day, it would have a disgusting echo.   [DI, 37]

December 26. Two and a half days I was, though not completely, alone, and already I am, if not transformed, at any rate on the way. Being alone has a power over me that never fails. My interior dissolves (for the time being only superficially) and is ready to release what lies deeper. A slight ordering of my interior begins to take place and I need nothing more, for disorder is the worst thing in small talents.

December 27. My strength no longer suffices for another sentence. Yes, if it were a question of words, if it were sufficient to set down one word and one could turn away in the calm consciousness of having entirely filled this word with oneself.

I slept part of the afternoon away, while I was awake I lay on the sofa, thought about several love experiences of my youth, lingered in a pique over a neglected opportunity (at the time I was lying in bed with a slight cold and my governess read me [Tolstoy's] *The Kreutzer Sonata* which enabled her to enjoy my agitation), imagined my vegetarian supper, was satisfied with my digestion, and worried whether my eyesight would last all my life.   [DI, 39]

1911

Bachelor's Ill Luck

It seems so dreadful to stay a bachelor, to become an old man struggling to keep one's dignity while begging for an invitation whenever one wants to spend an evening in company, to lie ill gazing for weeks into an empty room from the corner where one's bed is, always having to say goodnight at the front door, never to run up a stairway beside one's wife, to have only side doors in one's room leading into other people's living rooms, having to carry one's supper home in one's hand, having to admire other people's children and not even being allowed to go on saying: "I have none myself," modeling oneself in appearance and behavior on one or two bachelors remembered from one's youth.

That's how it will be, except that in reality, both today and later, one will stand there with a palpable body and a real head, a real forehead, that is, for smiting on with one's hand.

The Penal Colony, p. 30

January–February: Professional trip to Friedland and Reichenberg.

January 12. I haven't written down a great deal about myself during these days, partly because of laziness (I now sleep so much and so soundly during the day, I have greater weight while I sleep), but also partly because of the fear of betraying my self-perception. This fear is justified, for one should permit a self-perception to be established definitively in writing only when it can be done with the greatest completeness, with all the incidental consequences, as well as with entire truthfulness. For if this does not happen—and in any event I am not capable of it—then what is written down will, in accordance with its own purpose and with the superior power of the established, replace what has been felt only vaguely in such a way that the real feeling will disappear while the worthlessness of what has been noted down will be recognized too late.   [DI, 41]

A note by Brod, early 1911:

On Sundays Kafka goes for walks by himself, without any objective, without thinking. He says, "Every day I wish myself off the earth." "There is nothing wrong with me except myself." He has done no work. In the afternoons he sleeps or looks at the papers in the Arts and Crafts Museum. In company, he is cheerful, full of humor, as a critic, unsurpassable for his witty observations; with his conversation it is the same; it could and should all be written down. When asked what after all was responsible for his sad condition, and why he couldn't write, he said, "I have hundreds of wrong feelings—dreadful ones—the right ones won't come out—or if they do, only in rags; absolutely weak." I protest (in reply) that when one is writing one sometimes has to work one's way through one's first worthless ideas in order to come to the nobler thoughts that lie beneath them. He answers, "That's all right for you, but not for me—that would mean giving these wrong feelings the upper hand."

[B, 75]

January 17. Max read me the first act of [his] Abschied von der Jugend. How can I, as I am today, come up to this; I should have to look for a year before I found a true emotion in me, and am supposed, in the face of so great a work, in some way to have a right to remain seated in my chair in the coffeehouse late in the evening, plagued by the passing flatulence of a digestion which is bad in spite of everything.   [DI, 42]

January 19. Every day, since I seem to be completely finished—during the last year I did not wake up for more than five minutes at a time—I shall either have to wish myself off the earth or else, without my being able to see even the most moderate hope in it, I shall have to start afresh like a baby. Externally, this will be easier for me than before. For in those days I still strove with hardly a suspicion after a description in which every word would be linked to my life, which I would draw to my heart, and which would transport me out of myself. With what misery (of course, not to be compared with the present) I began ! What a chill pursued me all day long out of what I had written! How great the danger was and how uninterruptedly it worked, that I did not feel that chill at all, which indeed on the whole did not lessen my misfortune very much.   [DI, 42 f.]

February 19. When I wanted to get out of bed this morning I simply folded up. This has a very simple cause, I am completely overworked. Not by the office but by my other work. The office has an innocent share in it only to the extent that, if I did not have to go there, I could live calmly for my own work and should not have to waste these six hours a day which have tormented me to a degree that you cannot imagine, especially on Friday and Saturday, because I was full of my own things. In the final analysis, I know, that is just talk, the fault is mine and the office has a right to make the most definite and justified demands on me. But for me in particular it is a horrible double life from which there is probably no escape but insanity.   [DI, 44]

February 19. The special nature of my inspiration in which I, the most fortunate and unfortunate of men, now go to sleep at 2 A.M. (perhaps, if I can only bear the thought of it, it will remain, for it is loftier than all before) is such that I can do everything, and not only what is directed to a definite piece of work. If I write down the first sentence that comes into my head, for instance, "He looked out of the window," it already has perfection.   [DI, 45]

February 21. For the length of a moment I felt myself clad in steel. [DI, 46]

> *Mrs. Berta Fanta's home was a center of intellectuals. At the meetings, works of Kant, Hegel, Fichte, and others were read. Among the guests were Albert Einstein, mathematician Gerhart Kowalewski, philosopher Christian von Ehrenfels, physicist Philipp Frank, Felix Weltsch, Max Brod, and F.K. Mrs. Fanta, mother-in-law of Hugo Bergmann, leaned toward spiritism and theosophy; her husband favored Islam.*

> *From "My visit to Dr. [Rudolf] Steiner," the theosophist who gave lectures at Mrs. Fanta's on occult physiology:*

March 18. My happiness, my abilities, and every possibility of being useful in any way have always been in the literary field. And here I have, to be sure, experienced states (not many) that in my opinion correspond very closely to the clairvoyant states described by you, Herr Doktor, in which I completely dwelled in every idea, but also filled every idea, and in which I not only felt myself at my boundary, but at the boundary of the human in general. Only the calm of enthusiasm, which is probably characteristic of the clairvoyant, was still lacking in those states, even if not completely. I conclude this from the fact that I did not write the best of my works in those states. I cannot now devote myself completely to this literary field, as would be necessary and indeed for various reasons. Aside from my family relationships, I could not live by literature if only, to begin with, because of the slow maturing of my work and its special character; besides, I am prevented also by my health and my character from devoting myself to what is, in the most favorable case, an uncertain life. I have therefore become an official in a social insurance agency. Now these two professions can never be reconciled with one another and admit a common fortune. The smallest good fortune in one becomes a great misfortune in the other. If I have written something good one evening, I am afire the next day in the office and can bring nothing to completion. This back and forth continually becomes worse. Outwardly, I fulfill my duties satisfactorily in the office, not my inner duties, however, and every unfulfilled inner duty becomes a misfortune that never leaves. And to these two never-to-be-reconciled endeavors shall I now add theosophy as a third? Will it not disturb both the others and itself be disturbed by both? Will I, at present already so unhappy a person, be able to carry the three to completion? This is what I have come to ask you, Herr Doktor, for I have a presentiment that if you consider me capable of this, then I can really take it upon myself.

He listened very attentively without apparently looking at me at all, entirely devoted to my words. He nodded from time to time, which he seems to consider an aid to strict concentration. At first a quiet head cold disturbed him, his nose ran, he kept working his handkerchief deep into his nose, one finger at each nostril.   [DI, 58 f.]

F.K. does not tell what Dr. Steiner said to him.

August 15. The time that has just gone by and in which I haven't written a word has been so important for me because I have stopped being ashamed of my body in the swimming schools in Prague, Königssaal, and Czernoschitz. How late I make up for my education now, at the age of twenty-eight, a delayed start they would call it at the race track.

[DI, 60]

August 20. I have the unhappy belief that I haven't the time for the least bit of good work, for I really don't have time for a story, time to expand myself in every direction in the world, as I should have to do. But then I once more believe that my trip will turn out better, that I shall comprehend better if I am relaxed by a little writing, and so I try it again.

I have been reading about Dickens. Is it so difficult and can an outsider understand that you experience a story within yourself from its beginning, from the distant point up to the approaching locomotives of steel, coal, and steam, and you don't abandon it even now, but want to be pursued by it and have time for it, therefore are pursued by it and of your own volition run before it wherever it may thrust and wherever you may lure it.

I can't understand it and can't believe it. I live only here and there in a small word in whose vowel ("thrust" above, for instance) I lose my useless head for a moment. The first and last letters are the beginning and end of my fishlike emotion.   [DI, 61 f.]

> *August 26 to September 13: Zurich, Lugano, Milan, Paris (with Max Brod). Plans to work with Brod on a diary-novel, "Richard and Samuel." September 13–20: Alone in a sanatorium in Erlenbach, near Zurich.*

August 26. Tomorrow I am supposed to leave for Italy. Father has been unable to fall asleep these evenings because of excitement, since he has been completely caught up in his worries about the business and in his illness, which they have aggravated. A wet cloth on his heart, vomiting, suffocation, walking back and forth to the accompaniment of sighs. My mother in her anxiety finds new solace. He was always after all so energetic, he got over everything, and now . . . I say that all the misery over the business could after all last only another three months, then everything will have to be all right. He walks up and down, sighing and shaking his head. It is clear that from his point of view his worries will not be taken from his shoulders and will not even be made lighter by us, but even from our point of view they will not, even in our best intentions there is still something of the sad conviction that he must provide for his family.   [DI, 62 f.]

> *The diary of the trip follows at this point in the manuscript. It was published as an appendix to the second volume of* Diaries.

October 1. The Altneu Synagogue[1] yesterday. Kol Nidre.[2] Suppressed murmur of the stock market. In the entry, boxes with the inscription: "Merciful gifts secretly left assuage anger." Churchly inside. Three pious, apparently East European Jews. In socks. Bowed over their prayer books, their prayer shawls drawn over their heads, become as small as they possibly can. Two are crying, moved only by the holy day. One of them may only have sore eyes, perhaps, to which he fleetingly applies his still folded handkerchief, at once to lower his face to the text again. The words are not really, or chiefly, sung, but behind them arabesquelike melodies are heard that spin out the words as fine as hairs. The little boy without the slightest conception of it all and without any possibility of understanding, who, with the clamor in his ears, pushes himself among the thronging people and is pushed. The clerk (apparently) who shakes himself rapidly while he prays, which is to be understood only as an attempt at putting the strongest possible—even if possibly incomprehensible—emphasis on each word, by means of which the voice, which in any case could not attain a large, clear emphasis in the clamor, is spared. The family of a brothel owner. I was stirred immeasurably more deeply by Judaism in the Pinkas Synagogue. [3]   [DI, 72]

October 2. Sleepless night. The third in a row. I fall asleep soundly, but after an hour I wake up, as though I had laid my head in the wrong hole. I am completely awake, have the feeling that I have not slept at all or only under a thin skin, have before me anew the labor of falling asleep and feel myself rejected by sleep. And for the rest of the night, until about five, thus it remains, so that indeed I sleep but at the same time vivid dreams keep me awake. I sleep alongside myself, so to speak, while I myself must struggle with dreams. About five the last trace of sleep is exhausted, I just dream, which is more exhausting than wakefulness. In short, I spend the whole night in that state in which a healthy person finds himself for a short time before really falling asleep. When I awaken, all the dreams are gathered about me, but I am careful not to reflect on them. Toward morning I sigh into the pillow, because for this night all hope is gone. I think of those nights at the end of which I was raised out of deep sleep and awoke as though I had been folded in a nut.

I believe this sleeplessness comes only because I write. For no matter how little and how badly I write, I am still made sensitive by these minor shocks, feel, especially toward evening and even more in the morning, the approaching, the imminent possibility of great moments which would tear me open, which could make me capable of anything, and in the general uproar that is within me and which I have no time to command, find no rest. In the end this uproar is only a suppressed, restrained harmony, which, left free, would fill me completely, which could even widen me and yet still fill me. But now such a moment arouses only feeble hopes and does me harm, for my being does not have sufficient strength or the capacity to hold the present mixture, during the day the visible world helps me, during the night it cuts me to pieces unhindered. [. . .]

My consolation is—and with it I now go to bed—that I have not written for so long, that therefore this writing could find no right place within my present circumstances, that nevertheless, with a little fortitude, I'll succeed, at least temporarily.   [DI, 73 ff.]

October 3. The same sort of night, but fell asleep with even more difficulty. While falling asleep a vertically moving pain in my head over the bridge of the nose, as though from a wrinkle too sharply pressed into my forehead. To make myself as heavy as possible, which I consider good for falling asleep, I had crossed my arms and laid my hands on my shoulders, so that I lay there like a soldier with his pack. Again it was the power of my dreams, shining forth into wakefulness even before I fall asleep, that did not let me sleep. In the evening and the morning my consciousness of the creative abilities in me is more than I can encompass. I feel shaken to the core of my being and can get out of myself whatever I desire. Calling forth such powers, which are then not permitted to function, reminds me of my relationship with B. Here too there are effusions which are not released but must instead spend themselves in being repulsed, but here—this is the difference—it is a matter of more mysterious powers and of my ultimate being.

Finally I say it, but retain the great fear that everything within me is ready for a poetic work and such a work would be a heavenly enlightenment and a real coming-alive for me, while here, in the office, because of so wretched an official document, I must rob a body capable of such happiness of a piece of its flesh.   [DI, 75 ff.]

> *A Yiddish theater troupe from Lemberg, Galicia, performed in the small Café Savoy in Prague. F.K. and Brod were frequent visitors. F.K. became an enthusiastically involved devotee. The performances conveyed some genuine elements of living East European Judaism.*

October 5. Last night Café Savoy. Yiddish troupe. Mrs. K. [Klug], "male impersonator." In a caftan, short black trousers, white stockings, from the black vest a thin white woolen shirt emerges that is held in front at the throat by a knot and then flares into a wide, loose, long, spreading collar. On her head, confining her woman's hair but necessary anyhow and worn by her husband as well, a dark, brimless skull cap, over it a large, soft black hat with a turned-up brim.

I really don't know what sort of person it is that she and her husband represent. If I wanted to explain them to someone to whom I didn't want to confess my ignorance, I should find that I consider them sextons, employees of the temple, notorious lazybones with whom the community has come to terms, privileged shnorrers for some religious reason, people who, precisely as a result of their being set apart, are very close to the center of the community's life, know many songs as a result of their useless wandering about and spying, see clearly to the core the relationship of all the members of the community, but as a result of their lack of relatedness to the workaday world don't know what to do with this knowledge, people who are Jews in an especially pure form because they live only in the religion, but live in it without effort, understanding, or distress. They seem to make a fool of everyone, laugh immediately after the murder of a noble Jew, sell themselves to an apostate, dance with their hands on their earlocks in delight when the unmasked murderer poisons himself and calls upon God, and yet all this only because they are as light as a feather, sink to the ground under the slightest pressure, are sensitive, cry easily with dry faces (they cry themselves out in grimaces), but as soon as the pressure is removed haven't the slightest specific gravity but must bounce right back up in the air.

They must have caused a lot of difficulty in a serious play, such as *Der Meshumed* [*The Apostate*] by [Joseph] Lateiner is, for they are forever—large as life and often on tiptoe or with both feet in the air—at the front of the stage and do not unravel but rather cut apart the suspense of the play. The seriousness of the play spins itself out, however, in words so compact, carefully considered even where possibly improvised, so full of the tension of a unified emotion, that even when the plot is going along only at the rear of the stage, it always keeps its meaning. Rather, the two in caftans are suppressed now and then, which befits their nature, and despite their extended arms and snapping fingers one sees behind them only the murderer, who, the poison in him, his hand at his really too large collar, is staggering to the door.

The melodies are long, one's body is glad to confide itself to them. As a result of their long-drawn-out forward movement, the melodies are best expressed by a swaying of the hips, by raising and lowering extended arms in a calm rhythm, by bringing the palms close to the temples and taking care not to touch them. Suggests the [Czech folk dance] *šlapák*.

Some songs, the expression "yiddishe kinderlach," some of this woman's acting (who, on the stage, because she is a Jew, draws us listeners to her because we are Jews, without any longing for or curiosity about Christians) made my cheeks tremble. The representative of the government, with the exception of a waiter and two maids standing to the left of the stage, perhaps the only Christian in the hall, is a wretched person, afflicted with a facial tic that—especially on the left side of his face, but spreading also far onto the right—contracts and passes from his face with the almost merciful quickness, I mean the haste but also the regularity, of a second hand. When it reaches the left eye it almost obliterates it. For this contraction new, small, fresh muscles have developed in the otherwise quite wasted face.

The talmudic melody of minute questions, adjurations, or explanations: the air moves into a pipe and takes the pipe along, and a great screw, proud in its entirety, humble in its turns, twists from small, distant beginnings in the direction of the one who is questioned.

[DI, 79 ff.]

There follows a detailed description of the plot.

October 8. Would like to see a large Yiddish theater as the production may after all suffer because of the small cast and inadequate rehearsal. Also, would like to know Yiddish literature, which is obviously characterized by an uninterrupted tradition of national struggle that determines every work. A tradition, therefore, that pervades no other literature, not even that of the most oppressed people. It may be that other peoples in times of war make a success out of a pugnacious national literature, and that other works, standing at a greater remove, acquire from the enthusiasm of the audience a national character too, as is the case with [Friedrich Smetana's opera] *The Bartered Bride,* but here there appear to be only works of the first type, and indeed always.

[DI, 87]

October 10. Day before yesterday among the Jews in Café Savoy. *Die Sedernacht* [*The Seder Night*] by [Zigmund] Fei[n]mann. At times (at the moment the consciousness of this pierced me) we did not interfere in the plot only because we were too moved, not because we were mere spectators.

[DI, 91]

October 16. Strenuous Sunday yesterday. The whole staff gave Father notice. By soft words, cordiality, effective use of his illness, his size and former strength, his experience, his cleverness, he wins almost all of them back in group and individual discussions. An important clerk, F., wants time until Monday to think it over because he has given his word to our manager who is stepping out and would like to take the whole staff along into his newly-to-be-established business. On Sunday the bookkeeper writes he cannot remain after all, R. will not release him from his promise.

[DI, 97]

October 17. I finish nothing because I have no time and it presses so within me. If the whole day were free and this morning restlessness could mount within me until midday and wear itself out by evening, then I could sleep. This way, however, there is left for this restlessness only an evening twilight hour at most, it gets somewhat stronger, is then suppressed, and uselessly and injuriously undermines the night for me. Shall I be able to bear it long? And is there any purpose in bearing it, shall I, then, be given time?

[DI, 100]

F.K. was especially attracted by the Yiddish actor Yitzhak Löwy,
through whom he came to know some of Yiddish and Hebrew
literature and Jewish folklore.

October 20. The 18th at Max's; wrote about Paris. Wrote badly, without
really arriving at that freedom of true description which releases one's
foot from the experienced. I was also dull after the great exaltation of
the previous day that had ended with Löwy's lecture. [. . .]

Löwy read humorous sketches by Sholom Aleichem, then a story by
[Y. L.] Peretz, the *Lichtverkäuferin* [*The Candle Vendor*] by [Morris]
Rosenfeld, a poem by [H. N.] Bialik (the one instance where the poet
stooped from Hebrew to Yiddish, himself translating his original Hebrew poem into Yiddish, in order to popularize this poem which, by
making capital out of the Kishinev pogrom [of 1903], sought to further
the Jewish cause). A recurrent widening of the eyes, natural to the
actor, which are then left so for a while, framed by the arched eye-
brows. Complete truth of all the reading; the weak raising of the right
arm from the shoulder, the adjusting of the pince-nez that seems borrowed for the occasion, so poorly does it fit the nose; the position under
the table of the leg that is stretched out in such a way that the weak
joint between the upper and lower parts of the leg is particularly in
motion; the crook of the back, weak and wretched-looking since the
unbroken surface of a back cannot deceive an observer in the way that
a face does, with its eyes, the hollows and projections of its cheeks, or
even with some trifle, be it only a stubble of beard. After the reading,
while still on my way home, I felt all my abilities concentrated, and on
that account complained to my sisters, even to my mother, at home.

[DI, 100 ff.]

October 21. The Jewish actors. Mrs. Tschissik has protuberances on her
cheeks near her mouth. Caused in part by hollow cheeks as a result of
the pains of hunger, childbed, journeys, and acting, in part by the
relaxed unusual muscles she had to develop for the actor's movements
of her large, what originally must have been a heavy mouth. Most of the
time, as Sulamith [in the play of that name by Abraham Goldfaden],
she wore her hair loose, which covered her cheeks so that her face
sometimes looked like the face of a girl out of the past. She has a large,
bony, moderately robust body and is tightly laced. Her walk easily
takes on a solemnity since she has the habit of raising, stretching, and
slowly moving her long arms. Especially when she sang the Jewish
national anthem, gently rocked her large hips, and moved her arms,
bent parallel to her hips, up and down with hands cupped as though
she were playing with a slowly flying ball.   [DI, 106]

October 22. Yesterday with the Jews. *Kol Nidre [All Vows]* by [Abraham] Scharkansky, pretty bad play with a good, witty letter-writing scene, a prayer by the lovers standing up beside each other with hands clasped, the converted Grand Inquisitor pressing himself against the curtain of the Ark, he mounts the stairs and remains standing there, his head bowed, his lips against the curtain, holds the prayer book before his chattering teeth. For the first time on this fourth evening my distinct inability to get a clear impression. Our large company and the visits at my sisters' table were also responsible for it. Nevertheless, I needn't have been so weak. With my love for Mrs. Ts. [Tschissik], who only thanks to Max sat beside me, I behaved wretchedly. I'll recover again, however, even now I feel better. [DI, 106 f.]

October 22. The sympathy we have for these actors who are so good, who earn nothing, and who do not get nearly enough gratitude and fame is really only sympathy for the sad fate of many noble strivings, above all of our own. Therefore, too, it is so immoderately strong, because on the surface it is attached to strangers and in reality belongs to us. Nevertheless, in spite of everything, it is so closely bound up with the actors that I cannot disengage it even now. Because I recognize this and in spite of it this sympathy attaches itself even more closely to them. [DI, 108]

October 23. Until the age of twenty Löwy was a *bocher* [talmudic student] who studied and spent the money of his well-to-do father. There was a society of young people of the same age who met in a locked tavern precisely on Saturday and, dressed in their caftans, smoked and otherwise sinned against the Sabbath laws. [DI, 109 f.]

October 24. Mother works all day, is merry and sad as the fancy strikes her, without taking advantage of her own condition in the slightest, her voice is clear, too loud for ordinary speech but does you good when you are sad and suddenly hear it after some time. For a long time now I have been complaining that I am always ill, but never have any definite illness that would compel me to go to bed. This wish certainly goes back chiefly to the fact that I know how comforting Mother can be when, for example, she comes from the lighted living room into the twilight of the sickroom, or in the evening, when the day begins to change monotonously into night, returns from business and with her concerns and hurried instructions once more causes the day, already so late, to begin again and rouses the invalid to help her in this. I should wish that for myself once more, because then I should be weak, therefore convinced by everything my mother did, and could enjoy childish

pleasure with age's keener capacity for gratification. Yesterday it occurred to me that I did not always love my mother as she deserved and
as I could, only because the German language prevented it. The Jewish
mother is no "Mutter," to call her "Mutter" makes her a little comic (not
to herself, because we are in Germany), we give a Jewish woman the
name of a German mother, but forget the contradiction that sinks into
the emotions so much the more heavily, "Mutter" is peculiarly German
for the Jew, it unconsciously contains, together with the Christian
splendor, Christian coldness also, the Jewish woman who is called
"Mutter" therefore becomes not only comic but strange. Mama would
be a better name if only one didn't imagine "Mutter" behind it. I believe
that it is only the memories of the ghetto that still preserve the Jewish
family, for the word "Vater" too is far from meaning the Jewish father.

[DI, 110 f.]

November 1. Today, eagerly and happily began to read the *History of
the Jews* by [Heinrich] Graetz. Because my desire for it had far outrun
the reading, it was at first stranger to me than I thought, and I had to
stop here and there in order by resting to allow my Jewishness to collect
itself. Toward the end, however, I was already gripped by the imper-
fection of the first settlements in the newly conquered Canaan and the
faithful handing down of the imperfections of the popular heroes
(Joshua, the Judges, Elijah).   [DI, 125]

November 2. [Yitzhak] Löwy. My father about him: "Whoever lies
down with dogs gets up with fleas." I could not contain myself and said
something uncontrolled. To which Father with unusual quietness (to
be sure, after a long interval which was otherwise occupied): "You
know that I should not get excited and must be treated with consideration. And now you speak to me like that. I really have enough excitement, quite enough. So don't bother me with such talk." I say: "I make
every effort to restrain myself," and sense in my father, as always in
such extreme moments, the existence of a wisdom of which I can grasp
only a breath.

   Death of Löwy's grandfather, a man who had an open hand, knew
several languages, had made long journeys deep into Russia, and who
once on a Saturday refused to eat at the house of a wonder-rabbi in
Ekaterinoslav because the long hair and colored neckerchief of the
rabbi's son made him suspect the piety of the house.

   The bed was set up in the middle of the room, the candlesticks were
borrowed from friends and relatives, the room therefore full of the light
and smoke of the candles. Some forty men stood around his bed all day
to receive inspiration from the death of a pious man. He was conscious

until the end and at the right moment, his hand on his breast, he began
to repeat the death prayers. During his suffering and after his death the
grandmother, who was with the women gathered in the next room,
wept incessantly, but while he was dying she was completely calm
because it is a commandment to ease the death of the dying man as
much as one can. "With his own prayers he passed away." He was
much envied for this death that followed so pious a life.   [DI, 131 f.]

November 5. I want to write, with a constant trembling on my forehead.
I sit in my room in the very headquarters of the uproar of the entire
house. I hear all the doors close, because of their noise only the foot-
steps of those running between them are spared me, I hear even the
slamming of the oven door in the kitchen. My father bursts through the
doors of my room and passes through in his dragging dressing gown,
the ashes are scraped out of the stove in the next room, Valli asks,
shouting into the indefinite through the anteroom as though through a
Paris street, whether Father's hat has been brushed yet, a hushing that
claims to be friendly to me raises the shout of an answering voice. The
house door is unlatched and screeches as though from a catarrhal
throat, then opens wider with the brief singing of a woman's voice and
closes with a dull manly jerk that sounds most inconsiderate. My father
is gone, now begins the more delicate, more distracted, more hopeless
noise led by the voices of the two canaries. I had already thought of it
before, but with the canaries it comes back to me again, that I might
open the door a narrow crack, crawl into the next room like a snake,
and in that way, on the floor, beg my sisters and their governess for
quiet.   [DI, 133]

> *F.K. allowed this description to be published unchanged in
> Herderblätter, I (October 1912), 4–5.*

With reference to Mrs. Tschissik of the Yiddish theater:
November 5. I had hoped, by means of the bouquet of flowers, to
appease my love for her a little, it was quite useless. It is possible only
through literature or through intercourse. I write this not because I did
not know it, but rather because it is perhaps well to write down warnings frequently.

Should I be grateful or should I curse the fact that despite all misfortune I can still feel love, an unearthly love but still for earthly ob-
jects.   [DI, 137, 139]

November 11. I will try, gradually, to group everything certain in me,
later the credible, then the possible, etc. The greed for books is certain
in me. Not really to own or to read them, but rather to see them, to

convince myself of their actuality in the stalls of a bookseller. If there are several copies of the same book somewhere, each individual one delights me. It is as though this greed came from my stomach, as though it were a perverse appetite. Books that I own delight me less, but books belonging to my sisters do delight me. The desire to own them is incomparably less, it is almost absent.   [DI, 146]

November 14. To awaken on a cold autumn morning full of yellowish light. To force your way through the half-shut window and while still in front of the panes, before you fall, to hover, arms extended, belly arched, legs curved backward, like the figures on the bows of ships in old times.   [DI, 150]

November 15. Yesterday evening, already with a sense of foreboding, pulled the cover off the bed, lay down, and again became aware of all my abilities as though I were holding them in my hand; they tightened my chest, they set my head on fire, for a short while, to console myself for not getting up to work, I repeated: "That's not healthy, that's not healthy," and with almost visible purpose tried to draw sleep over my head. I kept thinking of a cap with a visor which, to protect myself, I pulled down hard over my forehead. How much did I lose yesterday, how the blood pounded in my tight head, capable of anything and restrained only by powers which are indispensable for my very life and are here being wasted.

It is certain that everything I have conceived in advance, even when I was in a good mood, whether word for word or just casually, but in specific words, appears dry, wrong, inflexible, embarrassing to everybody around me, timid, but above all incomplete when I try to write it down at my desk, although I have forgotten nothing of the original conception. This is naturally related in large part to the fact that I conceive something good away from paper only in a time of exaltation, a time more feared than longed for, much as I do long for it; but then the fullness is so great that I have to give up. Blindly and arbitrarily I snatch handfuls out of the stream so that when I write it down calmly, my acquisition is nothing in comparison with the fullness in which it lived, is incapable of restoring this fullness, and thus is bad and disturbing because it tempts to no purpose.   [DI, 151 f.]

Referring to the travel book planned by Brod and F.K. during the summer trip:
November 19. I and Max must really be different to the very core. Much as I admire his writings when they lie before me as a whole, resisting my and anyone else's encroachment (a few small book reviews even

today), still, every sentence he writes for "Richard and Samuel" [4] is bound up with a reluctant concession on my part which I feel painfully to my very depths. At least today.   [DI, 156]

November 21. My former governess, the one with the black-and-yellow face, with the square nose and a wart on her cheek which used to delight me so, was at our house today for the second time recently to see me. The first time I wasn't home, this time I wanted to be left in peace and to sleep and had them tell her I was out. Why did she bring me up so badly, after all I was obedient, she herself is saying so now to the cook and the governess in the anteroom, I was good and had a quiet disposition. Why didn't she use this to my advantage and prepare a better future for me? She is a married woman or a widow, has children, has a lively way of speaking that doesn't let me sleep, thinks I am a tall, healthy gentleman at the beautiful age of twenty-eight who likes to remember his youth and in general knows what to do with himself. Now, however, I lie here on the sofa, kicked out of the world, on the lookout for the sleep that refuses to come and will only graze me when it does, my joints ache with fatigue, my dried-up body trembles toward its own destruction in turmoils of which I dare not become fully conscious, in my head are astonishing convulsions. And there stand the three women before my door, one praises me as I was, two as I am. The cook says I shall go straight—she means without any detour—to heaven. Thus it shall be.   [DI, 158 f.]

November 22. It is certain that a major obstacle to my progress is my physical condition. Nothing can be accomplished with such a body. I shall have to get used to its perpetual balking. As a result of the last few nights spent in wild dreams but with scarcely a few snatches of sleep, I was so incoherent this morning, felt nothing but my forehead, saw a halfway bearable condition only far beyond my present one, and in sheer readiness to die would have been glad simply to have curled up in a ball on the cement floor of the corridor with the documents in my hand. My body is too long for its weakness, it hasn't the least bit of fat to engender a blessed warmth, to preserve an inner fire, no fat on which the spirit could occasionally nourish itself beyond its daily need without damage to the whole. How shall the weak heart that lately has troubled me so often be able to pound the blood through all the length of these legs. It would be labor enough to the knees, and from there it can only spill with a senile strength into the cold lower parts of my legs. But now it is already needed up above again, it is being waited for, while it is wasting itself down below. Everything is pulled apart throughout the length of my body. What could it accomplish then, when it perhaps wouldn't have enough strength for what I want to achieve even if it were shorter and more compact.   [DI, 160]

December 8. Friday, have not written for a long time, but this time it was really in part because of satisfaction, as I have finished the first chapter of "Richard and Samuel" and consider it, particularly the original description of the sleep in the train compartment, a success. Even more, I think that something is happening within me that is very close to Schiller's transformation of emotion into character. Despite all the resistance of my inner being I must write this down.   [DI, 169]

December 8. Even if I overlook all other obstacles (physical condition, parents, character), the following serves as a very good excuse for my not limiting myself to literature in spite of everything: I can take nothing on myself as long as I have not achieved a sustained work that satisfies me completely. That is of course irrefutable.

I have now, and have had since this afternoon, a great yearning to write all my anxiety entirely out of me, write it into the depths of the paper just as it comes out of the depths of me, or write it down in such a way that I could draw what I had written into me completely. This is no artistic yearning. Today, when [Yitzhak] Löwy spoke of his dissatisfaction with and of his indifference to everything that the troupe does, I explained his condition as due to homesickness, but in a sense did not give him this explanation even though I voiced it, instead kept it for myself and enjoyed it in passing as a sorrow of my own.   [DI, 173]

With reference to his sister Elli Hermann and her son Felix, born December 8:
December 10. Sunday. I must go to see my sister and her little boy. When my mother came home from my sister's at one o'clock at night the day before yesterday with the news of the boy's birth, my father marched through the house in his nightshirt, opened all the doors, woke me, the maid, and my sisters, and proclaimed the birth as though the child had not only been born, but as though it had already lived an honorable life and been buried too.   [DI, 174 f.]

December 13. When I begin to write after a rather long interval, I draw the words as if out of the empty air. If I capture one, then I have just this one alone and all the toil must begin anew.   [DI, 177]

December 14. My father reproached me at noon because I don't bother with the factory.[5] I explained that I had accepted a share because I expected profit but that I cannot take an active part so long as I am in the office. Father quarreled on, I stood silently at the window. This evening, however, I caught myself thinking, as a result of that noontime discussion, that I could put up with my present situation very contentedly, and that I only had to be careful not to have all my time free for literature. I had scarcely exposed this thought to a closer inspection when it became no longer astonishing and already appeared accustomed. I disputed my ability to devote all my time to literature. This conviction arose, of course, only from the momentary situation, but was stronger than it.

[DI, 177 f.]

December 16. In periods of transition such as the past week has been for me and as this moment at least still is, a sad but calm astonishment at my lack of feeling often grips me. I am divided from all things by a hollow space and I don't even push myself to the limits of it.

The moment I were set free from the office I would yield at once to my urge to write an autobiography. I would have to have some such decisive change before me as a preliminary goal when I began to write in order to be able to give some direction to the mass of events. But I cannot imagine any other inspiriting change than this, which is itself so terribly improbable. Then, however, the writing of the autobiography would be a great joy because it would move along as easily as the writing down of dreams, yet it would have an entirely different effect, a great one, which would influence me forever and would be accessible as well to the understanding and feeling of everyone else.   [DI, 180 f.]

> Writes "Measures for the Prevention of Accidents" [in factories and farms] and "Workers' Accident Insurance and Management."

December 18. I hate Werfel,[6] not because I envy him, but I envy him too. He is healthy, young, and rich, everything that I am not. Besides, gifted with a sense of music, he has done very good work early and easily, he has the happiest life behind him and before him, I work with weights I cannot get rid of, and I am entirely shut off from music.

I am not punctual because I do not feel the pains of waiting. I wait like an ox. For if I feel a purpose in my momentary existence, even a very uncertain one, I am so vain in my weakness that I would gladly bear anything for the sake of this purpose once it is before me. If I were in love, what couldn't I do then. How long I waited, years ago, under the arcades of the Ring until M. came by, even to see her walk by with her lover. I have been late for appointments partly out of carelessness, partly out of ignorance of the pains of waiting, but also partly in order to attain new, complicated purposes through a renewed, uncertain search for the people with whom I had made the appointments, and so to achieve the possibility of long, uncertain waiting. From the fact that as a child I had a great nervous fear of waiting, one could conclude that I was destined for something better and that I foresaw my future.   [DI, 182]

December 19. Mrs. Tschissik acted again [in *Davids Geige (David's Violin),* by Joseph Lateiner]. Yesterday her body was more beautiful than her face, which seemed narrower than usual so that the forehead, which is thrown into wrinkles at her first word, was too striking. The beautifully rounded, moderately strong, large body did not belong with her face yesterday, and she reminded me vaguely of hybrid beings like mermaids, sirens, centaurs. When she stood before me then, with her face distorted, her complexion spoiled by makeup, a stain on her dark-blue short-sleeved blouse, I felt as though I were speaking to a statue in a circle of pitiless onlookers. [. . .] Then while I was speaking with Mrs. Tschissik I observed that my love had not really grasped her, but only flitted about her, now nearer, now farther. Indeed, it can find no peace.

Today at breakfast I spoke with my mother by chance about children and marriage, only a few words, but for the first time saw clearly how untrue and childish is the conception of me that my mother builds up for herself. She considers me a healthy young man who suffers a little from the notion that he is ill. This notion will disappear by itself with time; marriage, of course, and having children would put an end to it best of all. Then my interest in literature would also be reduced to the degree that is perhaps necessary for an educated man. A matter-of-fact, undisturbed interest in my profession or in the factory or in whatever may come to hand will appear. Hence there is not the slightest, not the trace of a reason for permanent despair about my future. There is occasion for temporary despair, which is not very deep, however, whenever I think my stomach is upset, or when I can't sleep because I write too much. There are thousands of possible solutions. The most probable is that I shall suddenly fall in love with a girl and will never again want to do without her. Then I shall see how good their intentions toward me are and how little they will interfere with me. But if I remain a bachelor like my uncle [Alfred Löwy] in Madrid, that too will be no misfortune because with my cleverness I shall know how to make adjustments.   [DI, 183 ff.]

December 23. Saturday. When I look at my whole way of life going in a direction that is foreign and false to all my relatives and acquaintances, the apprehension arises, and my father expresses it, that I shall become a second Uncle Rudolf [Löwy], the fool of the new generation of the family, the fool somewhat altered to meet the needs of a different period; but from now on I'll be able to feel how my mother (whose opposition to this opinion grows continually weaker in the course of the years) sums up and enforces everything that speaks for me and against Uncle Rudolf, and that enters like a wedge between the conceptions entertained about the two of us.

One advantage in keeping a diary is that you become aware with reassuring clarity of the changes which you constantly suffer and which in a general way are naturally believed, surmised, and admitted by you, but which you'll unconsciously deny when it comes to the point of gaining hope or peace from such an admission. In the diary you find proof that in situations which today would seem unbearable, you lived, looked around, and wrote down observations, that this right hand moved then as it does today, when we may be wiser because we are able to look back upon our former condition, and for that very reason have got to admit the courage of our earlier striving in which we persisted even in sheer ignorance.

All yesterday morning my head was as if filled with steam from Werfel's poems. For a moment I feared the enthusiasm would carry me along straight into nonsense.   [DI, 185, 187 f.]

F.K. was present at the circumcision of his nephew, Felix Hermann (see entry of December 10).
December 24. Today when I heard the *moule*'s[7] assistant say the grace after meals and those present, aside from the two grandfathers, spent the time in dreams or boredom with a complete lack of understanding of the prayer, I saw West European Judaism before me in a transition whose end is clearly unpredictable and about which those most closely affected are not concerned, but, like all people truly in transition, bear what is imposed upon them. It is so indisputable that these religious forms which have reached their final end have merely a historical character, even as they are practiced today, that only a short time was needed this very morning to interest the people present in the outmoded custom of circumcision and its half-sung prayers by describing it to them as something out of history.   [DI, 190 f.]

December 25. A close-knit family life does not seem to be so very common among and characteristic of the Jews, especially those in Russia. Family life is also found among Christians, after all, and the fact that women are excluded from the study of the Talmud is really destructive of Jewish family life; when the man wants to discuss learned talmudic matters—the very core of his life—with guests, the women withdraw to the next room even if they need not do so—so it is even more characteristic of the Jews that they come together at every possible opportunity, whether to pray or to study or to discuss divine matters or to eat holiday meals whose basis is usually a religious one and at which alcohol is drunk only very moderately. They flee to one another, so to speak.   [DI, 196 f.]

December 26. It is unpleasant to listen to Father talk with incessant insinuations about the good fortune of people today and especially of his children, about the sufferings he had to endure in his youth. No one denies that for years, as a result of insufficient winter clothing, he had open sores on his legs, that he often went hungry, that when he was only ten he had to push a cart through the villages, even in winter and very early in the morning—but, and this is something he will not understand, these facts, taken together with the further fact that I have not gone through all this, by no means lead to the conclusion that I have been happier than he, that he may pride himself on these sores on his legs, which is something he assumes and asserts from the very beginning, that I cannot appreciate his past sufferings, and that, finally, just because I have not gone through the same sufferings I must be endlessly grateful to him. How gladly I would listen if he would talk on about his youth and parents, but to hear all this in a boastful and quarrelsome tone is torment. Over and over again he claps his hands together: "Who can understand that today! What do the children know! No one has gone through that! Does a child understand that today!"   [DI, 199 f.]

December 28. The agony that the factory causes me. Why didn't I object when they made me promise to work there in the afternoons. No one used force to make me do it, but my father compels me by his reproaches, Karl [husband of F.K.'s sister Elli] by his silence, and I by my guilty conscience. I know nothing about the factory, and this morning, when the committee made an inspection, I stood around uselessly with my tail between my legs. I deny that it is possible for me to fathom all the details of the operation of the factory. And if I should succeed in doing it by endlessly questioning and pestering all those concerned, what would I have achieved? I would be able to do nothing practical with this knowledge. I am fit only for cooking up something that looks all right, to which the sound common sense of my boss [in the Workers' Accident Insurance Institute] adds the salt that makes it look like a really good job. But through this empty effort spent on the factory I would, on the other hand, rob myself of the use of the few afternoon hours that belong to me, which would of necessity lead to the complete destruction of my existence, which, even apart from this, becomes more and more hedged in.   [DI, 201 f.]

December 29. The difficulties of bringing to an end even a short essay lie not in the fact that we feel the end of the piece demands a fire that the actual content up to that point has not been able to produce out of itself, they arise rather from the fact that even the shortest essay demands of the author a degree of self-satisfaction and of being lost in himself out of which it is difficult to step into the everyday air without great determination and an external incentive, so that, before the essay is rounded to a close and one might quietly slip away, one bolts, driven by unrest, and then the end must be completed from the outside with hands that must not only do the work but hold on as well.   [DI, 202 f.]

December 30. In the morning I felt so fresh for writing, but now the idea that I am to read to Max in the afternoon blocks me completely. This shows too how unfit I am for friendship, assuming that friendship in this sense is even possible. For since a friendship without interruption of one's daily life is unthinkable, a great many of its manifestations are blown away time and again, even if its core remains undamaged. From the undamaged core they are formed anew, but as every such formation requires time, and not everything that is expected succeeds, one can never, even aside from the change in one's personal moods, pick up again where one left off last time. Out of this, in friendships that have a deep foundation, an uneasiness must arise before every fresh meeting which need not be so great that it is felt as such, but which can disturb one's conversation and behavior to such a degree that one is consciously astonished, especially as one is not aware of, or cannot believe, the reason for it. So how am I to read to Max, or even think, while writing down what follows, that I shall read it to him.

Besides, I am disturbed by my having leafed through the diary this morning to see what I could read to Max. In this examination I have found neither that what I have written so far is especially valuable nor that it must simply be thrown away. My opinion lies between the two and closer to the first, yet it is not of such a nature that, judging by the value of what I have written, I must, in spite of my weakness, regard myself as exhausted. Despite that, the sight of the mass of what I had written diverted me almost irrecoverably from the fountainhead of my writing for the next hour, because my attention was to a certain extent lost downstream, as it were, in the same channel.   [DI, 204 f.]

From Brod's diary: "Nothing but Kafka's own dreams seem to interest him any more."

The Nature Theatre of Oklahoma

At a street corner Karl saw a placard with the following announcement: The Oklahoma Theatre will engage members for its company today at Clayton racecourse from six o'clock in the morning until midnight. The great Theatre of Oklahoma calls you! Today only and never again! If you miss your chance now you miss it forever! If you think of your future you are one of us! Everyone is welcome! If you want to be an artist, join our company! Our Theatre can find employment for everyone, a place for everyone! If you decide on an engagement we congratulate you here and now! But hurry, so that you get in before midnight! At twelve o'clock the doors will be shut and never opened again! Down with all those who do not believe in us!

Amerika, p. 272

January 3. It is easy to recognize a concentration in me of all my forces on writing. When it became clear in my organism that writing was the most productive direction for my being to take, everything rushed in that direction and left empty all those abilities that were directed toward the joys of sex, eating, drinking, philosophical reflection, and above all music. I atrophied in all these directions. This was necessary because the totality of my strengths was so slight that only collectively could they even halfway serve the purpose of my writing.

Naturally, I did not find this purpose independently and consciously, it found itself, and is now interfered with only by the office, but that interferes with it completely. In any case I shouldn't complain that I can't put up with a sweetheart, that I understand almost exactly as much of love as I do of music and have to resign myself to the most superficial effects I may pick up, that on New Year's Eve I dined on parsnips and spinach, washed down with a glass of Ceres, and that on Sunday I was unable to take part in Max's lecture on his philosophical work—the compensation for all this is clear as day.

My development is now complete and, so far as I can see, there is nothing left to sacrifice; I need only throw my work in the office out of this complex in order to begin my real life in which, with the progress of my work, my face will finally be able to age in a natural way. [DI, 211]

January 5. For two days I have noticed, whenever I choose to, an inner coolness and indifference. Yesterday evening, during my walk, every little street sound, every eye turned toward me, every picture in a showcase, was more important to me than myself. [DI, 213]

January 6. Yesterday *Vizekönig* [*The Vice-King* by Zigmund] Fei[n]-mann. My receptivity to the Jewishness in these plays deserts me because they are too monotonous and degenerate into a wailing that prides itself on isolated, violent outbreaks. When I saw the first plays it was possible for me to think that I had come upon a Judaism on which the beginnings of my own rested, a Judaism that was developing in my direction and so would enlighten and carry me farther along in my own clumsy Judaism, instead, it moves farther away from me the more I hear of it. The people remain, of course, and I hold fast to them. [DI, 215]

F.K.'s first serious studies of Judaism began at this time.

January 24. Wednesday. For the following reasons have not written for so long: I was angry with my boss and cleared it up only by means of a good letter; was in the factory several times; read, and indeed greedily, [M. I.] Pines' *L'histoire de la Littérature Judéo-Allemande,*[1] 500 pages, with such thoroughness, haste, and joy as I have never yet shown in the case of similar books; now I am reading [Jakob] Fromer, *Organismus des Judentums;*[2] finally I spent a lot of time with the Jewish actors, wrote letters for them, prevailed on the Zionist society to inquire of the Zionist societies of Bohemia whether they would like to have guest appearances of the troupe; I wrote the circular that was required and had it reproduced; saw *Sulamith* [by Abraham Goldfaden] once more and [Moses] Richter's *Herzele Meyiches* for the first time, was at the folksong evening of the Bar Kokhba Society,[3] and day before yesterday saw *Graf von Gleichen* by [Wilhelm] Schmidtbonn. [DI, 223]

F.K. promised Yitzhak Löwy to prepare a speech on the Yiddish language as an introduction to an evening of recitations by Löwy.

February 13. I am beginning to write the lecture for Löwy's performance. It is on Sunday, the 18th. I shall not have much time to prepare and am really striking up a kind of recitative here as though in an opera. The reason is only that an incessant excitement has been oppressing me for days and that, somewhat hesitant in the face of the actual beginning of the lecture, I want to write down a few words only for myself; in that way, given a little momentum, I shall be able to stand up before the audience. Cold and heat alternate in me with the successive words of the sentence, I dream melodic rises and falls, I read sentences of Goethe's as though my whole body were running down the stresses.   [DI, 232 f.]

February 18: Speech on the Yiddish language.

February 25. Hold fast to the diary from today on! Write regularly! Don't surrender! Even if no salvation should come, I want to be worthy of it at every moment. I spent this evening at the family table in complete indifference, my right hand on the arm of the chair in which my sister sat playing cards, my left hand weak in my lap. From time to time I tried to realize my unhappiness, I barely succeeded.

I have written nothing for so long because of having arranged an evening for Löwy in the banquet room of the Jewish Town Hall on February 18th, at which I delivered a little introductory speech on Yiddish. For two weeks I worried for fear that I could not produce the lecture. On the evening before the lecture I suddenly succeeded.

Preparations for the lecture: Conferences with the Bar Kokhba Society, getting up the program, tickets, hall, numbering the seats, key to the piano (Toynbee Hall), setting up the stage, pianist, costumes, selling tickets, newspaper notices, censorship by the police and the [Jewish] community office. [. . .]

Excitements: About the speech, one night twisted up in bed, hot and sleepless, hatred of Dr. B., fear of Weltsch (he will not be able to sell anything), Afike Yehuda,[4] the notices are not published in the papers the way in which they were expected to be, distraction in the office, the stage does not come, not enough tickets are sold, the color of the tickets upsets me, the lecture has to be interrupted because the pianist forgot his music at home in Košíř, a great deal of indifference toward Löwy, almost disgust.

Benefits: Joy in Löwy and confidence in him, proud, unearthly consciousness during my speech (coolness in the presence of the audience, only the lack of practice kept me from using enthusiastic gestures freely), strong voice, effortless memory, recognition, but above all the power with which I loudly, decisively, determinedly, faultlessly, irresistibly, with clear eyes, almost casually, put down the impudence of the three Town Hall porters and gave them, instead of the twelve kronen they demanded, only six kronen, and even these with a grand air. In all this are revealed powers to which I would gladly entrust myself if they would remain. (My parents were not there.)   [DI, 233 ff.]

March 2. Who is to confirm for me the truth or probability of this, that it is only because of my literary mission that I am uninterested in all other things and therefore heartless.   [DI, 245]

March 8. Read through some old notebooks. It takes all my strength to last it out. The unhappiness one must suffer when one interrupts oneself in a task that can never succeed except all at once, and this is what has always happened to me until now; in rereading one must reexperience this unhappiness in a more concentrated way though not as strongly as before.   [DI, 248]

March 11. Today burned many old, disgusting papers.   [DI, 250]

Spring: Beginnings of Amerika *(or,* The Man Who Disappeared).

March 16. Saturday. Again encouragement. Again I catch hold of myself, as one catches hold of a ball in its fall. Tomorrow, today, I'll begin an extensive work which, without being forced, will shape itself according to my abilities. I will not give it up as long as I can hold out at all. Rather be sleepless than live on in this way.   [DI, 254]

March 18. I was wise, if you like, because I was prepared for death at any moment, but not because I had taken care of everything that was given me to do, rather because I had done none of it and could not even hope ever to do any of it.   [DI, 257]

March 26. Only not to overestimate what I have written, for in that way I make what is to be written unattainable.   [DI, 258]

April 1. For the first time in a week an almost complete failure in writing. Why? Last week too I lived through various moods and kept their influence away from my writing; but I am afraid to write about it.
                    [DI, 259]

April 3. This is how a day passes—in the morning, the office, in the afternoon, the factory, now in the evening, shouting to the right and left of me at home, later brought my sister home from *Hamlet*—and I haven't been able to make use of a single moment.   [DI, 259]

April 8. Saturday before Easter. Complete knowledge of oneself. To be able to seize the whole of one's abilities like a little ball. To accept the greatest decline as something familiar and so still remain elastic in it.

Desire for a deeper sleep that dissolves more. The metaphysical urge is only the urge toward death. [DI, 259]

May 6. 11 o'clock. For the first time in a considerable while a complete failure in writing. The feeling of a tried man. [DI, 260]

May 9. Yesterday evening in the coffeehouse with [Otto] Pick. How I hold fast to my novel [Amerika] against all restlessness, like a figure on a monument that looks into the distance and holds fast to its pedestal.

Hopeless evening with the family today. My brother-in-law needs money for the factory, my father is upset because of my sister, because of the business, and because of his heart, my unhappy second sister, my mother unhappy about all of them, and I with my scribblings. [DI, 261]

June 6. I have just read in [Gustave] Flaubert's letters: "My novel is the cliff on which I am hanging, and I know nothing of what is going on in the world."—Like what I noted down about myself on May 9th.

Without weight, without bones, without body, walked through the streets for two hours considering what I overcame this afternoon while writing. [DI, 264]

> June 28 to July 29: Weimar (Goethe's town) with Max Brod. Then alone at Jungborn, Harz Mountains (Sanatorium Rudolf Just). On the way to Weimar, in Leipzig, Brod introduced F.K. to Rowohlt Verlag, managed jointly by Ernst Rowohlt and Kurt Wolff.

July 9. Nothing written for so long. Begin tomorrow. Otherwise I shall again get into a prolonged, irresistible dissatisfaction; I am really in it already. The nervous states are beginning. But if I can do something, then I can do it without superstitious precautions.

The invention of the devil. If we are possessed by the devil, it cannot be by one, for then we should live, at least here on earth, quietly, as with God, in unity, without contradiction, without reflection, always sure of the man behind us. His face would not frighten us, for as diabolical beings we would, if somewhat sensitive to the sight, be clever enough to prefer to sacrifice a hand in order to keep his face covered with it. If we were possessed by only a single devil, one who had a calm, untroubled view of our whole nature, and freedom to dispose of us at any moment, then that devil would also have enough power to hold us for the length of a human life high above the spirit of

God in us, and even to swing us to and fro, so that we should never get to see a glimmer of it and therefore should not be troubled from that quarter.

Only a crowd of devils could account for our earthly misfortunes. Why don't they exterminate one another until only a single one is left, or why don't they subordinate themselves to one great devil? Either way would be in accord with the diabolical principle of deceiving us as completely as possible. With unity lacking, of what use is the scrupulous attention all the devils pay us? It simply goes without saying that the falling of a human hair must matter more to the devil than to God, since the devil really loses that hair and God does not. But we still do not arrive at any state of well-being so long as the many devils are within us.   [DI, 264 f.]

From the travel diaries:
I was lying in the grass when the man from the "Christian Community" (tall, handsome body, sunburned, pointed beard, happy appearance) walked from the place where he reads to the dressing cabin; I followed him unsuspectingly with my eyes, but instead of returning to his place he came in my direction, I closed my eyes, but he was already introducing himself: H., land surveyor, and gave me four pamphlets as reading matter for Sunday. [. . .] I read in them and then went back to him and, hesitant because of the respect in which I held him, tried to make it clear why there was no prospect of grace for me at present. Exercising a beautiful mastery over every word, something that only sincerity makes possible, he discussed this with me for an hour and a half (toward the end an old, thin, white-haired, red-nosed man in linen joined in with several indistinct remarks). Unhappy Goethe, who made so many other people unhappy. A great many stories. How he, H., forbade his father to speak when he blasphemed God in his house. "Oh, Father, may you be stricken with horror by your own words and be too terrified to speak further, I wouldn't care one bit." How his father heard God's voice on his deathbed. He saw that I was close to grace. I interrupted all his arguments and referred him to the inner voice. Successfully.   [DII, 306 f.]

To Brod, from Jungborn, July 10:
Here it is beautiful enough, but I am rather incapable and sad. It doesn't have to be a permanent state, I know. At all events I'm nowhere near ready to write yet. The novel [*Amerika*] is so immense, as though it had been designed right across the sky (and as colorless and imprecise as the sky today), and I get tangled up in the very first sentence I try to write. At least I have realized that I mustn't be put off by the

dreariness of what I have already written and yesterday I derived much profit from that knowledge. [Br, 96]

To Brod, from Jungborn, July 22:
What I have written was written in a tepid bath, the perpetual torment of real writers is something I have not experienced, save in a few exceptional cases which, although they may have been infinitely strong, I am able to exclude from this assessment on account of their rarity and the weakness of the force with which they were toying.

I am also writing here, very little it is true, I complain and I rejoice; that is how pious women pray to God, although in the Bible stories God is seen differently. The fact that I will not be able to show you what I am writing for a long time to come, that you will have to accept, Max, if only to please me. It is being pieced together, consecutively rather than integrally, it will continue on this straightforward course for a long time before it turns to form the circle that I so long for; and then, in that moment, which I am working toward, far from everything becoming easier, it is probable that, having been unsure of myself until then, I will completely lose my head. Consequently, only when the first draft has been completed will it be a fit subject for discussion. [Br, 100]

On the volume Meditation:
August 7. Long torment. Finally wrote to Max that I cannot clear up the little pieces that still remain, do not want to force myself to it, and therefore will not publish the book. [DI, 265]

August 11. Nothing, nothing. How much time the publishing of the little book takes from me and how much harmful, ridiculous pride comes from reading old things with an eye to publication. Only that keeps me from writing. And yet in reality I have achieved nothing, the disturbance is the best proof of it. In any event, now, after the publication of the book, I will have to stay away from magazines and reviews even more than before, if I do not wish to be content with just sticking the tips of my fingers into the truth. How immovable I have become! Formerly, if I said only one word that opposed the direction of the moment, I at once flew over to the other side, now I simply look at myself and remain as I am. [DI, 266]

August 13: First encounter with Felice Bauer, on a visit from Berlin, in the house of Max Brod's father in Prague.

To Brod, August 14:
Good morning, dear Max. While I was arranging the pieces [for the

volume *Meditation*] yesterday, I was completely under the influence of
the girl [Felice Bauer], as a result it is quite possible that some stupidity
has crept in, some sequence that may strike one as comic only in secret.
Please see if this is so, and let me add my thanks for that, to all the great
thanks I owe you.   [B, 127; Br, 102]
   [*There follows a request for two alterations.*]

   August 14: Manuscript of Meditation *sent to the publisher. To
   Ernst Rowohlt:*
I am enclosing the little prose pieces you wanted to see; they will
probably be enough to make up a small book. While I was putting them
together toward this end, I sometimes had to choose between satisfying
my sense of responsibility and an eagerness to have a book among your
beautiful books. Certainly I did not in each instance make an entirely
clear-cut decision. But now I should naturally be happy if the things
pleased you sufficiently to print them. After all, even with the greatest
skill and the greatest understanding the bad in them is not discernible
at first sight. Isn't what is most universally individual in writers the fact
that each conceals his bad qualities in an entirely different way?

                                                             [DI, 266 f.; Br, 103]

August 15. Again read old diaries instead of keeping away from them. I
live as irrationally as is at all possible. And the publication of the
thirty-one pages is to blame for everything. Even more to blame, of
course, is my weakness, which permits a thing of this sort to influence
me. Instead of shaking myself, I sit here and consider how I could
express all this as insultingly as possible. But my horrible calm interferes with my inventiveness. I am curious as to how I shall find a way
out of this state. I don't permit others to push me, nor do I know which
is "the right path." So what will happen? Have I finally run aground, a
great mass in shallow water? In that case, however, I should at least be
able to turn my head. That's what I do, however.   [DI, 267]

August 20. If Rowohlt would send it back and I could lock it up again as
if it had all never happened, so that I should be only as unhappy as I
was before.

   Miss F.B. When I went to see Brod on August 13th, she was sitting at
the table and yet she looked to me like a domestic. I was not at all
curious about who she was, but rather took her for granted at once.
Bony, empty face that wore its emptiness openly. Bare throat. A blouse
thrown on. Looked very domestic in her dress although, as it later
turned out, she by no means was. (I alienate myself from her a little by

inspecting her so closely.) [. . .] Almost broken nose. Blond, somewhat straight, unattractive hair, strong chin. As I was taking my seat I took a good look at her for the first time, and by the time I was seated I had already formed an unshakable opinion. [DI, 268 f.]

September 15. The hollow that the work of genius has burned into our surroundings is a good place into which to put one's little light. Therefore the inspiration that emanates from genius, the universal inspiration that doesn't only drive one to imitation. [DI, 273]

> *First letter to Felice, from Prague, September 20:*
> My dear Fräulein Bauer,
>   In the likelihood that you no longer have even the remotest recollection of me, I am introducing myself once more: my name is Franz Kafka, and I am the person who greeted you for the first time that evening at Director Brod's [Adolf Brod, father of Max Brod] in Prague, the one who subsequently handed you across the table, one by one, photographs of a Thalia trip [probably a journey to Weimar], and who finally, with the very hand now striking the keys, held your hand, the one which confirmed a promise to accompany him next year to Palestine.
>   Now, if you still wish to undertake this journey—you said at the time you are not fickle, and I saw no signs of it in you—then it will be not only right but absolutely essential for us to start discussing this journey at once. For we shall have to make use of every minute of our holiday, which in any case is far too short, especially for a trip to Palestine, and this we can do only by preparing ourselves as thoroughly as possible and by agreeing on all preparations. [F, 5]

> *In a letter to Felice, October 27, F.K. recollects the first meeting in its minutest details (F, 13 ff.).*

> *The following diary entry is preceded in the manuscript by a draft of "The Judgment," the story that demonstrates the breakthrough of F.K.'s new style.*

September 23. This story, "The Judgment," I wrote at one sitting during the night of the 22nd–23rd, from ten o'clock at night to six o'clock in the morning. I was hardly able to pull my legs out from under the desk, they had got so stiff from sitting. The fearful strain and joy, how the story developed before me, as if I were advancing over water. Several times during this night I heaved my own weight on my back. How everything can be said, how for everything, for the strangest fancies, there waits a great fire in which they perish and rise up again. [. . .] The conviction verified that with my novel-writing [sketches for *Amerika*] I am in the shameful lowlands of writing. Only *in this way* can writing be done, only with such coherence, with such a complete flinging open of body and soul.   [DI, 275 f.]

September 24. My sister said: The house (in the story [*The Judgment*]) is very like ours. I said: How? In that case, then, Father would have to be living in the toilet.   [DI, 277]

    Gustav Janouch reports:
"*I have been reading 'The Judgment.'* "
  "Did you like it?"
  "*Like it? The book is horrifying!*"
  "You are perfectly right."
  "*I should like to know how you came to write it. The dedication, For F., is certainly not merely formal. Surely you wanted the book to say something to someone. I should like to know the context.*"
  F.K. smiled, embarrassed.
  "*I am being impertinent. Forgive me.*"
  "You mustn't apologize. One reads in order to ask questions. 'The Judgment' is the ghost of a night."
  "*What do you mean?*"
  "It is a ghost," *he repeated, with a hard look into the distance.*
  "*And yet you wrote it.*"
  "That is merely the verification, and so the complete exorcism, of the ghost."   [J, 34]

    Years later, to Milena Jesenská, on the occasion of her translation into Czech of "The Judgment":
The translation of the final sentence is very good. Each sentence in this story, each word, each—if I may say so—music is connected with "fear." On this occasion the wound broke open for the first time during one long night and in my opinion the translation catches the connection perfectly, with that magic hand which is yours.   [M, 191]

    On the first reading of "The Judgment":
September 25. Yesterday read at Baum's. [. . .] Toward the end my hand was moving uncontrollably about and actually before my face. There were tears in my eyes. The indubitability of the story was confirmed.
                                          [DI, 278]

See also the letter to Felice, December 4–5, 1912. "The Judgment"
appeared in 1916, in the series Der jüngste Tag. From October
1912 to May 2, 1913, there are (with three exceptions) no entries in
the diary.

Writing as a form of prayer.   [DF, 312]

September–October: Writes "The Stoker," which later became
the first chapter of Amerika.

From Brod's diary notes:
September 29: Kafka is in ecstasy, writes whole nights through. A
novel, set in America. October 1: Kafka in unbelievable ecstasy.
October 2: Kafka is still greatly inspired. One chapter finished. I am
happy about it. October 3: Kafka is doing well. On October 6 he read
me "The Judgment" and "The Stoker," the first chapter of his novel
Amerika.   [B, 128]

To Brod, from Prague, October 8, regarding the family-owned
asbestos factory:
So when mother once more began the same old story this evening, and,
apart from the reference to making my father unhappy and ill by my
behavior, produced the further reason of my brother-in-law's business
journey and the complete desertion of the factory, a wave of bitter-
ness—I don't know if it was only gall—passed through my whole body, I
saw perfectly that I had only the alternatives of either waiting until
everyone had gone to bed and then jumping out of the window, or of
going every day to the factory and sitting in my brother-in-law's office
every day for the next fourteen days. The former would have given me
the opportunity of rejecting all responsibility both for interrupting my
writing and for deserting the factory, the latter would have interrupted
my writing without any doubt—I can't just rub fourteen nights' sleep
out of my eyes—and would leave me, if I had enough strength of will
and hope, the prospect of perhaps being able to begin again where I
stopped today, fourteen days later.
  So I didn't jump out through the window, and also the temptation to
make this letter a letter of farewell (my motives for writing it lie in quite
a different direction) is not very strong. I stood at the window a long
time, and pressed my face against the glass, and I more than once felt
like frightening the toll collector on the bridge by my fall. But I felt too
firm a hold on myself the whole time for the decision to dash myself to
pieces on the pavement to be able to depress me to the necessary level.
It also seemed to me that by staying alive I should interrupt my writing

less—even if one does nothing, nothing, but talk of interruptions—than by dying, and that between the beginning of my novel and its continuation after a fortnight, I might somehow in the factory, in full view of my satisfied parents, move and have my being in the heart of my novel.

My dearest Max, I am putting the whole case before you, not because I want you to judge it, for you are not in a position to have any judgment on it, but since I had firmly decided to jump from my window without writing a letter of farewell—after all, one has the right to be tired just before the end—now that I am going to walk back into my room again as its occupant, I wanted to celebrate it by writing you a long letter of meeting again, and here it is.

And now a last kiss and goodnight, so that tomorrow I can do what they want of me, and be the boss of the factory.   [B, 92 f.; Br, 108 f.]

Brod helped F.K. to be relieved of duties at the factory.

To Felice, October 24:

Undoubtedly these preparations will not help me to overcome the difficulties which writing to you creates, and which again last night kept passing through my head in ever-changing forms. They do not consist of an inability to write what I want to say, which are but the simplest things, but there are so many of them that I cannot accommodate them in either time or space. In recognition of this fact there are times—although only at night—when I long to drop everything, stop writing, and perish by not writing rather than by writing.   [F, 11]

To Felice, November 1:

My life consists, and basically always has consisted, of attempts at writing, mostly unsuccessful. But when I didn't write, I was at once flat on the floor, fit for the dustbin. My energies have always been pitifully weak; even though I didn't quite realize it, it soon became evident that I had to spare myself on all sides, renounce a little everywhere, in order to retain just enough strength for what seemed to me my main purpose. When I didn't do so (oh God, even on a holiday such as this, when I am acting as duty officer, there is no peace, just visitor after visitor, like a little hell let loose) but tried to reach beyond my strength, I was automatically forced back, wounded, humbled, forever weakened; yet this very fact which made me temporarily unhappy is precisely what gave me confidence in the long run, and I began to think that somewhere, however difficult to find, there must be a lucky star under which it would be possible to go on living. I once drew up a detailed list of the things I have sacrificed to writing, as well as the things that were taken from me for the sake of writing, or rather whose loss was only made bearable by this explanation.

Just as I am thin, and I am the thinnest person I know (and that's saying something, for I am no stranger to sanatoria), there is also nothing to me which, in relation to writing, one could call superfluous, superfluous in the sense of overflowing. If there is a higher power that wishes to use me, or does use me, then I am at its mercy, if no more than as a well-prepared instrument. If not, I am nothing, and will suddenly be abandoned in a dreadful void.

Now I have expanded my life to accommodate my thoughts about you, and there is hardly a quarter of an hour of my waking time when I haven't thought about you, and many quarter-hours when I do nothing else. But even this is related to my writing, my life is determined by nothing but the ups and downs of writing, and certainly during a barren period I should never have had the courage to turn to you. This is just as true as it is true that since that evening I have felt as though I had an opening in my chest through which there was an unrestrained drawing-in and drawing-out until one evening in bed, when, by calling to mind a story from the Bible, the necessity of this sensation, as well as the truth of the Bible story, were simultaneously confirmed.

Lately I have found to my amazement how intimately you have now become associated with my writing, although until recently I believed that the only time I did not think about you at all was while I was writing. In one short paragraph I had written, there were, among others, the following references to you and your letters: Someone was given a bar of chocolate. There was talk of small diversions someone had during working hours. Then there was a telephone call. And finally somebody urged someone to go to bed, and threatened to take him straight to his room if he did not obey, which was certainly prompted by the recollection of your mother's annoyance when you stayed so late at the office.—Such passages are especially dear to me; in them I take hold of you, without your feeling it, and therefore without your having to resist. And even if you were to read some of my writings, these little details would surely escape you. But believe me, probably nowhere in the world could you let yourself be caught with greater unconcern than here.

My mode of life is devised solely for writing, and if there are any changes, then only for the sake of perhaps fitting in better with my writing; for time is short, my strength is limited, the office is a horror, the apartment is noisy, and if a pleasant, straightforward life is not possible then one must try to wriggle through by subtle maneuvers. The satisfaction gained by maneuvering one's timetable successfully cannot be compared to the permanent misery of knowing that fatigue of any kind shows itself better and more clearly in writing than anything one is really trying to say. For the past six weeks, with some interruptions in the last few days, due to unbearable weakness, my timetable has been as follows: from 8 to 2 or 2:30 in the office, then lunch till 3 or 3:30, after that sleep in bed (usually only attempts: for a whole week I saw nothing but Montenegrins in my sleep, in extremely disagreeable clarity, which gave me headaches, I saw every detail of their complicated dress) till 7:30, then ten minutes of exercises, naked at the open window, then an hour's walk—alone, with Max, or with another friend, then dinner with my family (I have three sisters, one married, one engaged; the single one, without prejudicing my affection for the others, is easily my favorite); then at 10:30 (but often not till 11:30) I sit down to write, and I go on, depending on my strength, inclination, and luck, until 1, 2, or 3 o'clock, once even till 6 in the morning. Then again exercises, as above, but of course avoiding all exertions, a wash, and then, usually with a slight pain in my heart and twitching stomach muscles, to bed. Then every imaginable effort to get to sleep—i.e., to achieve the impossible, for one cannot sleep (Herr K. even demands dreamless sleep) and at the same time be thinking about one's work and trying to solve with certainty the one question that certainly is insoluble, namely, whether there will be a letter from you the next day, and at what time. Thus the night consists of two parts: one wakeful, the other sleepless, and if I were to tell you about it at length and you were prepared to listen, I should never finish. So it is hardly surprising if, at the office the next morning, I only just manage to start work with what little strength is left. In one of the corridors along which I always walk to reach my typist, there used to be a coffinlike trolley for the moving of files and documents, and each time I passed it I felt as though it had been made for me, and was waiting for me.   [F, 20 ff.]

To Felice, November 3:
You actually told me then, and I don't understand how I could have forgotten, that staying alone in a hotel made you feel uncomfortable. I probably replied that I on the contrary felt very much at ease in a hotel room. This really is a fact; I noticed it particularly last year, when I had to travel for some time in the depths of winter through towns and villages in northern Bohemia. To have to oneself the expanse of a hotel room with its easily surveyed four walls and a door that can be locked; the knowledge that specific items of one's belongings are tucked away into specific corners of cupboards, on tables and coat hangers, always gives me a vague sensation of a new, unspent existence charged with vigor and destined for better things, which may of course be nothing but a despair driven beyond itself and finding itself at home in the cold grave of a hotel room. In any case, I have always felt at ease in them,

and of almost all hotel rooms I have stayed in I have nothing but good
to report.   [F, 25]

To Felice, November 5:
Above all, you would take a different view of my writing and my
attitude to writing, and would no longer advise moderation. Human
weakness alone provides enough moderation. Shouldn't I stake all I
have on the one thing I can do? What a hopeless fool I should be if I
didn't! My writing may be worthless; in which case, I am definitely and
without doubt utterly worthless. If I spare myself in this respect, I am
not really sparing myself, I am committing suicide. By the way, how old
do you think I am? There may have been some talk about it that
evening, I don't know, but perhaps you did not notice.   [F, 28]

To Felice, November 9:
You are not to write to me again, nor will I write to you. I would be
bound to make you unhappy by writing to you, and as for me I am
beyond help. To realize this I need not have counted the striking of the
clock all through the night; I was well aware of it before writing my first
letter to you. If I attempted, nevertheless, to tie myself to you I should
deserve to be cursed, were I not cursed already.—If you want me to
return your letters, of course I shall do so, much as I should like to keep
them. But if you insist on having them, send me a blank postcard as a
sign that you do. I on the other hand beg you to keep my letters.—Now
quickly forget the ghost that I am, and go on living happily and peacefully as before.   [F, 33 f.]
    *F.K. did not send this letter; the draft was found among his
    papers.*

To Felice, November 11:
I am going to write only short letters from now on (on Sundays, however, I shall always allow myself the luxury of an enormous letter), but
also because I want to spend every ounce of myself on my novel, which
after all belongs to you as well, or rather it should give you a clearer
idea of the good in me than the mere hints in the longest letters of the
longest lifetime. The story I am writing, designed, I fear, in such a
manner that it will never be completed, is called, to give you an ap-
proximate idea, "The Man Who Disappeared" [*Amerika*], and takes
place entirely in the United States of America. So far 5 chapters are
completed, the 6th almost. [. . .] After 15 years of despairing effort
(except for rare moments), this is the first major work in which, for the
past 6 weeks, I have felt confidence. It must be completed, as I feel sure
you will agree, and so, with your blessing, I would like to transfer the

brief periods I otherwise spend on writing inaccurate, alarmingly incomplete, imprudent, dangerous letters to you, to this task around
which, until now at any rate, everything, no matter what and from
where it came, has calmed down and taken the right turning. Do you
agree? And you won't abandon me to the terrible loneliness I feel in
spite of all this? Dearest Fräulein Felice, what would I not give to be
able to look into your eyes at this moment!   [F, 35 f.]

To Felice, November 11:
I am now going to ask you a favor which sounds quite crazy, and which
I should regard as such, were I the one to receive the letter. It is also the
very greatest test that even the kindest person could be put to. Well,
this is it:
Write to me only once a week, so that your letter arrives on Sunday—for I cannot endure your daily letters, I am incapable of enduring
them. For instance, I answer one of your letters, then lie in bed in
apparent calm, but my heart beats through my entire body and is
conscious only of you. I belong to you; there is really no other way of
expressing it, and that is not strong enough. But for this very reason I
don't want to know what you are wearing; it confuses me so much that
I cannot deal with life; and that's why I don't want to know that you are
fond of me. If I did, how could I, fool that I am, go on sitting in my office,
or here at home, instead of leaping onto a train with my eyes shut and
opening them only when I am with you? Oh, there is a sad, sad reason
for not doing so. To make it short: My health is only just good enough
for myself alone, not good enough for marriage, let alone fatherhood.
Yet when I read your letter, I feel I could overlook even what cannot
possibly be overlooked.   [F, 37]

Brod to Felice, November 15:
*All I ask is that you should make allowances for Franz and his often
pathological sensitivity. He responds entirely to the mood of the moment. Altogether he is a man who wants nothing but the absolute, the
ultimate in all things. He is never prepared to compromise. For example, when he does not feel fully in possession of all his faculties for
work, he is capable of not writing a single line for months on end rather
than content himself with work he considers second best. And as with
his writing, so with everything else. That is why he often appears
moody, eccentric, etc. But from my profound knowledge of his character I know that this is not the case. When it comes to the point he is
even very clever and sensible in practical matters. But when it comes
to ideals he cannot take things lightly; in such matters he is terribly
severe, above all with himself; and since he is physically not very*

strong and the circumstances of his daily life (the office!!) are not favorable, conflicts arise which one must try and help him to overcome with understanding and kindness, aware that such a unique and wonderful human being deserves to be treated in a different way from the millions of banal and commonplace people.   [F, 43]

November–December: Writing The Metamorphosis; the first indication occurs in a letter to Felice. In the letters up to December 6–7, "story" refers to this work.

To Felice, November 17:
Once again I haven't answered anything, but answers have to be given orally; in writing one doesn't achieve much, at most a foretaste of happiness. Anyway, I shall be writing to you again today, though I still have to do a lot of running around, not to mention a short story that occurred to me in bed in my misery, and now troubles me and demands to be written.   [F, 47]

To Felice, November 18:
My dearest, it's 1:30 at night, the story I mentioned is by no means finished, not a line of the novel has been written today, and I go to bed with little enthusiasm. If only the night were free to keep pen to paper and I could write straight through to the morning! That would be a good night.   [F, 47]

To Felice, November 18:
I am just sitting down to yesterday's story with an overwhelming desire to pour myself into it, which obviously springs from despair. Beset by many problems, uncertain of you, quite incapable of coping at the office, my novel [Amerika] at a standstill for a day, with a fierce longing to continue the new, equally demanding story, all but total insomnia for the last few days and nights, as well as some minor but nevertheless worrying and irritating things going around in my head.   [F, 49]

To Felice, November 21:
I have always looked upon my parents as persecutors; until about a year ago I was indifferent to them and perhaps to the world at large, as some kind of lifeless thing, but I see now it was only suppressed fear, worry, and unhappiness. All parents want to do is drag one down to them, back to the old days from which one longs to free oneself and escape; they do it out of love, of course, and that's what makes it so horrible.   [F, 55]

Brod to Felice, November 22:

Franz's mother loves him very much, but she has not the faintest idea who her son is and what his needs are. Literature is a "pastime"! My God! As though it did not eat our hearts out, willing victims though we are.—Frau Kafka and I have often had words over this. All the love in the world is useless when there is total lack of understanding. [. . .]

If his parents love him so much, why don't they give him 30,000 gulden as they would to a daughter, so that he could leave the office, go off to some cheap little place on the Riviera to create those works that God, using Franz's brain, wishes the world to have.—So long as Franz is not in a position to do this, he will never be entirely happy. His whole disposition cries out for a peaceful, trouble-free existence dedicated to writing. In the present circumstances his life is a kind of vegetating, with a few bright moments.—You will now more readily understand his nervousness.   [F, 57]

To Felice, November 23:

Dearest, oh God, how I love you! It is very late at night; I have put aside my little story, on which I really haven't worked at all these last two evenings, and which is quietly developing into a much bigger story. How could I give it to you to read, even if it were finished? It is rather illegible, and even if that weren't an obstacle—up to now I certainly haven't spoiled you with beautiful writing—I don't want to send you anything to read. I want to read it to you. Yes, that would be lovely, to read this story to you, while I would have to hold your hand, for the story is a little frightening. It is called *Metamorphosis*, and it would thoroughly scare you, you might not want to hear a word of it, for alas! I scare you enough every day with my letters.   [F, 57 f.]

November 24: *A reading of parts of the still unfinished* The Metamorphosis *at Oskar Baum's.*

To Felice, November 24:

Dearest, once again I am putting aside this exceptionally repulsive story in order to refresh myself by thinking of you. By now it is more than half finished, and on the whole I am not too dissatisfied; but it is infinitely repulsive, and these things, you see, spring from the same heart in which you dwell and which you tolerate as a dwelling place. But don't be unhappy about it, for who knows, the more I write and the more I liberate myself, the cleaner and the worthier of you I may become, but no doubt there is a great deal more to be got rid of, and the nights can never be long enough for this business which, incidentally, is highly voluptuous.   [F, 58]

To Felice, November 28:

I am especially frightened of tears. I cannot cry. To me other people's tears are a strange, incomprehensible phenomenon. In the course of many years I have cried only once, that was two or three months ago; but then I was literally shaking in my armchair, twice in quick succession; I was afraid my uncontrollable sobs would wake my parents next door; it happened at night and was brought about by a particular passage in my novel.   [F, 72]

To Felice, night of November 29–30:

My work moreover has been so bad that I don't deserve any sleep, and should be condemned to spend the rest of the night looking out of the window. Can you understand this, dearest: to write badly, yet feel compelled to write, or abandon oneself to total despair! To have to atone for the joys of good writing in this terrible way! In fact, not to be really unhappy, not to be pierced by a fresh stab of unhappiness, but to see the pages being covered endlessly with things one hates, that fill one with loathing, or at any rate with dull indifference, that nevertheless have to be written down in order that one shall live. Disgusting! If only I could destroy the pages I have written in the last 4 days, as though they had never been.   [F, 76]

With an invitation to a reading at the Herder Association in Prague, to Felice, November 30:

I enclose an invitation to a reading. I shall be reading your short story ["The Judgment"]. Believe me, you will be there, even if you stay in Berlin. To appear in public with your story, and thus as it were with you, will be a strange feeling. The story is sad and painful, and no one will be able to explain my happy face during the reading.   [F, 78]

To Felice, December 3:

Dearest, I really should have gone on writing all night. It would have been my duty, for I am nearing the end of my little story, and uniformity and the fire of consecutive hours would do this end an immense amount of good. And who knows whether I shall be able to write tomorrow after the reading—I curse it now. Nevertheless, I am stopping, I dare not risk it. It is not so long since I started writing regularly and continuously, but since then I have turned from a by no means exemplary, but in some ways rather useful employee (my present rank is Draftsman) into a nightmare to my chief. My desk at the office was certainly never tidy, but now it is littered with a chaotic pile of papers and files; I may just know the things that lie on top, but lower down I suspect nothing but horrors. Sometimes I think I can almost hear myself being ground down, by my writing on the one hand, by the office on the other. At other times I keep them both reasonably well balanced, especially when my writing at home has gone badly, but this ability (not the ability to write badly) is, I'm afraid, gradually declining.   [F. 84]

To Felice, night of December 4–5:
You don't even know your little story ["The Judgment"] yet. It is somewhat wild and meaningless and if it didn't express some inner truth (which can never be universally established, but has to be accepted or denied every time by each reader or listener in turn), it would be nothing. It is also hard to imagine how, being so short (17 typewritten pages), it could have so many faults; and I really don't know what right I have to dedicate to you such a very doubtful creation. But we each give what we can, I the little story with myself as an appendage, you the immense gift of your love. Oh dearest, how happy I am through you; tears of happiness mingled with the single tear the end of your story brought to my eyes.   [F. 86 f.]

To Felice, December 6–7 (or, probably, December 5–6):
Cry, dearest, cry, the time for crying has come! The hero of my story died a little while ago. To comfort you, I want you to know that he died peacefully enough and reconciled to all. The story itself is still not quite finished; I am not in the right mood just now, and am leaving the end until tomorrow. Moreover, it's very late; it took me so long to recover from yesterday's disturbance. It's a pity that in some passages of the story my state of exhaustion and other interruptions and extraneous worries are so apparent; I know it could have been done more neatly; this is particularly conspicuous in the more tender passages. That is the ever-gnawing realization: in more favorable circumstances, with the creative powers I feel within me, and quite apart from their strength and endurance, I could have achieved a neater, more telling, better-constructed piece of work than the one that now exists. This is a feeling which no amount of reasoning can dispel, though of course it is reason, too, that is right in saying that since there are no circumstances other than real ones, one cannot take any others into account, either. However that may be, I hope to finish the story tomorrow, and to return to the novel the following day.   [F. 89]

At the conclusion of The Metamorphosis, *to Felice, December 6–7:*
Dearest, now listen, my little story is finished, but today's ending does not please me at all, it really could have been better, there is no doubt about this. The thought that immediately follows upon my distress is

inevitably: I have still got you, dearest, a second justification for living, but then it is shameful to draw one's justification for living entirely from the existence of one's beloved.   [F, 91]

To Felice, December 9–10:
Please don't look upon me as some kind of prodigy; for our love's sake, don't do it. For it would look as though you wished to push me away from yourself. Insofar as I have to rely upon myself, and as long as you are nowhere near me, I am basically a very feeble and unhappy man; the things that are unusual about me are largely bad and sad, and consist mainly—as you rightly suspected at the beginning of your letter, without thinking it through to its conclusion—of the fact that, although able to go on a pointless trip to Leitmeritz, I am unable to come to Berlin with the most definite objective. Dearest, draw me as close to you as this unfortunate peculiarity of mine permits. And don't talk about the greatness hidden in me, or do you think there is something great about spending a two-day interruption of my writing in permanent fear of never being able to write again, a fear, by the way, that this evening has proved to be not altogether unfounded?   [F, 97]

To Felice, December 11, with a copy of Meditation:
Please be kind to my poor book! It consists of the very pages you saw me putting in order that evening. At the time you were not "considered worthy" to inspect them, you dear, crazy, vindictive one! Now it belongs to you exclusively; only jealousy could make me snatch it from your hand, so as to be the only one to be held by you and not to have to share my place with an unimportant old book. I wonder if you notice how the various pieces differ in age. One of them for example is certainly 8 to 10 years old. Show the book to as few people as possible, so as to avoid having your mind about me changed.
    Goodnight, dearest, goodnight.   [F, 100]
    Twice more F.K. refers to this work; there was no noticeable reaction on the part of Felice.

To Felice, night of December 11–12:
Anyway I was in complete discord with myself today, owing to having done no writing for so long, and did not write to you this afternoon partly for lack of time, but also because you will get my book at 10 o'clock, and also because the calm exchange of one letter a day would be best for both of us—but above all because of my terrible general disinclination and lassitude—due to not writing—and because I said to myself that it shouldn't be necessary to pour out in one long stream every momentary unhappiness, you much-tormented girl. But now,

this evening, I had the chance to write, which my whole nature has been irrefutably demanding—if not directly, then with an inward-spreading despair; but I write barely enough to let me survive another day, and remain lazily sitting back, in comfortable lassitude, as though slowly bleeding to death. How gloomily I should have gone to bed if it weren't for you, dearest, to whom I can direct my feeble words, and from whom I shall get them back ten times as strong. However, from now on I shall not leave my work for a single evening, and from tomorrow will immerse myself more deeply.   [F, 101]

To Felice, night of December 15–16:
Well, dearest, the doors are shut, all is quiet, I am with you once more. How many things does "to be with you" mean by now? I have not slept all day, and while I duly went about all the afternoon and early evening with a heavy head and a befogged brain, now, as night sets in, I am almost excited, feel within me a tremendous desire to write; the demon inhabiting the writing urge begins to stir at most inopportune moments. Let him, I'll go to bed. But if I could spend Christmas writing and sleeping, dearest, that would be wonderful!   [F, 107]

To Felice, December 20–21:
Tomorrow I shall start to write again, I want to delve into it with all my strength; when not writing I feel myself being pushed out of life by unyielding hands. And perhaps tomorrow I shall have a more cheerful letter than today's *but an equally truthful one:* for considerateness hurts me more than the truth.   [F, 116]

To Felice, December 29–30:
Not to write, and yet to have an urge, an urge, a screaming urge to write!
    By the way, now I know more precisely why yesterday's letter made me so jealous: You don't like my book [*Meditation*] any more than you liked my photograph. This really wouldn't matter, for what is written there is largely old stuff, but nevertheless still a part of me, hence a part of me unknown to you. But this wouldn't matter at all, I feel your presence so acutely in everything else that I should be quite pre-pared—provided you are very close to me—to be the *first* to kick the little book aside with *my* foot. If you love me in the present, the past can abide where it will, if necessary as far removed as fears for the future. But why don't you tell me, tell me in two words, that you don't like it!—You wouldn't have to say you don't like it (which probably wouldn't be true anyway), but simply that you can't make head or tail of it. It really is full of hopeless confusion, or rather there are glimpses into endless perplexities, and one has to come very close to see any-

thing at all. And so it would be quite understandable if you did not like the book, but hope would remain that at some favorable and weak moment it might yet entice you. In any case, no one will know what to make of it, that is and was perfectly clear to me; the trouble the spendthrift publisher took and the money he lost, both utterly wasted, prey on my mind too. Its publication came about quite by chance, perhaps I will tell you about it some time; it would never have occurred to me on my own. I am telling you all this simply to make it clear to you that an uncertain opinion on your part would have seemed quite natural to me. [. . .] Dearest. look, I do want to feel that you turn to me with everything; nothing, not the slightest thing should be withheld, for we belong—or so I thought—together; I may not like a favorite blouse of yours as such, but because you are wearing it, I will like it; you don't like my book as such, but insofar as it is I who wrote it you will surely like it—well, then one should say so, and say *both*.

[. . .] It's not like that here; my mother is my father's devoted slave, and my father her devoted tyrant, which is fundamentally why there has always been perfect harmony, and the sorrows we have all shared, particularly in the last few years, are due entirely to my father's ill health; he suffers from hardening of the arteries, but because of the existing harmony this could not really touch the innermost core of the family.

At this very moment my father next door is turning over violently in bed. He is a big, strong man; fortunately he has been feeling better recently, but his illness is an ever-threatening one. The family's harmony is really upset only by me, and more so as the years go by; very often I don't know what to do, and feel a great sense of guilt toward my parents and everyone else. Thus I too have my share of suffering, my dearest distant girl, within and through my family, except that I deserve it more than you. On more than one occasion in the past, I have stood by the window at night playing with the catch, feeling it almost my duty to open the window and throw myself out. But that is long past, and now the knowledge of your love has made me a more confident person than I have ever been before.   [F, 132 f.]

To Felice, December 31, 1912, to January 1, 1913:
In your last letter there is a sentence you have written once before, and so have I: "We belong together unconditionally." That, dearest, is true a thousandfold; now, for instance, in these first hours of the New Year I could have no greater and no crazier wish than that we should be bound together inseparably by the wrists of your left and my right hand. I don't quite know why this should occur to me; perhaps because

a book on the French Revolution, with contemporary accounts, is lying in front of me, and it may be possible after all—not that I have read or heard of it anywhere—that a couple thus bound together were once led to the scaffold.—But what is all this that's racing through my head which, by the way, has remained completely closed to my poor novel today? That's the 13 in the new year's date. But the finest 13 won't prevent me from drawing you, my dearest, closer, closer, closer to me. Where are you at this moment? From whose company am I drawing you away?

[F, 136 f.]

Diary, December 25, 1915, looking back upon 1912:
Always this one principal anguish: If I had gone away in 1912, in full possession of all my forces, with a clear head, not eaten by the strain of keeping down living forces!

[DII, 145]

1913

From "The Judgment"

"Because she lifted up her skirts," his father began to flute, "because she lifted her skirts like this, the nasty creature," and mimicking her he lifted his shirt so high that one could see the scar on his thigh from his war wound, "because she lifted her skirts like this and this you made up to her, and in order to make free with her undisturbed you have disgraced your mother's memory, betrayed your friend, and stuck your father into bed so that he can't move. But he can move, or can't he?"

The Penal Colony, p. 60

January: Publication of Meditation, *F.K.'s first publication in book form. He continues working on* Amerika.

To Felice, January 2–3:
Dearest, whatever happens I implore you, with hands raised in supplication, not to be jealous of my novel. If the people in my novel get wind of your jealousy, they will run away from me; as it is, I am holding on to them only by the ends of their sleeves. And imagine, if they run away from me I shall have to run after them, even as far as the underworld, where of course they really are at home. The novel is me, my stories are me—where, I ask you, would there be the tiniest corner for jealousy? In any case, when everything else goes well, all my characters come running arm in arm toward you, ultimately to serve you alone. I would certainly not detach myself from my novel even in your presence; it wouldn't do me any good if I could, for it is through writing that I keep a hold on life [. . .]. Bear in mind, dearest Felice, once I lose my writing, I am bound to lose you and everything else.   [F, 138]

To Felice, January 7:
In any case, ever since my childhood a minor, fleeting illness has always been a much coveted but rarely achieved pleasure. It breaks the inexorable passage of time, and bestows on this worn-out, dragged-out, dragged-along being that one is a minor rebirth, which I am now really beginning to crave.   [F, 145]

To Felice, January 8–9:

I can also laugh, Felice, have no doubt about this; I am even known as a great laugher, although in this respect I used to be far crazier than I am now. It even happened to me once, at a solemn meeting with our [Institute's] president [Dr. Otto Příbram]—it was two years ago, but the story will outlive me at the office—that I started to laugh, and how! It would be too involved to describe to you this man's importance; but believe me, it is very great: an ordinary employee thinks of this man as not on this earth, but in the clouds. And as we usually have little opportunity of talking to the Emperor, contact with this man is for the average clerk—a situation common of course to all large organizations—tantamount to meeting the Emperor. Needless to say, like anyone exposed to clear and general scrutiny whose position does not quite correspond to his achievements, this man invites ridicule; but to allow oneself to be carried away by laughter at something so commonplace and, what's more, in the presence of the great man himself, one must be out of one's mind. At that time we, two colleagues and I, had just been promoted, and in our formal black suits had to express our thanks to the president—here I must not forget to add that for a special reason I owed the president special gratitude. The most dignified of us (I was the youngest) made the speech of thanks—short, sensible, dashing, in accordance with his character. The president listened in his usual posture adopted for solemn occasions, somewhat reminiscent of our Emperor when giving audience—which, if one happens to be in a certain mood, is a terribly funny pose. Legs lightly crossed, left hand clenched and resting on the very corner of the table, head lowered so that the long white beard curves on his chest, and, on top of all this, his not excessively large but nevertheless protruding stomach gently swaying. I must have been in a very uncontrolled mood at the time, for I knew this posture well enough, and it was quite unreasonable for me to be attacked by fits of the giggles (albeit with interruptions), which so far however could easily be taken as due to a tickle in the throat, especially as the president did not look up. My colleague's clear voice, eyes fixed straight ahead—he was no doubt aware of my condition, without being affected by it—still kept me in check. But at the end of my colleague's speech the president raised his head, and then for a moment I was seized with terror, without laughter, for now he could see my expression and easily ascertain that the sound unfortunately escaping from my mouth was definitely not a cough. But when he began his speech, again the usual one, all too familiar, in the imperial mold, delivered with great conviction, a totally meaningless and unnecessary speech; and when my colleague with sidelong glances tried to warn me (I was doing everything in my power to control myself), and in so doing reminded me vividly of the joys of my earlier laughter, I could no longer restrain myself and all hope that I should ever be able to do so vanished. At first I laughed only at the president's occasional delicate little jokes; but while it is a rule only to contort one's features respectfully at these little jokes, I was already laughing out loud; observing my colleagues' alarm at being infected by it, I felt more sorry for them than for myself, but I couldn't help it; I didn't even try to avert or cover my face, but in my helplessness continued to stare straight at the president, incapable of turning my head, probably on the instinctive assumption that everything could only get worse rather than better, and that therefore it would be best to avoid any change. And now that I was in full spate, I was of course laughing not only at the current jokes, but at those of the past and the future and the whole lot together, and by then no one knew what I was really laughing about. A general embarrassment set in; only the president remained relatively unconcerned, as behooves a great man accustomed to the ways of the world and to whom the possibility of irreverence toward his person would not even occur. Had we been able to slip out at this moment (the president had evidently shortened his speech a little), everything might still have gone fairly well; no doubt my behavior would have remained discourteous, but this discourtesy would not have been mentioned, and the whole affair, as sometimes happens with apparently impossible situations, might have been dealt with by a conspiracy of silence between the four of us. But unfortunately my colleague, the one hitherto unmentioned (a man close to 40, a heavy beer drinker with a round, childish, but bearded face), started to make a totally unexpected little speech. At that moment this struck me as quite incomprehensible; my laughter had made him lose his composure, he had stood there with cheeks blown out with suppressed laughter—and now he embarked on a serious speech. Actually this was quite consistent with his character. Empty-headed and impetuous, he is capable of defending generally accepted statements, passionately and at length, and the boredom of this kind of speech, without the absurd but engaging passion, would be intolerable. Now, the president in all innocence had said something to which this colleague of mine took exception. In addition, influenced by my continuous laughter, he may have forgotten where he was; in short, he assumed the moment had come to air his particular views and to convince the president (a man utterly indifferent to other people's opinions). So now, as he started to hold forth, brandishing his arms, about something absurdly childish (even in general, but here in particular), it was too much for me: the world, the semblance of the world which hitherto I had seen before me, dissolved completely, and I burst into loud and uninhibited laughter of such heartiness as perhaps only schoolchildren at their desks are capable of. A silence fell, and now at last my laughter and I were the acknowledged center of attention. While I laughed my knees of course shook with fear, and my colleagues on their part could join in to their hearts' content, but they could never match the full horror of my long-rehearsed and -practiced laughter, and thus they remained comparatively unnoticed. Beating my breast with my right hand, partly in awareness of my sin (remembering the Day of Atonement), and partly to drive out all the suppressed laughter, I produced innumerable excuses for my behavior, all of which might have been very convincing had not the renewed outbursts of laughter rendered them completely unintelligible. By now of course even the president was disconcerted; and in a manner typical only of people born with an instinct for smoothing things out, he found some phrase that offered some reasonable explanation for my howls—I think an allusion to a joke he had made a long time before. He then hastily dismissed us. Undefeated, roaring with laughter yet desperately unhappy, I was the first to stagger out of the hall.—By writing a letter to the president immediately afterwards and through the good offices of one of the president's sons whom I know well, and thanks also to the passage of time, the whole thing calmed down considerably. Needless to say, I did not achieve complete absolution, nor shall I ever achieve it. But this matters little; I may have behaved in this fashion at the time simply in order to prove to you later that I am capable of laughter.

[F, 146 ff.]

To Felice, January 10–11 (or, probably, January 9–10):
My poor dearest writing sales letters! Do I get one too, though I'm not a buyer? Although, if anything, I am fundamentally frightened of Parlographs? A machine with its silent, serious demands strikes me as exercising a greater, more cruel compulsion on one's capacities than any human being. How insignificant, how easy to control, to send away, to shout down, upbraid, question, or stare at, a living typist is! He who dictates is master, but faced with a Parlograph he is degraded and becomes a factory worker whose brain has to serve a whirring machine. Think how a long chain of thought is forced out of the poor, naturally slow-working brain! You're lucky, dearest, not to have to reply to these objections in your sales letter; they are irrefutable. That the speed of the machine is easy to regulate, that one can put it away when one doesn't feel like dictating, etc., is no refutation of this argument, for the fact that all this does not help is part of the nature of the man who makes these objections.   [F, 149]

January 12: Marriage of Valli Kafka to Josef Pollak. To Felice, January 10–11:

At the very moment you read this letter I may be driving to the syna-gogue—wearing my old tailcoat, cracked patent-leather shoes, a top hat far too small for me, and with an unusually pale* face (because nowa-days I always take so long to get to sleep) in my position as an usher sitting next to a pleasant, pretty, elegant, and above all very consider-ate and modest cousin—where the marriage will be solemnized with that tremendous solemnity that upsets me every time. Because the Jewish public in general, here at any rate, have limited the religious ceremonies to weddings and funerals, these two occasions have drawn grimly close to each other, and one can virtually see the reproachful glances of a withering faith.

* ["unusually pale" crossed out. Between the lines] This is just co-quetry, I look exactly as I always do and as I did last August.   [F, 151]

To Felice, January 14–15:

You once said you would like to sit beside me while I write. Listen, in that case I could not write (I can't do much, anyway), but in that case I could not write at all. For writing means revealing onself to excess; that utmost of self-revelation and surrender, in which a human being, when involved with others, would feel he was losing himself, and from which, therefore, he will always shrink as long as he is in his right mind—for everyone wants to live as long as he is alive—even that degree of self-revelation and surrender is not enough for writing. Writing that springs from the surface of existence—when there is no other way and the deeper wells have dried up—is nothing, and col-lapses the moment a truer emotion makes that surface shake. This is why one can never be alone enough when one writes, why there can never be enough silence around one when one writes, why even night is not night enough. This is why there is never enough time at one's disposal, for the roads are long and it is easy to go astray, there are even times when one becomes afraid and has the desire—even without any constraint or enticement—to run back (a desire always severely pun-ished later on), how much more so if one were suddenly to receive a kiss from the most beloved lips! I have often thought that the best mode of life for me would be to sit in the innermost room of a spacious locked cellar with my writing things and a lamp. Food would be brought and always put down far away from my room, outside the cellar's outermost door. The walk to my food, in my dressing gown, through the vaulted cellars, would be my only exercise. I would then return to my table, eat slowly and with deliberation, then start writing again at once. And how I would write! From what depths I would drag it up! Without effort! For extreme concentration knows no effort. The trouble is that I might not be able to keep it up for long, and at the first failure—which perhaps even in these circumstances could not be avoided—would be bound to end in a grandiose fit of madness.   [F, 155 f.]

To Felice, January 15–16:

It is still comparatively early today, but I do want to lie down soon, for I had to pay for yesterday's relatively good work with headaches lasting all day (these headaches are actually an invention of the past two months, if not entirely of the year 1913) and with dreams exploding in my uneasy sleep. It's a long time since I managed to write well on two successive evenings. What a mass of erratic writing this novel [Amerika] will be! Once the first draft is completed, what a difficult, perhaps impossible, task it will be to bring the dead sections at least partially to life! And much that is wrong will have to remain, for no help is forthcoming from out of the depths.   [F, 156]

To Felice, January 16:

The thing is that [Martin] Buber is lecturing on the Jewish Myth;[1] it would take more than Buber to get me out of my room, I have heard him before, I find him dreary; no matter what he says, something is missing. (No doubt he knows a lot, there were some Chinese Ghost and Love Stories,[2] which are wonderful, at least the ones I know.) But after Buber, [Gertrud] Eysoldt will be reading, and it is entirely on her account that I am going. Have you ever heard her?   [F, 157 f.]

To Felice, January 19:

Dearest, take me to you, hold me, don't lose faith; the days cast me back and forth; you must realize that you will never get unadulterated happiness from me; only as much unadulterated suffering as one could wish for, and yet—don't send me away. I am tied to you not by love alone, love would not be much, love begins, love comes, passes, and comes again; but this need, by which I am utterly chained to your being, this remains. So you too, dearest, must remain. And don't write any more letters like the last but one. [. . .]

I also talked to Buber yesterday; as a person he is lively and simple and remarkable, and seems to have no connection with the tepid things he has written.   [F, 161]

To Felice, January 21:

This morning before getting up and after a very fitful night's sleep, I was so sad that in my sadness I longed not to throw myself (that would have been too high-spirited for my sadness) but to spill myself out of the window.

But now that I have your letter I hasten to propose to you, dearest, that we never again hold anything against each other, since neither of us can be held responsible. The distance is so great, the perpetual overcoming of it so tormenting, that one sometimes lets oneself go and for a moment cannot pull oneself together. Then add to this my wretched disposition which knows but three possibilities: to burst forth, collapse, or pine away. And my life consists of a succession of these three possibilities. My poor admirable dearest, who has got herself involved in such a turmoil! I belong to you entirely; this much I can say as a result of surveying my 30 years of life.   [F. 164]

To Felice, for January 26:
I want you to know, dearest, that I think of you with such love and concern, as though God had entrusted you to me in most unequivocal terms.   [F. 171]

To Felice, January 28-29:
My powers of reasoning are incredibly limited; to sense the development in the results, that I can do; but to ascend from the development to the results or step by step to reconstruct it from the results, that is not given to me. It is as though I were falling down upon these things, and caught sight of them only in the confusion of my fall.
                                                    [F, 174 f.]

February to July 1913: Lacuna in productivity.

To Felice, February 9-10 (or, probably, February 7-8):
I am sitting down to write in a state of some confusion; I have been reading a lot of different things that are merging into one another, and if one hopes to find a solution for oneself by this kind of reading, one is mistaken; one comes up against a wall, and cannot proceed. Your life is so very different, dearest. Except in relation to your fellow men, have you ever known uncertainty? Have you ever observed how, within yourself and independent of other people, diverse possibilities open up in several directions, thereby actually creating a ban on your every movement? Have you ever, without giving the slightest thought to anyone else, been in despair simply about yourself? Desperate enough to throw yourself on the ground and remain there beyond the Day of Judgment? How devout are you? You go to the synagogue; but I dare say you have not been recently. And what is it that sustains you, the idea of Judaism or of God? Are you aware, and this is the most important thing, of a continuous relationship between yourself and a reassuringly distant, if possibly infinite height or depth? He who feels this

continuously has no need to roam about like a lost dog, mutely gazing around with imploring eyes; he never need yearn to slip into a grave as if it were a warm sleeping bag and life a cold winter night; and when climbing the stairs to his office he never need imagine that he is careering down the well of the staircase, flickering in the uncertain light, twisting from the speed of his fall, shaking his head with impatience.

[F, 185 f.]

To Felice, February 9–10, on Kleist's Michael Kohlhaas: This is a story I read with true piety; it carries me along on waves of wonder, and if it weren't for the rather weak, in part carelessly written ending, it would be a thing of perfection, the kind of perfection I like to maintain does not exist. (For I believe that even the greatest works of literature have a little tail of human frailty which, if one is on the lookout for it, begins to wag slightly and disturbs the sublime, godlike quality of the whole.)

[F, 187]

February 11. While I read the proofs of "The Judgment," I'll write down all the relationships that have become clear to me in the story as far as I now remember them. This is necessary because the story came out of me like a real birth, covered with filth and slime, and only I have the hand that can reach to the body itself and that cares to do so:

The friend is the link between father and son, he is their strongest common bond. Sitting alone at his window, Georg takes a sensual pleasure in this consciousness of what they have in common, believes he has his father within him, and would be at peace with everything if it were not for a fleeting, sad hesitation. In the course of the story the father, with the strengthened position that the other, lesser things they share in common give him—the mother's love and devotion, loyalty to her memory, the clientele that he (the father) had been the first to acquire for the business—uses the common bond of the friend to set himself up as Georg's antagonist. Georg has nothing; the bride, who lives in the story only in relation to the friend, that is, to what father and son have in common, is easily driven away by the father since no marriage has yet taken place, and so she cannot penetrate the circle of blood relationship that is drawn around father and son. What they have in common is built up entirely around the father, Georg can feel it only as something foreign, something that has become independent, that he has never given enough protection, that is exposed to Russian revolutions, and only because he himself has lost everything except his awareness of the father does the judgment, which closes off his father from him completely, have so strong an effect on him.

Georg has the same number of letters as Franz. In Bendemann,

"mann" is a strengthening of "Bende" [bonds] to provide for all the as yet unforeseen possibilities in the story. But Bende has the same number of letters as Kafka, and the vowel e occurs in the same places as does the vowel a in Kafka.

Frieda has as many letters as F. and the same initial, Brandenfeld has the same initial as B., and in the word "Feld" a certain connection in meaning, as well. Perhaps even the thought of Berlin was not without influence and the recollection of the Brandenburg province perhaps had some influence.   [DI, 278 f.]

To Felice, February 12–13, on the poetess Else Lasker-Schüler:
Finally in yesterday's letter Lasker-Schüler was mentioned, and today you ask about her. I cannot bear her poems; their emptiness makes me feel nothing but boredom, and their contrived verbosity nothing but antipathy. Her prose I find just as tiresome and for the same reasons; it is the work of an indiscriminate brain twitching in the head of an overwrought city-dweller. But I may be quite wrong; many people love her, including Werfel, who talks of her with genuine enthusiasm. Yes, she is in a bad way; I believe her second husband has left her; they are collecting for her here, too; I had to give 5 kronen, without feeling the slightest sympathy for her. I don't quite know why, but I always imagine her simply as a drunk, dragging herself through the coffeehouses at night.   [F, 191]

To Felice, February 14–15, on Brod's review of Meditation:
This afternoon I could have done with a hole to disappear into; for in the current issue of *März* I read Max's review of my book; I knew it was coming out, but had not seen it. A few reviews have already appeared, needless to say all of them by friends, valueless in their exaggerated praise, valueless in their comments, and explicable only as a sign of misguided friendship, an overrating of the printed word, a misunderstanding of the general public's attitude to literature. Ultimately that is what, on the whole, they have in common with the majority of reviews, and if they did not act as a sad though quickly spent spur to one's vanity, one might easily accept them. But Max's review is more than excessive. Just because his friendship for me, in its most human aspect, has roots far deeper than those of literature, and for this reason is effective long before literature gets a chance, he overestimates me to a degree that makes me feel embarrassed, and vain, and conceited, whereas with his literary experience and powers of discernment, he has at his disposal vast reserves of genuine judgment, which is nothing but judgment. Nevertheless, that is how he writes. If I myself were working, were in

the flow of work and borne along by it, I wouldn't have to give a thought to the review; in my mind I could kiss Max for his love, and the review itself would not affect me in any way! But as things are—And the dreadful thing is that I have to say to myself that my attitude to Max's work is no different than his to mine, except that sometimes I am aware of it, whereas he never is.   [F, 194]

To Felice, February 17–18:

And what hand, in what dream, made you write that I have won you completely? Dearest, that's what you believe for a brief moment, at a distance. To win you at close quarters, and for good, requires greater strength than the play of muscles that drives my pen. Don't you yourself believe this, when you think about it? It does seem to me sometimes that this communication by letter, beyond which I have an almost constant longing for reality, is the only kind of communication in keeping with my wretchedness (my wretchedness which of course I do not always feel as wretchedness), and that the transgression of this limit imposed on me would lead us both to disaster.   [F, 197]

To Felice, February 18–19:

Help me, dearest, I beg you, to put right the damage I have done in the last few days. Perhaps in fact nothing whatever has happened, and you wouldn't have noticed anything if I hadn't shouted about it, but I am driven by this feeling of anxiety in the midst of my lethargy, and I write, or fear I may at any moment write, irresponsible things. The wrong sentences lie in wait about my pen, twine themselves around its point, and are dragged along into the letters. I am not of the opinion that one can ever lack the power to express perfectly what one wants to write or say. Observations on the weakness of language, and comparisons between the limitations of words and the infinity of feelings, are quite fallacious. The infinite feeling continues to be as infinite in words as it was in the heart. What is clear within is bound to become so in words as well. This is why one need never worry about language, but at sight of words may often worry about oneself. After all, who knows within himself how things really are with him? This tempestuous or floundering or morasslike inner self is what we really are, but by the secret process by which words are forced out of us, our self-knowledge is brought to light, and though it may still be veiled, yet it is there before us, wonderful or terrible to behold.

So protect me, dearest, from these horrible words of which I have recently been delivering myself. Tell me that you understand it all, and yet go on loving me.   [F, 198]

To Felice, February 19–20:

In the past, when I had less insight into myself and thought I could not disregard the world for a single moment, on the childish assumption that this was where the danger lay, and that the "I" would adjust automatically, without trouble or hesitation, according to the observations made in the outside world—at that time, no, not really even then, it was rather that I was always sunk within myself, then as now. The only difference is that today there are moments (a substitute for the past erroneous assumptions) when I imagine myself writing these things at the foot and in the shadow of a mountain, whose summit I may one day be allowed to reach by climbing or soaring.   [F, 199]

To Felice, February 23:

As seemed fitting (for I should be either in bed or in Dresden), I spent most of the day in bed, and the only two, though terrible, adventures were caused by my father who gradually, and despite all resistance, dragged me firmly out of my morning sleep back into this bleak world with his insane, monotonous, incessant shouting, singing, and hand-clapping, which he repeated over and over again with renewed force to amuse a great-nephew, while in the afternoon he carried on in the same way to entertain his grandson. Dearest one, it takes considerable virtue to endure these goings-on without unfilial oaths, although it may be understandable (it's my father's only pleasure), but in one's soul quite incomprehensible (to me tribal dances are less incomprehensible). Imagine battering at someone like that! In the afternoon especially, every shout was like a punch in the eye. And then to think that many years ago I was being entertained in the same way. In those days, however, there was no one next door being made to suffer from it. And yet it may not even be the shouting that puts such a strain on me; altogether it requires strength to tolerate children in the apartment. I can't do it, I can't forget myself, my blood refuses to flow, it becomes congealed, and this desire of the blood, after all, is supposed to represent love for children. I am wondering whether to leave home and take a room somewhere on account of my nephew's and my niece's occasional presence; after all, they are growing up and getting noisier and noisier. Once, years ago, though for different reasons, I came very close to moving out, but in the end I let them stop me.   [F, 202]

To Felice, February 28 to March 1, on Amerika:

The other day I was walking along Eisengasse when beside me someone said: "What is Karl doing?" I turn; I see a man who, without taking any notice of me, walks along talking to himself, and had also asked himself this question. But it so happens that the principal character in my ill-fated novel is called Karl, and it was this harmless passerby's function to jeer at me, for I can hardly consider it an encouragement.

The other day in connection with my uncle's letter you asked me about my plans and prospects. I was amazed by your question, and am now reminded of it again by this stranger's question. Needless to say I have no plans, no prospects; I cannot step into the future; I can crash into the future, grind into the future, stumble into the future, this I can do; but best of all I can lie still. Plans and prospects, however—honestly, I have none; when things go well, I am entirely absorbed by the present; when things go badly, I curse even the present, let alone the future!

[F, 208 f.]

March 1: Promotion to vice secretary of the Workers' Accident Insurance Institute. Reading of The Metamorphosis *at Brod's.*

To Felice, March 1:

If one bolts the doors and windows against the world, one can from time to time create the semblance and almost the beginning of the reality of a beautiful life.

[F, 209]

To Felice, March 3-4:

I have the feeling of being outside a locked door behind which you live, and which will never be opened. Knocking is the only way of communicating, and now all is silent behind the door. But there is one thing I can do [. . .], which is to wait. [. . .]

For me impatience is only one way of passing the time while waiting; the strength required for waiting is not weakened by it, though of course it is not strength at all, but weakness, and the relaxing—at the slightest suggestion—of those feeble powers that had been active. This characteristic of mine, dearest, exposes you to the greatest dangers—this I add as a postscript to yesterday's letter. Because I for my part would never leave you, not even if it were my lot—worse things could happen to me—to have with you an inner relationship that corresponded to an outer circumstance such as having nothing to do but wait forever outside the side entrance to your house, while you passed in and out through the front door.

When judging me, don't let this mislead you, and however low I may bend over your hand, speak your true mind over and above my head! Anyway, nothing you say will surprise me. I am now a different person to the one I was during the first 2 months of our correspondence; it is not a transformation into a new state, rather a relapse into an old and no doubt lasting one. If you felt drawn to that person, you must, you must inevitably abhor this one. If you conceal this fact, you do so out of compassion and from misleading recollections. The fact that this different person—so greatly altered in every way—continues to cling to you, if anything more tenaciously than before, cannot fail, if you will admit it to yourself, to make him even more abhorrent to you.   [F, 212]

To Felice, March 4-5:
The trouble is, I am not at peace with myself; I am not always "something," and if for once I am "something," I pay for it by "being nothing" for months on end. And of course if I don't collect myself in time, my judgment of people and of the world in general suffers from it, too; my view of the hopelessness of the world is due largely to this distorted judgment which could no doubt be straightened out automatically by reflecting, but only for a single useless moment.   [F, 213]

To Felice, March 13-14:
No matter how little happens, how pointless it may be, how great my indifference to it all, I miss not keeping a diary.[3] But unless you were to read it, it wouldn't be a diary to me. And the changes and omissions necessary in a diary meant for you would surely be all the more beneficial and instructive for me. Do you agree? The difference as compared to my letters will be that the pages of my diary may sometimes contain more substance, but will certainly be even more boring and even more brutal than my letters. But don't be too alarmed; my love for you will not be absent from them.   [F, 221]

To Felice, March 19, before going to Berlin:
I am going to Berlin for no other reason than to tell and show you—you who have been misled by my letters—who I really am. Shall I be able to make it clearer in person than I could in writing? In writing I failed, because I thwarted my purpose, consciously and unconsciously; but when I am actually there, little can be concealed, even if I made an effort to do so. Presence is irrefutable.   [F, 226]

The brief meeting, the first after the initial acquaintance on August 13, 1912, took place on Easter, March 23.

To Felice, March 28:
I lack all confidence. I have it only when I write well, otherwise the world goes its inexorable way against me.   [F, 231]

To Felice, April 1:
My one fear—surely nothing worse can either be said or listened to—is

that I shall never be able to possess you. At best I would be confined, like an unthinkingly faithful dog, to kissing your casually proffered hand, which would not be a sign of love, but of the despair of the animal condemned to silence and eternal separation. I would sit beside you and, as has happened, feel the breath and life of your body at my side, yet in reality be further from you than now, here in my room. I would never be able to attract your attention, and it would be lost to me altogether when you look out of the window, or lay your head in your hands. You and I would ride past the entire world, hand in hand, seemingly united, and none of it would be true. In short, though you might lean toward me far enough for you to be in danger, I would be excluded from you forever.   [F, 233]

To Brod, April 3:
Yesterday [the day before yesterday] I wrote to Berlin the great confession. She is a true martyr and I undermine the ground on which she lived before, happily and in harmony with the whole world.   [Br, 115]
Felice failed to react to F.K.'s letter.

To Kurt Wolff, April 11:
I have only one request. [. . .] "The Stoker," *The Metamorphosis* (which is about one and a half times as long as "The Stoker"), and "The Judgment" belong together both internally and externally; there is a manifest and, what is even more important, a secret link between them, whose presentation in a single volume under some such general title as *The Sons* I would not willingly forego. [. . .] I attach as much importance to the unity of the three stories as to the unity of one of them.
                                                              [Br, 116]

To Felice, April 20:
If only I could write, Felice! I am consumed with the desire to do so. Above all, if only I were free enough, and fit enough! I don't think you have properly taken in that writing is the only thing that makes my inner existence possible. No wonder, I always express myself so badly; I am awake only among my imaginary characters, but on this subject I can neither write nor talk convincingly. Nor would this be necessary, provided I had everything else.   [F, 245]

To Felice, April 29–30:
What a lovely feeling to be in your safekeeping when confronted by this fearful world which I venture to take on only during nights of writing. Today I thought that one had nothing to complain of so long as one lived with this dual feeling: that someone one loves is well dis-

posed toward one, and that at the same time one had boundless possibilities of doing away with oneself at any moment.   [F, 249]

To Felice, May 1:
I ought to be writing, says the doctor within. Write, though my head is
so unsteady, and though a short time ago I had occasion to recognize
the inadequacy of my writing. Yes, I haven't told you yet that a very
short book of mine (47 pages) is to be published next month, the page
proofs are right here. It is called *The Stoker: A Fragment,* and is the first
chapter of that unfortunate novel [*Amerika*]. It will appear in an inexpensive series which Wolff is publishing and which will be given the
somewhat ludicrous title "The Day of Judgment," 80 pfennigs each volume.   [F, 250]
The Stoker appeared in May 1913.

May 2. It has become very necessary to keep a diary again. The uncertainty of my thoughts, F., the ruin in the office, the physical impossibility of writing and the inner need for it.   [DI, 284 f.]

May 3. The terrible uncertainty of my inner existence.   [DI, 286]

May 11–12 (Whitsun holidays): Second visit to Felice in Berlin;
meets Felice's family.

To Felice, May 15:
How is your family? My impressions of them are very confused,
probably due to the fact that your family presented an aspect of total
resignation so far as I am concerned. I felt so very small while they all
stood around me like giants with such fatalistic expressions on their
faces (with the exception of your sister Erna, to whom I instantly felt
drawn). It was entirely in keeping with the situation: you are theirs, so
they are big, you are not mine, so I was small; but surely that was only
the way *I,* not they, saw it; so how—despite all their kindness and
hospitality—did they come to adopt this attitude? I must have made a
very nasty impression on them; I don't want to know about it; all I want
to know is what your sister Erna said, even if it was very critical or
malicious. Will you tell me that?   [F, 257]

To Felice, May 18, with reference to his love affair with an
unnamed woman in Zuckmantel (Silesia) in the summers of 1905
and 1906:
Had I but known you 8 or 10 years ago (the past is as undeniable as it is
lost), how happy we might be today—no miserable prevarications, no

sighs, no hopeless silences. Instead—all this was years ago—there were girls I fell in love with easily, was gay with, and left with even greater ease, or who left me without causing the slightest pain. (It is only the plural that makes them sound so numerous, because I don't give their names, and because it is all so long ago.) There may have been one woman I loved enough to feel shaken to my very depths, that is now 7 or 8 years ago. Since then, though by no means as a result, I have been almost completely detached from everything, more and more confined to myself; my wretched physical state, which—how shall I put it?—preceded or followed my dissolution, helped to submerge me still further, until—when I had almost reached the end—I met you.   [F, 258 f.]

May 24. In high spirits because I consider "The Stoker" so good. This evening I read it to my parents, there is no better critic than I when I read to my father, who listens with the most extreme reluctance. Many shallow passages followed by unfathomable depths.   [DI, 287]

To Felice, June 1:
What will become of us, my poor dearest? You know, if [Yitzhak] Löwy weren't here and I didn't have to organize a recital for the poor fellow (a notice, suggested by me and written by [Otto] Pick, is enclosed, and there are other things of this kind to be done), and didn't have to sell tickets and busy myself about the hall, and finally if Löwy's unquenchable fire hadn't infected me and given me a semblance of speed and activity—I don't know how I should have got through these last few days. After all, we do belong together, there seems to be no doubt about that, but equally there is no doubt that we are immensely different, that you are healthy in every sense of the word, and as a result calm in your innermost being; whereas I am ill, perhaps not so much in the generally accepted sense, but consequently in the worst possible sense of the word, hence I am restive, absentminded, and listless.   [F. 264]
  The performance was a failure. See Letters to Felice, *June 10, 1913.*

June 5. The inner advantages that mediocre literary works derive from the fact that their authors are still alive and present behind them. The real sense of growing old.   [DI, 287]

Early June: "The Judgment" published in the yearbook Arkadia.

To Felice, June 10:
The "Judgment" cannot be explained. Perhaps one day I'll show you some entries in my diary about it. The story is full of abstractions,

though they are never admitted. The friend is hardly a real person,
perhaps he is more whatever the father and Georg have in common.
The story may be a journey around father and son, and the friend's
changing shape may be a change in perspective in the relationship
between father and son. But I am not quite sure of this, either.

Today I am sending you the *Stoker*. Receive the little lad kindly, sit
him down beside you and praise him, as he longs for you to do.   [F, 267]

To Felice, June 15, in despair over her silence:
Dear Felice, I find it difficult to write today, not because it is late, but
because the letter that will arrive tomorrow—will it in fact arrive?—was
extracted by force; I forced it from you with my telegram. Your guardian angel kept you from writing, even on that endless Sunday, and I
wrestled with your guardian angel. A shameful victory—if, in fact, it is
one. What do I want from you? What makes me persecute you? Why
don't I desist, or heed the signs? On the pretext of wanting to free you of
me, I force myself upon you. Is there no limit, no way out? The moment
I am forced to believe that you are lost to me, a simple optical illusion
occurs at once, and the somehow-somewhere-existing, minute, barely
visible, never-to-be-discovered way out takes on proportions of won-
drous size and beauty, and once again I plunge into pursuit, and
promptly stop short again. And I experience not only my own suffering,
but even more that which I inflict upon you.   [F, 268 f.]

*To Felice, June 16, asking her for her hand; F.K., who called this
    letter "a treatise" (letter, June 10), worked on it for several days.*
Now consider, Felice, in view of this uncertainty, it is difficult to say the
word, and indeed it is bound to sound rather strange. Clearly, it's too
soon to say it. But afterwards, it would be too late: there wouldn't be
any time to discuss matters of the kind you mentioned in your last
letter. But there also isn't time for endless hesitations, at least this is
what I feel about it, and so I ask: In view of the above—alas, irremediable—conditions, will you consider whether you wish to be my wife?
Will you do that?

I stopped at this point a few days ago, and have not resumed since. I
can well understand why I was unable to. Because, fundamentally, this
is a criminal question I am putting to you (your letter of today confirms
this), but in the conflict of forces, those that have to pose this question
are victorious.

What you say about being equals, etc.—*provided it is not a cover
(needless to say an unconscious one) for other things*—is pure fantasy. I
am nothing, absolutely nothing. I am "further ahead in every way"
than you? Some capacity for understanding people, and for putting

myself in their place—this I have, but I don't believe I have ever met a single person who in the long run in his ordinary human relationships, in normal everyday life (and what else is it all about?), could be more hopeless than I.

I have no memory, either for things learned or things read, either for things experienced or things heard, either for people or events; I feel as though I had experienced nothing, learned nothing, and in fact I know less about most things than the average schoolboy; and what I know, I know so superficially that even the second question is beyond me.

I am unable to reason, my reasoning constantly comes up against a blank wall; certain isolated matters I can grasp in a flash, but I am quite incapable of coherent, consecutive reasoning. Nor can I tell a story properly; in fact I can hardly even talk; when I am telling a story I usually have the kind of feeling small children probably experience when attempting their first steps—not, however, because they themselves feel the need to walk, but because the grownups, who can walk perfectly, expect them to. And you, Felice, don't feel equal to such a man, you who are gay, lively, sure of yourself, and healthy? All I possess are certain powers which, at a depth almost inaccessible under normal conditions, shape themselves into literature, powers to which, however, in my present professional as well as physical state, I dare not commit myself, because for every inner exhortation of these powers there are as many, if not more, inner warnings. Could I but commit myself to them they would undoubtedly, of this I am convinced, lift me out of my inner misery in an instant.

Apropos the theoretical aspect of equality—for in practice, as I said, it doesn't arise, not at any rate in your sense—I only want to add that the degree of similarity in education, knowledge, higher aspirations, and ideals, which you seem to demand as prerequisites to a happy marriage, is in my opinion almost impossible, secondly unimportant, and thirdly not even advantageous or desirable. What is essential to marriage is personal harmony, a harmony far deeper than that of opinions, a harmony that cannot be analyzed but only felt—i.e., the necessity for personal proximity. But this doesn't mean that the freedom of either party is in any way endangered; it is endangered only by unnecessary human proximity which constitutes the greatest part of our lives.

You say it is conceivable that I might not be able to stand life with you. Here you almost touch on the truth, but from an angle totally different from the one you have in mind. I really do believe I am lost to all social intercourse. I am quite incapable of conducting a prolonged, vigorously developed conversation with any individual, except in certain exceptional, appallingly exceptional cases. For example, during the long years we have known each other I have, after all, been alone with Max on many occasions, for days on end, when traveling even for weeks on end and almost continuously, yet I do not remember—and had it happened, I would certainly remember—ever having had a long coherent conversation involving my entire being, as should inevitably follow when two people with a great fund of independent and lively ideas and experiences are thrown together. [. . .]

I am at my most bearable in familiar surroundings with 2 or 3 friends; then I am free, am not forced to be continually attentive and coopera-tive, but can take part in what's going on if and when I feel like it, as much or as little as I wish; no one misses me, no one is made uneasy by my presence. If there is a stranger present who happens to get under my skin, all the better, for then, on borrowed strength, I seem to be able to become quite animated. But if I am in an unfamiliar place, among a number of strange people, or people whom I feel to be strangers, then the whole room presses on my chest and I am unable to move, my whole personality seems virtually to get under their skins, and every-thing becomes hopeless. [. . .]

Now consider, Felice, the change that marriage would bring about for us, what each would lose and each would gain. I should lose my (for the most part) terrible loneliness, and you, whom I love above all others, would be my gain. Whereas you would lose the life you have lived hitherto, with which you were almost completely satisfied. You would lose Berlin, the office you enjoy, your girl friends, the small pleasures of life, the prospect of marrying a decent, cheerful, healthy man, of having beautiful, healthy children for whom, if you think about it, you clearly long. In place of these incalculable losses, you would gain a sick, weak, unsociable, taciturn, gloomy, stiff, almost hopeless man who possibly has but one virtue, which is that he loves you. Instead of sacrificing yourself for real children, which would be in accordance with your nature as a healthy girl, you would have to sacrifice yourself for this man who is childish, but childish in the worst sense, and who at best might learn from you, letter by letter, the ways of human speech. And you would lose in all the small things, all of them.

My income may not be more than yours; I have precisely 4,588 kronen a year, am however entitled to a pension, but my income, as in any employment similar to the civil service, can increase only very slightly; from my parents I have no great expectations, from literature none. So you would have to live far more modestly than you do now. Would you really do this and stand it for my sake, for the sake of the man described above?

And now, Felice, you speak. Think over everything I have said in all my letters from the beginning. I don't believe the statements about myself could ever have varied a great deal. Hardly anything would have been exaggerated, about some things too little may have been said. You need say nothing about the external account, this is plain enough, and strictly prohibits a "Yes." What remains is only the internal account. How does it stand? Will you reply in great detail? Or not in great detail if you haven't much time, but clearly, as befits your basically clear nature, only slightly muddied by me.   [F, 269 ff.]

June 21. The tremendous world I have in my head. But how free myself and free it without being torn to pieces. And a thousand times rather be torn to pieces than retain it in me or bury it. That, indeed, is what I am here for, that is quite clear to me.   [DI, 288]

To Felice, June 21-23:

Dearest, this too, and perhaps this above all, you do not take into account sufficiently in your considerations, though we have written a great deal about it: namely, that writing is actually the good part of my nature. If there is anything good about me, it is that. Without this world in my head, this world straining to be released, I would never have dared to think of wanting to win you. It is not so much a question of what you think of my writing now, but, should we live together, you would soon realize that if willingly or unwillingly you do not come to love my writing, there would be absolutely nothing for you to hold on to. In which case you would be terribly lonely, Felice; you would not realize how much I love you, and I should hardly be able to prove my love, even though then I might feel myself especially yours, then as now.

[F, 275]

To Felice, June 26:

What I need for my writing is seclusion, not "like a hermit," that would not be enough, but like the dead. Writing, in this sense, is a sleep deeper than that of death, and just as one would not and cannot tear the dead from their graves, so I must not and cannot be torn from my desk at night. This has no immediate bearing on my relationship with people; it is simply that I can write only in this regular, continuous, and rigorous fashion, and therefore can live only in this way too. But as you say, for you it will be "rather difficult." I have always had this fear of people, not actually of the people themselves, but of their intrusion upon my weak nature; for even the most intimate friend to set foot in my room fills me with terror, and is more than just a symbol of this fear.   [F, 279]

June 28: First meeting in Prague with Ernst Weiss, physician and writer.

July 1. The wish for an unthinking, reckless solitude. To have only myself to face. Perhaps I shall find it in Riva.   [DI, 288]

July 3. When I say something it immediately and finally loses its importance, when I write it down it loses it too, but sometimes gains a new one.   [DI, 289]

To Felice, June 7 (July 7):

I cannot live with people; I absolutely hate all my relatives, not because they are my relatives, not because they are wicked, not because I don't think well of them (which by no means diminishes my "terrible timidity," as you suggest), but simply because they are the people with whom I live in close proximity. It is just that I cannot abide communal life; what's more, I hardly have the energy to regard it as a misfortune. [. . .]

Felice, beware of thinking of life as commonplace, if by commonplace you mean monotonous, simple, petty. Life is merely terrible; I feel it as few others do. Often—and in my inmost self perhaps all the time—I doubt whether I am a human being.   [F, 287]

To Felice, July 9:

Dearest Felice, if you are unable to write to me, don't write to me, but let me write to you and repeat day by day what you already know: that I love you as much as I have any power to love, and that I wish to serve you and must serve you, as long as I live.   [F, 288]

To Felice, July 10:

If only I were with you, Felice, and had the capacity to make things clear to you, or rather the capacity just to see things clearly. It's all my fault. After all, we have never been as united as we are now; this Yes on both sides has tremendous power. But I am held back by what is almost a command from heaven; an apprehension that cannot be appeased; everything that used to be of the greatest importance to me—my health, my small income, my miserable disposition, all this for which there would be some justification—vanishes, is as nothing compared to this apprehension, and seems to be used only as a pretext. To be quite frank (as I have always been with you as far as my self-knowledge at the moment allows) and at long last to be recognized by you as the madman I am, it is my *dread of the union* even with the most beloved woman, above all with her. How can I explain to you what to me is so clear that I long to cover it, to stop it blinding me! And then of course it becomes less clear again when I read your sweet, trusting letter; then everything appears to be perfectly all right, and happiness seems to await us both.

Can you understand this, Felice, if only from a distance? I have a definite feeling that through marriage, *through the union, through the dissolution* of this nothingness that I am, I shall perish, and not alone but with my wife, and that the more I love her the swifter and more terrible it will be. Now you tell me what we should do, for I believe we are now so close to each other that neither of us, without the other's corroboration, could do anything on his own. Think carefully, too, about all that has been left unsaid! *Ask questions, I shall answer every one.* God, it really is about time to ease the pressure, and there surely isn't a girl who has been loved as I love you, and been tortured as I find it necessary to torture you.   [F, 288 f.]

Almost immediately after he asked Felice for her hand, F.K. felt doubts about engagement and marriage.

July 21. Summary of all the arguments for and against my marriage:

1. Inability to bear living alone, which does not imply inability to live, quite the contrary, it is even improbable that I know how to live with anyone, but I am incapable, alone, of bearing the onslaught of my own life, the demands of my own person, the attacks of time and old age, the vague pressure of the desire to write, sleeplessness, the nearness of madness—I cannot bear all this alone. I naturally add a "perhaps" to this. The connection with F. will give my existence more strength to resist.

2. Everything immediately starts me thinking. Every joke in the comic papers, every memory of Flaubert and Grillparzer, the sight of the nightshirts on my parents' beds, laid out for the night, Max's marriage. Yesterday my sister said, "All the married people (that we know) are happy, I don't understand it," this remark started me thinking, I became afraid again.

3. I must be alone a great deal. What I accomplished was only the result of being alone.

4. I hate everything that does not relate to literature, conversations bore me (even if they relate to literature), to visit people bores me, the sorrows and joys of my relatives bore me to the very soul. Conversation takes the importance, the seriousness, the truth out of everything I think.

5. The fear of being tied to anyone, of passing into the other. Then I'll never be alone any more.

6. In the past, especially, the person I am in the company of my sisters has been entirely different from the person I am in the company of other people. Fearless, strong, surprising, carried away, as I otherwise am only when I write. If through the intermediation of my wife I could

be like that in the presence of everyone! But then would it not be at the expense of my writing? Not that, not that!

7. Alone, I could perhaps some day really give up my job. Married, it will never be possible.   [DI, 292 f.]

July 21. Don't despair, not even over the fact that you don't despair. Just when everything seems over with, new forces come marching up, and precisely that means that you are alive. And if they don't, then everything is over with here, once and for all.   [DI, 290 f.]

July 21. Miserable creature that I am!   [DI, 293]

Nothing, nothing, nothing. Weakness, self-destruction, tip of a flame of hell piercing the floor.   [DI, 294]

> *To Felice, August 12:*
> It fills me with horror, Felice, when I imagine that on a lovely morning, after a reasonably good night, you sit at breakfast in anticipation of a pleasant day ahead, and morning after morning you are handed my infernal letters, like messages from the underworld. But what can I do, Felice? In your last letters and postcards I get no feeling of your nearness to me, your help, your definite determination, and unless I can be sure of that, I can effect no contact with your parents, since you, you alone create my only valid connection with people, and *you alone will be the one to create it in future.* So I shall have to await your reply to yesterday's letter. Don't you understand my position, Felice? My own suffering is far greater than the suffering I inflict—but this, though it means a great deal, does not in itself exonerate me in any way.   [F, 303]

August 13. Perhaps it is now all over and the letter I wrote yesterday [to Felice] was the last one. That would certainly be the best. What I shall suffer, what she will suffer—that cannot be compared with the mutual suffering that would result. I shall gradually pull myself together, she will marry, that is the only way out among the living. We cannot beat a path into the rock for the two of us, it is enough that we wept and tortured ourselves for a year trying to do so. She will see that from my last letters. If not, then I will certainly have to marry her, for I am too weak to resist her opinion about our mutual happiness and am unable not to carry out, so far as I can, something she considers possible.

                                    [DI, 295]

August 14. The opposite has happened. There were three letters. The last letter I could not resist. I love her as far as I am capable of it, but the

love lies buried to the point of suffocation under fear and self-re-
proaches.

Conclusion for my case from "The Judgment." I am indirectly in her
debt for the story. But Georg goes to pieces because of his fiancée.

Coitus as punishment for the happiness of being together. Live as
ascetically as possible, more ascetically than a bachelor, that is the
only possible way for me to endure marriage. But she?   [DI, 295 f.]

August 15. Agonies in bed toward morning. Saw only solution in
jumping out of the window. My mother came to my bedside and asked
whether I had sent off the letter [to F.'s parents] and whether it was my
original text. I said it was the original text, but made even sharper. She
said she does not understand me. I answered, she most certainly does
not understand me, and by no means only in this matter. Later she
asked me if I were going to write to Uncle Alfred [Löwy, of Madrid], he
deserved it. I asked why he deserved it. He has telegraphed, he has
written, he has your welfare so much at heart. "These are simply
formalities," I said, "he is a complete stranger to me, he mis-
understands me entirely, he does not know what I want and need, I
have nothing in common with him."

"So no one understands you," my mother said, "I suppose I am a
stranger to you too, and your father as well. We all want only what is
bad for you."

"Certainly, you are all strangers to me, it is only blood that connects
us, but that never shows itself. Of course you don't want what is bad
for me."

Through this and several other observations of myself I have come to
believe that there are possibilities in my ever-increasing inner determination and confidence which may enable me to pass the test of
marriage in spite of everything, and even to steer it in a direction
favorable to my vocation. Of course, to a certain extent this is a belief
that I grasp at when I am already on the windowsill.

I'll shut myself off from everyone to the point of insensibility. I shall
set myself at enmity with everybody, speak to no one.   [DI, 296 f.]

Brod's notes on a conversation on August 18:
*Franz on the subject of his marriage. He has proposed. His unhappi-
ness. Everything or nothing. His justification, pure emotion, without
analysis, without the possibility or need for analysis. A complicated
situation, which engages my deepest attention. He talks of Radešovice
[a summer resort near Prague], where the married women are bursting*

with sexuality, with children, the unborn too, who rule everything. He
counsels complete retirement from the world.   [B, 143]

To Felice, August 20:

Talking is altogether against my nature. Whatever I may say is wrong, in my sense. For me, speech robs everything I say of its seriousness and importance. To me it seems impossible that it should be otherwise, since speech is continuously influenced by a thousand external factors and a thousand external constraints. Hence I am silent not only from necessity, but likewise from conviction. Writing is the only appropriate form of expression for me, and will continue to be so even when we are together. But for you, dependent as you are by nature on speaking and listening, will my writing—whatever may be granted to me—suffice as my main, my only means of communication (though probably addressed to no one but you)?   [F, 307]

August 21. Today I got [the] Kierkegaard [anthology] *Buch des Richters.* As I suspected, his case [his relationship to Regine Ohlsen], despite essential differences, is very similar to mine, at least he is on the same side of the world. He bears me out like a friend.   [DI, 298]

To Felice, August 22:

The life that awaits you is not that of the happy couples you see strolling along before you in Westerland, no lighthearted chatter arm in arm, *but a monastic life at the side of a man who is peevish, miserable, silent, discontented, and sickly;* a man who, and this will seem to you akin to madness, is chained to invisible literature by invisible chains and screams when approached because, so he claims, someone is touching those chains.   [F, 308]

To Felice, August 24:

The moment I had read your letter today I went next door, where my parents always have their brief game of cards after luncheon, and asked at once: "Father, so what do you think about my wanting to get married?" These were the first words I had uttered to my father about you. Needless to say, my mother has told him everything she knows. Have I already told you that I admire my father? You know that he is my enemy, and I his, as is determined by our temperaments, but apart from this my admiration for him as a man is perhaps as great as my fear of him. I can manage to avoid him; but ignore him, never. Like every one of our conversations (but it wasn't a conversation; like all our so-called conversations it consisted of uncontrolled remarks on my side, and powerful orations on his)—like every one of our conversations this one started with irritable remarks on his side, and the registering of his irritability on mine. I feel unable at present, too weak, to describe the whole thing, not that I had been especially unnerved by this conversation; after all, I am well aware of my inferiority vis-à-vis my father, I realize it, and it certainly affects my father more than it affects me. The substance of his oration centered around the difficulties in which, by marrying, I would find myself with regard to my income—-difficulties that, owing to my lack of purpose (here came horrible accusations about my having persuaded him to invest in the unsuccessful asbestos factory, to which I no longer paid any attention), I would not be able to endure, let alone resolve. As an additional argument, with some bearing on my affairs which is no longer quite clear to me now, he addressed his reproaches partly to thin air, partly to my mother, and partly to me as well, for my second sister's marriage with which, from the financial point of view, he is (and with good reason) dissatisfied. About half an hour passed in this fashion. Finally, as is usual toward the end of these scenes, he becomes gentle, not really gentle, but relatively gentle, so that one is helpless when confronted by him, above all I myself, who haven't a word to say to him that is genuinely felt. (But perhaps the strangest of all in my relationship with him is that I am capable of feeling and suffering to the utmost not with him, but within him.) And in the end he said (the transitions are omitted from my description) he was prepared, if I so wished, to go to Berlin, see your family, advance what in his opinion are irrefutable objections, and, if a marriage were agreed upon in spite of these objections, he would say no more.   [F, 309 f.]

To Felice, presumably during the night of August 24–25:
Dearest Felice, I may not have put things quite accurately this afternoon. I rely so much on the moment and its influences. So try to understand me! What my father said is consent, after his fashion, as far as he can give his consent to anything I want. He talks about his children's happiness being close to his heart, and he hardly ever tells a deliberate lie, he has too strong a character for that. But the fears that lie behind it—that's another matter. In this respect he may be rather like your mother: he foresees catastrophe everywhere. When he was younger and still had complete confidence in himself and his health, these fears were not so pronounced, least of all when dealing with anything he had started and carried out himself. But today he fears everything, and, horrible as it may be, these fears, at any rate in important matters, are invariably confirmed. These constant warnings mean no more in the end than that happiness is a rare thing, and this, after all, is a fact. But then my father has worked hard all his life, and

from nothing has made, comparatively speaking, something. This progress, however, came to an end years ago, when his daughters were
grown up, and now, owing to their marriages, it has turned into a
frightful never-ending decline. My father has the feeling that his
sons-in-law as well as his own children, save for me at present, are
permanently around his neck. This feeling, alas, is completely justified,
and enormously intensified by my father's illness, a hardening of the
arteries. Now he reasons as follows: if I marry, I who so far have not
been included in these worries, I am bound to get into financial difficulties, if not at once, then certainly in 2 years' time; and then, however
much I may deny it now, I would come to him, almost paralyzed with
worry as he is, for help; or, if I didn't, he would still try somehow to
provide it, thus hastening his own ruin and the ruin of all those whom
he believes to be dependent on him. You should see him in this light,
Felice.   [F, 311]

  To Carl Bauer, Felice's father, August 28:
You know your own daughter: she is a gay, healthy, self-confident girl,
who in order to live should be surrounded by gay, healthy, and lively
people. You know me only from my visit (I was about to add that this
should be enough), and I cannot repeat what I have told your daughter
about myself in some 500 letters. But please consider this one important
fact: my whole being is directed toward literature; I have followed this
direction unswervingly until my 30th year, and the moment I abandon
it I cease to live. Everything I am, and am not, is a result of this. I am
taciturn, unsociable, morose, selfish, a hypochondriac, and actually in
poor health. Fundamentally I deplore none of this: it is the earthly
reflection of a higher necessity. (What I am really capable of is not the
problem here, and has no connection with it.)
  I live within my family, among the kindest, most affectionate
people—and am more strange than a stranger. In recent years I have
spoken hardly more than twenty words a day to my mother, and I
exchange little more than a daily greeting with my father. To my
married sisters and brothers-in-law I do not speak at all, although I
have nothing against them. I lack all sense of family life.
  And is your daughter, whose healthy nature has destined her for a
happy married life, to live with this kind of man? Is she to tolerate a
monastic existence with a person who, though he loves her as he can
never love anyone else, spends most of his time in his room or wandering about by himself—simply because of his irrevocable vocation?
Is she to tolerate a life utterly divorced from her parents, her family,
and almost any other social contact—because I, who would lock my
door against my best friend, cannot imagine any other kind of married

life? Could she stand this? And what for? For my writing, which is
highly problematic in her eyes and perhaps even in mine? And for this
she is to live alone in a foreign town, in a marriage that may turn out to
be a relationship of love and friendship rather than a real marriage?

[F, 313]

*Felice did not deliver this letter to her father. See the draft of a
similar letter in DI, 298 ff.*

To Felice, August 30:
What is stopping me can hardly be said to be facts; it is fear, an
insurmountable fear, fear of achieving happiness, a desire and a command to torment myself for some higher purpose. That you, dearest,
should be forced to land under the wheels of this carriage, which is
destined for me alone, is really terrible. I am consigned to darkness by
my inner voice, yet in reality am drawn to you; this is irreconcilable;
yet even if we were to try, the blows would fall alike on you and me.

[F, 314]

August 30. Where am I to find rescue? How many untruths I no longer
even knew about will be brought to the surface. If they are going to
pervade our marriage as they pervaded the goodbye, then I have certainly done the right thing. In me, by myself, without human relationship, there are no visible lies. The limited circle is pure.   [DI, 300]

There are no entries in the diary during the next six weeks.

To Felice, September 2:
Dearest, everything you say to me, I say almost all the time; the slightest
detachment from you makes me smart; whatever happens between us
is repeated with renewed intensity inside myself; faced with your
letters, faced by your pictures, I succumb. And yet—of the four men I
consider to be my true blood-relations (without comparing myself to
them either in power or in range), Grillparzer, Dostoevski, Kleist, and
Flaubert, Dostoevski was the only one to get married, and perhaps
Kleist, when compelled by outer and inner necessity to shoot himself
on the Wannsee, was the only one to find the right solution. All this
might be entirely irrelevant as far as we are concerned; after all, each
one of us lives life anew—even if I were standing in the very center of
the shadow they cast upon our own time. But this is a fundamental
question of life and faith in general, and from this point of view
interpreting the behavior of these four men makes more sense.   [F, 315 f.]

There is an obvious strain in the relationship between F.K. and
Felice at this time.

To Felice, September 6:
The question of the diary is at the same time the question of the whole,
contains all impossibilities pertaining to the whole. Considered this in
the train during my conversation with P. It is impossible to say everything, and it is impossible not to say everything. Impossible to preserve one's freedom, impossible not to preserve it. Impossible to lead
the only possible kind of life, i.e., to live together, each one to be free,
each one for himself, not to be married, neither outwardly nor actually,
simply to be together and by so doing to have taken the last possible
step beyond the friendship between men, right up to the limit set for
myself where one foot is already raised. But after all, this too is impossible.   [F, 318 f.]

September: Journey to Vienna to attend the Second Interna-
tional Congress for First Aid and Accident Prevention and the
Eleventh Zionist Congress. In mid-September he travels to Ven-
ice, then to Riva on Lake Garda. In a sanatorium in Riva he has
a love affair with "the Swiss girl" ("W." or "G. W."), aged eigh-
teen. They promise each other to keep their affair secret.

To Felice, September 9:
I went to the Zionist Congress this morning. I have no real contact. I
feel it in certain respects, also for the entire concept, but not for the
essential part.   [F, 317]

To Brod, September 16:
I was sitting there as if at an utterly strange performance.   [Br, 120]

To Felix Weltsch, from the sanatorium in Riva, September:
No, Felix, it will not turn out well, nothing will turn out well for me.
There are times when I think that I am no longer in this world, that I am
wandering about somewhere in purgatory. You think my sense of guilt
is a crutch, a way out; no, I have a sense of guilt simply because for me
it is the most perfect form of repentance, but you do not have to look
very closely to discover that this sense of guilt is really only a longing
for the past. And no sooner has this been established than a feeling of
freedom, of liberation, and of relative satisfaction rises up, transcend-
ing all forms of repentance, and instilling a far greater sense of fear.

                                                                          [Br, 122 f.]

Brod's note:
In September 1913 he took refuge in Riva, at the Hartungen
sanatorium. "The very idea of a honeymoon fills me with horror," he
writes to me. He experiences the curious episode with a Swiss girl. It
remains obscure. "Everything struggles against its being set on paper.
Were I sure that her command not to say anything about it had any
influence on this—I have obeyed her command strictly, almost without
effort—I should be satisfied."   [B, 144]

October 15. The stay in Riva was very important to me. For the first
time I understood a Christian girl and lived almost entirely within the
sphere of her influence.   [DI, 301]

> *There is no communication between F.K. and Felice from mid-*
> *September to the end of October.*

October 15. Perhaps I have caught hold of myself again, perhaps I
secretly took the shorter way again, and now I, who already despair in
loneliness, have pulled myself up again. But the headaches, the
sleeplessness! Well, it is worth the struggle, or rather, I have no choice.

In despair. Today, in the half-sleep during the afternoon: In the end
the pain will really burst my head. And at the temples. What I saw
when I pictured this to myself was really a gunshot wound, but around
the hole the jagged edges were bent straight back, as in the case of a tin
can violently torn open.   [DI, 301 ff.]

October 20. I am now reading *The Metamorphosis* at home and find it
bad. Perhaps I am really lost, the sadness of this morning will return
again, I shall not be able to resist it for long, it deprives me of all hope. I
don't even have the desire to keep a diary, perhaps because there is
already too much lacking in it, perhaps because I should perpetually
have to describe incomplete—by all appearances *necessarily*
incomplete—actions, perhaps because writing itself adds to my sadness.

I would gladly write fairy tales (why do I hate the word so?) that
could please W. ["the Swiss girl"] and that she might sometimes keep
under the table at meals, read between courses, and blush fearfully
when she noticed that the sanatorium doctor has been standing behind
her for a little while now and watching her. Her excitement sometimes—or really all of the time—when she hears stories.

I notice that I am afraid of the almost physical strain of the effort to
remember, afraid of the pain beneath which the floor of the thoughtless

vacuum of the mind slowly opens up, or even merely heaves up a little in preparation. All things resist being written down. If I knew that her commandment not to mention her were at work here (I have kept it faithfully, almost without effort), then I should be satisfied, but it is nothing but inability. Besides, what am I to think of the fact that this evening, for a long while, I was pondering what the acquaintance with W. had cost me in pleasures with the Russian woman, who at night perhaps (this is by no means impossible) might have let me into her room, which was diagonally across from mine. While my evening's communication with W. was carried on in a language of knocks whose meaning we never definitely agreed upon. I knocked on the ceiling of my room below hers, received her answer, leaned out of the window, greeted her, once let myself be blessed by her, once snatched at a ribbon she let down, sat on the windowsill for hours, heard every one of her steps above, mistakenly regarded every chance knock to be the sign of an understanding, heard her coughing, her singing before she fell asleep.   [DI, 303 f.]

October 22. Too late. The sweetness of sorrow and of love. To be smiled at by her in the boat. That was the most beautiful thing of all. Always only the longing to die and yet keeping oneself alive; this alone is love.

Yesterday's observation. The most appropriate situation for me: To listen to a conversation between two people who are discussing a matter that concerns them closely while I have only a very remote interest in it which is in addition completely selfless.   [DI, 305]

End of October: Felice sends her friend Grete Bloch to Prague to intermediate between her and the silent F.K.

To Felice, November 6:
Well, I'll be coming on Saturday, Felice, leaving here at 3 P.M., and will have to leave Berlin on Sunday between 4 and 5. I will be staying at the Askanische Hof.

I do realize that it is absolutely essential for us to meet. Originally, I had not meant to come until Christmas, but when your letter and your girl friend [Grete Bloch] arrived I decided to come this Saturday; and then, when your friend left and I had no letter from you, and minor obstacles arose, I intended to postpone my journey until two weeks from Saturday (Max is going to Berlin a week from Saturday, and I wanted to go alone). But owing to the discoveries I have made about myself during this past week—I feel utterly futile—and now that I have your letter, I am coming on Saturday. Should something suddenly prevent me, I'll send a telegram.

Have you any real hope, Felice, that our meeting will make things
clear to us? I agree that it is absolutely essential, but will it in fact make
things clear? No matter where I am, things are not clear. Don't you
remember that after each meeting you have felt more doubtful than
ever? That it was only in letters that all doubts were resolved, in letters
comprising the better part of my self?

Well, we'll see, and let heaven look upon us with understanding.

[F, 325]

*November 8–9: Visits Felice in Berlin. Begins correspondence
with Grete Bloch; an intimate friendship develops.*

November 18. I will write again, but how many doubts have I
meanwhile had about my writing. At bottom I am an incapable, ignorant person who, if he had not been compelled—without any effort
on his own part and scarcely aware of the compulsion—to go to school,
would be fit only to crouch in a kennel, to leap out when food is offered
him and to leap back when he has swallowed it.   [DI, 308]

November 19. The reading of the diary moves me. Is it because I no
longer have the slightest confidence now? Everything appears to me to
be an artificial construction of the mind. Every remark by someone
else, every chance look throws everything in me over on the other side,
even what has been forgotten, even what is entirely insignificant. I am
more uncertain than I ever was, I feel only the power of life. And I am
senselessly empty. I am really like a lost sheep in the night and in the
mountains, or like a sheep that is running after this sheep. To be so lost
and not have the strength to regret it.

I intentionally walk through the streets where there are whores.
Walking past them excites me, the remote but nevertheless existent
possibility of going with one. Is that grossness? But I know no better,
and doing this seems basically innocent to me and causes me almost no
regret. I want only the stout, older ones, with outmoded clothes that
have, however, a certain luxuriousness because of various adorn-
ments. One woman probably knows me by now. I met her this afternoon, she was not yet in her working clothes, her hair was still flat
against her head, she was wearing no hat, a work blouse like a cook's,
and was carrying a bundle of some sort, perhaps to the laundress. No
one would have found anything exciting in her, only I. We looked at
each other fleetingly. Now, in the evening, it had meanwhile grown
cold, I saw her, wearing a tight-fitting, yellowish-brown coat, on the
other side of the narrow street that branches off from Zeltnerstrasse,

where she has her beat. I looked back at her twice, she caught the glance too, but then I really ran away from her.

This uncertainty is surely the result of thinking about F.   [DI, 309]

November 27. I must stop without actually being shaken off. Nor do I feel any danger that I might get lost, still, I feel helpless and an outsider. The firmness, however, that the most insignificant writing brings about in me is beyond doubt and wonderful. The comprehensive view I had of everything on my walk yesterday!   [DI, 314]

December 4. Viewed from the outside it is terrible for a young but mature person to die, or worse, to kill himself. Hopelessly to depart in a complete confusion that would make sense only within a further development, or with the sole hope that in the great account this appearance in life will be considered as not having taken place. Such would be my plight now. To die would mean nothing else than to surrender a nothing to the nothing, but that would be impossible to conceive, for how could a person, even only as a nothing, consciously surrender himself to the nothing, and not merely to an empty nothing but rather to a roaring nothing whose nothingness consists only in its incomprehensibility.

The unity of mankind, now and then doubted, even if only emotionally, by everyone, even by the most approachable and adaptable person, on the other hand also reveals itself to everyone, or seems to reveal itself, in the complete harmony, discernible time and again, between the development of mankind as a whole and of the individual man. Even in the most secret emotions of the individual.

Wonderful, entirely self-contradictory idea that someone who died at 3 A.M., for instance, immediately thereafter, about dawn, enters into a higher life. What incompatibility there is between the visibly human and everything else! How out of one mystery there always comes a greater one! In the first moment the breath leaves the human calculator. Really one should be afraid to step out of one's house.   [DI, 316 f.]

December 16. I sat in the rocking chair at [Felix] Weltsch's, we spoke of the disorder of our lives, he always with a certain confidence ("One must want the impossible"), I without it, eying my fingers with the feeling that I was the representative of my inner emptiness, an emptiness that replaces everything else and is not even very great.   [DI, 323]

December 20. The effect of a peaceful fate, calm speech, especially

when exercised by a strange person one hasn't seen through yet. The
voice of God out of a human mouth.   [DI, 324]

   To Felice, December 29:
I think I must now be completely truthful and tell you something that
no one in fact has so far heard from me. At the sanatorium [in Riva,
mid-September] I fell in love with a girl, a child, about 18 years old; she
is Swiss, but lives in Italy, near Genoa, thus by blood as alien to me as
can be; still immature but remarkable and despite her illness a real
person with great depth. A girl far less remarkable than she could have
captivated me at that time in my empty, hopeless state; you've got my
notes from Desenzano, they were written about 10 days before. It was
as clear to me as it was to her that we did not really belong together,
and that once the 10 days available to us had expired everything would
have to end, and that no letters, not a single line would be exchanged.
Nevertheless, we meant a great deal to each other, and I had to make all
kinds of arrangements to prevent her bursting into tears in front of
everyone when we said goodbye, and I felt much the same. With my
departure it was all over.   [F, 335]

   *In the same letter F.K. expresses his desire to marry Felice. For a
   long while Felice remained indifferent. Mid-December: Ernst
   Weiss visits Felice, and on F.K.'s behalf asks for an explanation
   of her silence.*

From "Before the Law"

The doorkeeper has to bend low toward him, for the difference in height between them has altered much to the man's disadvantage. "What do you want to know now?" asks the doorkeeper; "you are insatiable." "Everyone strives to reach the Law," says the man, "so how does it happen that for all these many years no one but myself has ever begged for admittance?" The doorkeeper recognizes that the man has reached his end, and, to let his failing senses catch the words, roars in his ear: "No one else could ever be admitted here, since this gate was made only for you. I am now going to shut it."   *The Penal Colony,* pp. 149 f.

Early January: F.K. renews his request for Felice's hand; she answers evasively.

January 8. Uncertainty, aridity, peace—all things will resolve themselves into these and pass away.

What have I in common with Jews? I have hardly anything in common with myself and should stand very quietly in a corner, content that I can breathe.

Description of inexplicable emotions. A.: Since that happened, the sight of women has been painful to me; it is neither sexual excitement nor pure sadness, it is simply pain. That's the way it was too before I felt sure of Liesl.   [DII, 11]

January 12. Clear night on the way home; distinctly aware of what in me is mere dull apathy, so far removed from a great clarity expanding without hindrance.

There are possibilities for me, certainly; but under what stone do they lie?

Youth's meaninglessness. Fear of youth, fear of meaninglessness, of the meaningless rise of an inhuman life.   [DII, 11 f.]

January 19. Anxiety alternating with self-assurance at the office. Otherwise more confident. Great antipathy to *Metamorphosis.* Unreadable ending. Imperfect almost to its very marrow. It would have turned out much better if I had not been interrupted at the time by the business trip.   [DII, 12]

January 23. "It wasn't your fate," my mother's lame consolation. The bad part of it is that at the moment it is almost all the consolation that I need. There is my weak point and will remain my weak point; otherwise the regular, hardly varying, semiactive life I have led these last days, [. . . among other things] proofreading *Metamorphosis,* has really pulled me together and instilled some resolution and hope in me.
                                                                [DII, 13]

January 24. Incapable of writing a few lines to Miss Bl. [Bloch], two letters already remain unanswered, today the third came. I grasp nothing correctly and at the same time feel quite hale, though hollow. Recently, when I got out of the elevator at my usual hour, it occurred to me that my life, whose days more and more repeat themselves down to the smallest detail, resembles that punishment in which each pupil must according to his offense write down the same meaningless (in repetition, at least) sentence ten times, a hundred times, or even oftener; except that in my case the punishment is given me with only this limitation: "as many times as you can stand it."   [DII, 13 f.]

January 26. The way I almost insulted my mother just now because she had lent [F.K.'s sister] Elli *Die böse Unschuld* [by Oskar Baum], which I had myself intended to offer her only yesterday. "Leave me my books! I have nothing else." Speeches of this kind in a real rage.   [DII, 15]

February 11. Hastily read through [Wilhelm] Dilthey's *Goethe;* tumultuous impression, carries one along, why couldn't one set oneself afire and be destroyed in the flames? Or obey, even if one hears no command? Or sit on a chair in the middle of one's empty room and look at the floor? Or shout "Forward!" in a mountain defile and hear answering shouts and see people emerge from all the bypaths in the cliffs.   [DII, 18]

February 14. There will certainly be no one to blame if I should kill myself, even if the immediate cause should for instance appear to be F.'s [Felice's] behavior. Once, half asleep, I pictured the scene that would ensue if, in anticipation of the end, the letter of farewell in my pocket, I should come to her house, should be rejected as a suitor, lay the letter on the table, go to the balcony, break away from all those who run up to hold me back, and, forcing one hand after another to let go its grip, jump over the ledge. The letter, however, would say that I was jumping because of F., but that even if my proposal had been accepted nothing essential would have been changed for me. My place is down below, I can find no other solution, F. simply happens to be the one through whom my fate is made manifest; I can't live without her and must jump, yet—and this F. suspects—I couldn't live with her either. Why not use tonight for the purpose, I can already see before me the people talking at the parents' gathering this evening, talking of life and the conditions that have to be created for it—but I cling to abstractions, I live completely entangled in life, I won't do it, I am cold, am sad that a shirt collar is pinching my neck, am damned, gasp for breath in the mist.   [DII, 20]

February 22. In spite of my drowsy head, whose upper left side is near aching with restlessness, perhaps I am still able quietly to build up some greater whole wherein I might forget everything and be conscious only of the good in one.   [DII, 22]

February 23. I am on my way. Letter from [Robert] Musil.[1] Pleases me and depresses me, for I have nothing.   [DII, 22]

> *February 28 to March 1: Meets Felice in Berlin; her arguments against their marriage.*

> *To Grete Bloch, March 2:*

The result of all this was as follows: F. quite likes me, but in her opinion this is not enough for marriage, for this particular marriage; she has insurmountable fears about a joint future; she might not be able to put up with my idiosyncrasies; she might not be able to forego Berlin; she is afraid of having to dispense with nice clothes, of traveling third class, sitting in cheaper seats in the theater (this sounds ridiculous only when put on paper), etc.

On the other hand she is friendly toward me (not in conversation, of course; she doesn't answer); in the streets we walk arm in arm like the happiest of engaged couples; we say *"Du"* to each other even in front of Dr. [Ernst] Weiss whom we happened to run into; my picture, as F. showed me, is in a locket she was given in November; she claims she wouldn't marry anyone else; she would never dispose of my letters, nor wish to return my photographs, nor ask for hers to be returned; while she would like to go on writing, she would be equally willing to stop writing altogether.   [F, 353]

March 8. It happened that when Grandmother died only the nurse was with her. She said that just before Grandmother died she lifted herself up a little from the pillow so that she seemed to be looking for someone, and then peacefully lay back again and died.

There is no doubt that I am hemmed in all around, though by something that has certainly not yet fixed itself in my flesh, that I occasionally feel slackening, and that could be burst asunder. There are two remedies, marriage or Berlin; the second is surer, the first more immediately attractive.   [DII, 22 f.]

March 9. I am too tired, I must try to rest and sleep, otherwise I am lost in every respect. What an effort to keep alive! Erecting a monument does not require the expenditure of so much strength.

The general argument: I am completely lost in F.

Yes, that much I can judge of: I am almost thirty-one years old, have known F. for almost two years, must therefore have some perspective by now. Besides, my way of life here is such that I can't forget, even if F. didn't have such significance for me. The uniformity, regularity, comfort, and dependence of my way of life keep me unresistingly fixed wherever I happen to be. Moreover, I have a more than ordinary inclination toward a comfortable and dependent life, and so even strengthen everything that is pernicious to me. Finally, I am getting older, any change becomes more and more difficult. But in all this I foresee a great misfortune for myself, one without end and without hope; I should be dragging through the years up the ladder of my job, growing ever sadder and more alone as long as I could endure it at all.

But you wanted that sort of life for yourself, didn't you?

An official's life could benefit me if I were married. It would in every way be a support to me against society, against my wife, against writing, without demanding too many sacrifices, and without on the other hand degenerating into indolence and dependence, for as a married man I should not have to fear that. But I cannot live out such a life as a bachelor.

But you could have married, couldn't you?

I couldn't marry then; everything in me revolted against it, much as I always loved F. It was chiefly concern over my literary work that prevented me, for I thought marriage would jeopardize it. I may have been right, but in any case it is destroyed by my present bachelor's life. I have written nothing for a year, nor shall I be able to write anything in the future; in my head there is and remains the one single thought, and I am devoured by it. I wasn't able to consider it all at the time. Moreover, as a result of my dependence, which is at least encouraged by this way of life, I approach everything hesitantly and complete nothing at the first stroke. That was what happened here too.

Why do you give up all hope eventually of having F.?

I have already tried every kind of self-humiliation. In the Tiergarten I once said: "Say 'yes'; even if you consider your feeling for me insufficient to warrant marriage, my love for you is great enough to make up the insufficiency, and strong enough in general to take everything on itself." In the course of a long correspondence I had alarmed F. by my peculiarities, and these now seemed to make her uneasy. I said: "I love you enough to rid myself of anything that might trouble you. I will become another person." Now, when everything must be cleared up, I can confess that even at the time when our relationship was at its most affectionate, I often had forebodings, and fears, founded on trifling occurrences, that F. did not love me very much, not with all the force of the love she was capable of. F. has now realized this too, though not without my assistance. I am almost afraid that after my last two visits F. even feels a certain disgust for me, despite the fact that outwardly we are friendly, call each other *"Du,"* walk arm in arm together. The last thing I remember of her is the quite hostile grimace she made in the entrance hall of her house when I was not satisfied to kiss her glove but pulled it open and kissed her hand. Added to this there is the fact that, despite her promise to be punctual in the future in her correspondence, she hasn't answered two of my letters, merely telegraphed to promise letters but hasn't kept her promise; indeed, she hasn't even so much as answered my mother. There can be no doubt of the hopelessness in all this.

One should really never say that. Didn't your previous behavior likewise seem hopeless from F.'s point of view?

That was something else. I always freely confessed my love for her, even during what appeared to be our final farewell in the summer; I was never so cruelly silent; I had reasons for my behavior which, if they could not be approved, could yet be discussed. F.'s only reason is the complete insufficiency of her love. Nevertheless, it is true that I could wait. But I cannot wait in double hopelessness: I cannot see F. more and more slipping from my grasp, and myself more and more unable to escape. It would be the greatest gamble I could take with myself, although—or because—it would best suit all the overpowering evil forces within me. "You never know what will happen" is no argument against the intolerableness of an existing state of affairs.

Then what do you want to do?

Leave Prague. Counter the greatest personal injury that has ever befallen me with the strongest antidote at my disposal.

Leave your job?

In light of the above, my job is only a part of the general intolerableness. I should be losing only what is intolerable in any case. The security, the lifelong provision, the good salary, the fact that it doesn't demand all my strength—after all, so long as I am a bachelor all these things mean nothing to me and are transformed into torments.

Then what do you want to do?

I could answer all such questions at once by saying: I have nothing to lose; every day, each tiniest success, is a gift; whatever I do is all to the good. But I can also give a more precise answer: as an Austrian lawyer, which, speaking seriously, I of course am not, I have no prospects; the best thing I might achieve for myself in this direction I already possess in my present post, and it is of no use to me. Moreover, in the quite impossible event I should want to make some money out of my legal training, there are only two cities that could be considered: Prague, which I must leave, and Vienna, which I hate and where I should inevitably grow unhappy because I should go there with the deepest conviction of that inevitability. I therefore have to leave Austria and—since I have no talent for languages and would do poorly at physical labor or at a business job—go to Germany, at least at first, and in Germany to Berlin, where the chances of earning a living are best. Also, there, in journalism, I can make best and directest use of my ability to write, and so find a means of livelihood at least partially suited to me. Whether in addition I shall be capable of inspired work, that I cannot say at present with any degree of certainty. But I think I know definitely that from the independence and freedom I should have in Berlin (however miserable I otherwise would be) I should derive the only feeling of happiness I am still able to experience.

But you are spoiled.

No, I need a room and a vegetarian diet, almost nothing more.

Aren't you going there because of F.?

No, I choose Berlin only for the above reasons, although I love it and perhaps I love it because of F. and because of the aura of thoughts that surrounds F.; but that I can't help. It is also probable that I shall meet F. in Berlin. If our being together will help me to get F. out of my blood, so much the better, it is an additional advantage Berlin has.

Are you healthy?

No—heart, sleep, digestion.   [DII, 23 ff.]

March 15. Only this everlasting waiting, eternal helplessness.   [DII, 29]

To Felice, March 25:

To your final question, however, whether it is possible for me to take you as though nothing had happened, I can only say that it is not possible. But what is possible, and in fact necessary, is for me to take you with all that has happened, and to hold on to you to the point of delirium.   [F, 373]

April 5. If only it were possible to go to Berlin, to become independent, to live from one day to the next, even to go hungry, but to let all one's strength gush forth instead of conserving it here, or rather—instead of one's turning away into nothingness! If only F. wanted it, if she would stand by me!   [DII, 31]

April 8. Yesterday incapable of writing even one word. Today no better. Who will save me? And the turmoil in me, deep down, scarcely visible; I am like a living latticework, a lattice that is solidly planted and would like to tumble down.   [DII, 31]

April 12-13 (Easter): In Berlin. Unofficial engagement to Felice. The friendship with Grete Bloch continues.

To Grete Bloch, April 14:
I wouldn't have written to you today, Fräulein Grete, for I am very tired, had hardly any sleep in Berlin, had to use all my remaining energy for my work at the office today, not forgetting that I have several more hours' work to do—but there is one thing I can't tell you soon enough and that's this: Our relationship, which for me at least holds delightful and altogether indispensable possibilities, is in no way changed by my engagement or my marriage. Is this a fact, and will it remain so? I repeat, in case it hasn't been made clear already: All this is independent of anything that I and F. (so far as I, the bridegroom, can say this) owe to you in our affairs.   [F, 385]

To Grete Bloch, April 15:
Dear Fräulein Grete, I feel an unmistakable and true longing for you.
                                                                                                        [F, 386]

To Grete Bloch, April 18:
I have no control over my capacity for writing. It comes and goes like a phantom. I haven't written anything for a year, nor can I, as far as I know.   [F, 390]

To Felice, April 20:
Lately, in spite of my superficial loquacity (as yet you are not familiar with this vice, nor is it one of yours, which is yet another reason why I

love you), I have become more and more taciturn, more and more unsociable; in spite of this inner urge to be loquacious, and even a more legitimate desire to impart information, I cannot break out of myself; it is not actually shyness, rather a feeling of discomfort in the presence of people, an inability to establish complete, lasting relationships; I so rarely lose the detached eye (can you understand that?); I venture to claim that it is rare for anyone to have, as I have, silently from a distance, without being directly compel— final interruption: 2 uncles have arrived, one from Triesch in Moravia, the other, an eccentric, lives here in Prague; I must stop, but if only to prevent you from worrying about the half-finished sentence, worrying unnecessarily, believe me, we do trust each other, don't we? Well, to prevent you worrying, I complete the sentence —led to do so, the faculty of grasping the essence of people so completely that it frightens even me. That I have. This faculty, however, is almost a danger to me when I am not writing. But nothing is a danger to me now that I have you, and for you too, dearest, there should be no dangers. [F. 392 f.]

To Grete Bloch, April 21:
Whether you should be looking forward to the "story" [*The Metamorphosis*]? I don't know, you didn't like the "Stoker." Anyway, the "story" is looking forward to you, there's no doubt about that. Incidentally, the heroine's name is Grete and she doesn't discredit you, at least not in the first section. Later on, though, when the agony becomes too great, she withdraws, embarks on a life of her own, and leaves the one who needs her. An old story, by the way, more than a year old; at that time I hadn't begun to appreciate the name Grete, learned to do so only during the process of writing. [F. 394 f.]

May 1: Felice in Prague; search for an apartment.

May 6. My parents seem to have found a beautiful apartment for F. and me; I ran around for nothing one entire beautiful afternoon. I wonder whether they will lay me in my grave too, after a life made happy by their solicitude.

The horror in the merely schematic. [DII, 31, 33]

I have never discovered what the rule is. [DF, 206]

May 27. Mother and sister in Berlin. I shall be alone with my father in the evening. I think he is afraid to come up. Should I play cards [*Karten*] with him? (I find the letter K offensive, almost nauseating, and

yet I write it down; it must be very characteristic of me.) How Father
acted when I touched F.   [DII, 33 f.]

May 27. A heavy downpour. Stand and face the rain, let its iron rays
pierce you; drift with the water that wants to sweep you away but yet
stand fast, and upright in this way abide the sudden and endless
shining of the sun.   [DII, 36]

May 28. Day after tomorrow I leave for Berlin. In spite of insomnia,
headaches, and worries, perhaps in a better state than ever before.
                                                            [DII, 38 f.]

May 29. Tomorrow to Berlin. Is it a nervous or a real, trustworthy
security that I feel? How is that possible? Is it true that if one once
acquires a confidence in one's ability to write, nothing can miscarry,
nothing is wholly lost, while at the same time only seldom will something rise up to a more than ordinary height? Is this because of my
approaching marriage to F.? Strange condition, though not entirely
unknown to me when I think back.   [DII, 40]

*May 30: F.K. in Berlin for the official engagement. June 1: The
Bauer family's reception; Grete Bloch was present.*

June 6. Back from Berlin. Was bound like a criminal. Had they sat me
down in a corner bound in real chains, placed policemen in front of me,
and let me look on simply like that, it could not have been worse. And
that was my engagement; everybody made an effort to bring me to life,
and when they couldn't, to put up with me as I was. F. least of all, of
course, with complete justification, for she suffered the most. What was
merely a passing occurrence to the others, to her was a threat.   [DII, 42]

To Grete Bloch, June 6:
Dear Fräulein Grete, yesterday was another of those days when I felt
completely tied down, incapable of moving, incapable of writing you
the letter that everything still alive within me urged me to write. At
times—and for the moment you are the only one to know—I really don't
know how I, being what I am, can bear the responsibility of marriage. A
marriage erected on the woman's fortitude? Bound to be a crooked
edifice, don't you think? It will collapse and in so doing rip the foundations from the earth.
    Oh God, I did understand what you meant, Fräulein Grete, by your
evaluation of my writing. But even if understood, your opinion is not
correct, even though it is being considered. Each of us has his own way

of emerging from the underworld, mine is by writing. That's why the only way I can keep going, if at all, is by writing, not through rest and sleep. I am far more likely to achieve peace of mind through writing than the capacity to write through peace.

But I keep talking about myself, which in itself is an indication of the state I am in. I think this is what I did in Berlin as well, although I surely ought to have known that I am visible and alive only when I suppress as much as possible all things concerning myself.   [F. 420 f.]

To Grete Bloch, June 8:

In July I shall move somewhere into the woods and try to improve myself as best I can in the short time. Parents here are in the habit of saying that it's the children who make one realize how old one is getting. If one has no children, it's one's ghosts that make one realize it, and they do it all the more thoroughly. I know that when I was young I tried to lure them out, they barely showed themselves; I tried harder, I was bored without them, they wouldn't come, and I began to think they would never come. For this reason I was often on the point of cursing my life. Later on they did appear, only now and then, always as exalted visitors, one had to bow to them though they were still very small; quite often it wasn't them at all, it merely looked or sounded as if it were. But when they did come they were seldom fierce, one couldn't be very proud of them, at best they pounced on one like the lion cub on the bitch; they did bite, but this was noticeable only if one placed one's finger on the bitten spot and pressed hard with one's fingernail. Later, however, they grew bigger, they came and stayed at will, delicate birds' backs turned into the backs of monumental giants, they came in through every door, forcing those that were shut; huge, bony ghosts they were, nameless in their multitude; a single ghost could be fought, but not all those by which one was surrounded. If one were writing, they were all benevolent spirits; when not writing, they were demons, and pressed so close that all one could do was raise a hand to declare one's presence. Presumably one was not responsible for the way one strained the raised hand.   [F. 421 f.]

To Grete Bloch, June 11:

Owing to circumstances as well as to his own temperament, a completely antisocial man in an indifferent state of health hard to determine at the moment, excluded from every great soul-sustaining community on account of his non-Zionist (I admire Zionism and am nauseated by it), nonpracticing Judaism; the most precious part of his nature continually and most agonizingly upset by the enforced labor of his office—a man of this kind, certainly under the deepest inner compulsion, decides to get married—to undertake, in other words, the most social of acts. For a man of this kind, that strikes me as no mean venture.   [F, 423]

June 14. How I calmly walk along while my head twitches and a branch feebly rustles overhead, causing me the worst discomfort. I have in me the same calm, the same assurance as other people, but somehow or other inverted.   [DII, 61]

June 19. How the two of us, Ottla and I, explode in rage against every kind of human relationship.   [DII, 62]

Before traveling to Berlin for the formal breaking-off of the engagement with Felice:
July 5. To have to bear and to be the cause of such suffering!   [DII, 65]

To his sister Ottla, July 10:
I write not as I speak, I speak not as I think, I think not as I ought to think, and so it goes on into the deepest darkness.
    Give my love to everyone. You are not to show this letter to anyone, nor leave it lying around. The best thing would be to tear it up and scatter the little pieces from the *pavlatche* for the hens in the yard, I haven't any secrets from them.   [Br, 130]

July 12: F.K. in Berlin. Family meeting at the hotel Askanische Hof, in the presence of Grete Bloch and Felice's sister Erna. Engagement broken off.
    July 13: Two weeks' vacation, first in Travemünde (on the Baltic), then with Ernst Weiss at the Danish seaside resort Marienlyst. On July 26 F.K. returns to Prague.

End of July, to Brod and Felix Weltsch:
I should have written before, I know. But wait till you hear what has happened to me. I have broken off my engagement, I was in Berlin for three days, everybody was very friendly to me, I was very friendly to everybody; incidentally, I am quite certain that this is the best solution, and consequently, since the need for action was so obvious, I am less disturbed by this business than might have been expected. In other ways, however, things are not so good.   [Br, 130 f.]

Draft of a letter to his parents, written in Marienlyst:
I have not finished with Berlin, however, insofar as I believe that the whole business, for your good and for mine (for they are certainly one

and the same thing), prevents me from going on living as I have done. Look, really serious pain I have probably never caused you till now, unless it were that this breaking-off of my engagement is one, at this distance I can't judge it as such. But really lasting pleasure I have given you still less, and that, believe me, solely for the reason that I couldn't give myself this pleasure continuously. Why that is so, just you, Father, although you cannot recognize the real thing I want, will understand the easiest! You sometimes relate how badly things went with you when you were making your first beginnings. Don't you think it is a good training for self-respect and satisfaction? Don't you think—anyway you have already told me so in so many words—that I have had things too easy? So far I have grown up in complete dependence and outward well-being. Don't you think that that was not at all a good thing for a nature like mine, kind and loving as it was on the part of all who saw to it that it was so? Of course there are men who know how to ensure their independence anywhere, but I am not one of them. You must admit that there are also people who never lose their dependence, but to put it to the test as to whether I don't perhaps belong to that class, seems to me an attempt that must be made. Even the objection that I am too old for such an attempt doesn't hold water. I am younger than would appear. The only good result of dependence is that it keeps one young. That of course only in the case that it comes to an end.

In the office I shall never be able to achieve this improvement. Not anywhere at all in Prague. Here everything is arranged to keep me, a man that fundamentally asks for dependence, in that state. Everything is so nicely laid to my hand. The office I find very burdensome and often unbearable, but at bottom, all the same, easy. In this easy way I earn more than I need. What for? Whom for? I shall go up in the scale of salaries. To what purpose? If this work doesn't suit me and doesn't even bring me independence as a reward, why should I not throw it up? I have nothing to risk and everything to gain if I hand in my resignation and go away from Prague. I risk nothing, because my life in Prague leads to nothing good. Sometimes you say I am like Uncle R. [Rudolf]. But my way of life will not lead me so far apart from his if I stay in Prague. I shall presumably have more money, more interests, and less faith than he has; I shall be correspondingly more dissatisfied, because other differences there will hardly be. Away from Prague I can gain everything, that is to say, become an independent man at peace with himself, who is employing all his faculties, and as a reward for good and genuine work gets the feeling of really being alive, and of lasting contentment. A man like this—this will not be the smallest gain—will also behave better toward you. You will have a son whose every single action you will not perhaps approve of, but in whom, as a whole, you will be well pleased, because you will be obliged to say, "He does his best." This feeling you have not now, and rightly.

The way to carry out my plan I imagine is this: I have 5,000 kronen. That enables me to live somewhere in Germany, in Berlin or in Munich, for two years, if needs must, without earning anything. These two years will enable me to go on with my literary work, and to produce from out of myself that which I cannot produce in the same clarity, wealth, and coherence in Prague, what between inner lethargy and outer disturbances. This literary work will enable me, after these two years, to live, however modestly, on what I earn myself. But let it be as modest as you like, it will be incomparably better than the life I am now leading in Prague, and that which awaits me there in future. You will object that I am mistaken in my abilities and in the possibility of making a living out of these abilities. That's certainly not out of the question. Only the answer to that is that I am thirty-one, and mistakes of that kind cannot be taken into account at that age, otherwise it would make any accounting impossible. A further answer to it is that I have already written a certain amount, little though it be, which has half succeeded in meeting with recognition, but the objection is finally answered by the fact that I am not in the least lazy, and have fairly few pretensions, and therefore, even if this hope should fail, can find other ways of earning my living, and in any case should not make any claims on you; for that would anyhow, both in its effects on me, as well as on you, make things still worse than my present life in Prague is, in fact it would be completely unbearable.

My position therefore seems clear enough to me, and I am anxious to hear what you will have to say about it. For even if I am convinced that this is the only right way, and that if I miss putting this plan into action I shall miss something of decisive importance, yet it is naturally very important for me to know what you have to say to it all.   [B. 147 ff.]

With reference to the meeting at the Askanische Hof:
July 23. The tribunal in the hotel. Trip in the cab. F.'s face. She patted her hair with her hand, wiped her nose, yawned. Suddenly she gathered herself together and said very studied, hostile things she had long been saving up. The trip back with Miss Bl. [Grete Bloch]. The room in the hotel; heat reflected from the wall across the street. Afternoon sun, in addition. Energetic waiter, almost an East European Jew in his manner. The courtyard noisy as a boiler factory. Bad smells. Bedbug. Crushing it a difficult decision. Chambermaid astonished: There are no bedbugs anywhere; once only did a guest find one in the corridor.

At her parents'. Her mother's occasional tears. I told the whole story. Her father understood the thing from every side. Made a special trip from Malmö to meet me, traveled all night; sat there in his shirt sleeves. They admit that I was right, there was nothing, or not much, that could be said against me. Diabolical in all innocence. Miss Bl.'s apparent guilt. [. . .]

In the Restaurant Belvedere on the Strahlau Brücke with E. [Felice's sister Erna]. She still hopes it will end well, or acts as if she does. Drank wine. Tears in her eyes. Ships leave for Grünau, for Schwertau. A lot of people. Music. E. consoled me, though I wasn't sad; that is, my sadness has to do only with myself, but as such it is inconsolable. [. . .]

Why did her parents and aunt wave after me? Why did F. sit in the hotel and not stir in spite of the fact that everything was already settled? Why did she telegraph me: "Expecting you, but must leave on business Tuesday"? Was I expected to do something? Nothing could have been more natural.   [DII, 65 f.]

During "the tribunal" F.K. listened to the accusations against him and kept silent.

July 27. The next day didn't visit her parents again. Merely sent a messenger with a letter of farewell. Letter dishonest and coquettish. "Don't think badly of me." Speech from the place of execution.   [DII, 66]

July 28. I am more and more unable to think, to observe, to determine the truth of things, to remember, to speak, to share an experience; I am turning to stone, this is the truth. I am more and more unable even in the office. If I can't take refuge in some work, I am lost. Is my knowledge of this as clear as the thing itself? I shun people not because I want to live quietly, but rather in order to be able to die quietly. I think of the walk we, Erna and I, took from the trolley to the Lehrter railroad station. Neither of us spoke, I thought nothing but that each step taken was that much of a gain for me. And Erna is nice to me, believes in me for some incomprehensible reason, in spite of having seen me before the tribunal; now and then I even feel the effect of this faith in me, without, however, fully believing in the feeling.

The first time in many months that I felt any life stir in me in the presence of other people was in the compartment on the return trip from Berlin, opposite the Swiss woman. She reminded me of G.W. ["the Swiss girl"]. Once she even exclaimed: Children! She had headaches, her blood gave her so much trouble. Ugly, neglected little body; bad, cheap dress from a Paris department store. Freckles on her face. But small feet; a body completely under control because of its diminutive size, and despite its clumsiness, round, firm cheeks, sparkling, inextinguishable eyes.   [DII, 68 f.]

July 31. General mobilization. K. and P. have been called up. Now I receive the reward for living alone. But it is hardly a reward; living alone ends only with punishment. Still, as a consequence, I am little affected by all the misery and am firmer in my resolve than ever. I shall have to spend my afternoons in the factory; I won't live at home, for [F.K.'s sister] Elli and the two children are moving in with us.² But I will write in spite of everything, absolutely; it is my struggle for self-preservation.

August 2. Germany has declared war on Russia.—Swimming in the afternoon. [DII, 75]

August: F.K. leaves his parents' home, where he lived until then, and rents a room at Bilekgasse 10.

August 3. In one month I was to have been married. The saying hurts: You've made your bed, now lie in it. You find yourself painfully pushed against the wall, apprehensively lower your eyes to see whose hand it is that pushes you, and, with a new pain in which the old is forgotten, recognize your own contorted hand holding you with a strength it never had for good work. You raise your head, again feel the first pain, again lower your gaze; this up-and-down motion of your head goes on without pause. [DII, 76]

August 6. I discover in myself nothing but pettiness, indecision, envy and hatred against those who are fighting and whom I passionately wish everything evil.

What will be my fate as a writer is very simple. My preoccupation with portraying my dreamlike inner life has thrust all other matters into the background; my life has dwindled dreadfully, nor will it cease to dwindle. Nothing else will ever make me happy. But the strength I can muster for that portrayal is not to be counted upon: perhaps it has already vanished forever, perhaps it will come back to me once again, although the circumstances of my life are not favorable to it. Thus I waver, continually fly to the summit of the mountain, but then fall back in a moment. Others waver too, but in lower regions, with greater strength; if they are in danger of falling, they are caught up by the kinsman who walks beside them for that very purpose. But I waver on the heights; it is not death, alas, but the eternal torments of dying. [DII, 77]

August 7. Yesterday and today wrote four pages, trivialities difficult to surpass.

[August] Strindberg is tremendous. This rage, these pages won by fist-fighting.   [DII, 78]

In August, shortly after terminating his engagement, F.K. began to write The Trial *and "Memoirs of the Kalda Railroad."*

August 15. I have been writing these past few days, may it continue. Today I am not so completely protected by and wrapped up in my work as I was two years ago, nevertheless have the feeling that my regular, empty, mad bachelor's life has some justification. I can once more carry on a dialogue with myself, and don't stare so into complete emptiness. Only in this way can I ever get better.   [DII, 79]

August 29. The end of one chapter [of *The Trial*] a failure; another chapter, which began beautifully, I shall hardly—or rather certainly not—be able to continue as beautifully, while at the time, during the night, I should certainly have succeeded with it. But I must not forsake myself, I am entirely alone.   [DII, 91]

August 30. Cold and empty. I feel only too strongly the limits of my abilities, narrow limits, doubtless, unless I am completely inspired. And I believe that even in the grip of inspiration I am swept along only within these narrow limits, which, however, I then no longer feel because I am being swept along. Nevertheless, within these limits there is room to live, and for this reason I shall probably exploit them to a despicable degree.   [DII, 91]

September 1. In complete helplessness barely wrote two pages. I fell back a great deal today, though I slept well. Yet if I wish to transcend the initial pangs of writing (as well as the inhibiting effect of my way of life) and rise up into the freedom that perhaps awaits me, I know that I must not yield. My old apathy hasn't completely deserted me yet, as I can see, and my coldness of heart perhaps never. That I recoil from no ignominy can as well indicate hopelessness as give hope.   [DII, 92]

September 13. Again barely two pages [of *The Trial*]. At first I thought my sorrow over the Austrian defeats and my anxiety for the future (anxiety that appears ridiculous to me at bottom, and base too) would prevent me from doing any writing. But that wasn't it, it was only an apathy that forever comes back and forever has to be put down again.
    [DII, 92]

October 7. I have taken a week's vacation to push the novel on. Until today—it is Wednesday night, my vacation ends Monday—it has been a failure. I have written little and feebly. Even last week I was on the decline, but could not foresee that it would prove so bad. Are these three days enough to warrant the conclusion that I am unworthy of living without the office?   [DII, 92 f.]

October 5-19: Vacation; continuation of work on The Trial *and* Amerika; *writes "In the Penal Colony."*

October 15. Two weeks of good work; full insight into my situation occasionally. Today, Thursday (Monday my vacation is over, I have taken an additional week), a letter from Miss Bl. [Bloch]. I don't know what to do about it, I know it is certain that I shall live on alone (if I live at all—which is *not* certain), I also don't know whether I love F. (I remember the aversion I felt at the sight of her dancing with her severe eyes lowered, or when she ran her hand over her nose and hair in the Askanische Hof shortly before she left, and the numberless moments of complete estrangement); but in spite of everything the enormous temptation returns again, I played with the letter all through the evening; I don't work though I could (even if I've had excruciating headaches this whole past week). I'm noting down from memory the letter I wrote to Miss Bl.

"What a strange coincidence, Grete, that it was just today I received your letter. I will not say with what it coincided, that concerns only me and the things that were troubling me tonight as I went to bed, about three. (Suicide; letter full of instructions to Max.)

"Your letter was a great surprise to me. Not because you wrote to me. Why shouldn't you write to me? Though you do say that I hate you; but it isn't true. Were the whole world to hate you, I still shouldn't, and not only because I have no right to do so. You sat as a judge over me in the Askanische Hof—it was awful for you, for me, for everyone—but it only *seemed* so; in reality all the time I was sitting in your place and sit there to this day.

"You are completely mistaken about F. I don't say this to worm details from you. I can think of no detail—and my imagination has so often gone back and forth across this ground that I can trust it—I say I can think of no detail that could persuade me you are not mistaken. What you suggest is completely impossible; it makes me unhappy to think that F. should perhaps be deceiving herself for some undiscoverable reason. But that is also impossible.

"I have always believed your interest to be honest and free from any personal consideration. Nor was your last letter an easy one to write. I warmly thank you for it."

What did this accomplish? The letter sounds unyielding, but only because I was ashamed, because I considered it irresponsible, because I was afraid to be yielding; by no means because I did not want to yield. That was the only thing I did want. It would be best for all of us if she would not answer, but she will answer and I shall wait for her answer.

[DII, 93 f.]

The letter to Grete Bloch (October 15, 1914) appears in Letters to Felice, *436.*

October 15 (?) . . .[3] I have now lived calmly for two months without any real contact with F. (except through the correspondence with E. [Erna]), have dreamed of F. as though of someone who was dead and could never live again, and now, when I am offered a chance to come near her, she is at once the center of everything again. She is probably also interfering with my work. How very much a stranger she has sometimes seemed to me these latter days when I would think of her, of all the people I had ever met the most remote; though at the same time I told myself that this was simply because F. had been closer to me than any other person, or at least had been thrust so close to me by other people.

Leafed through the diary a little. Got a kind of inkling of the way a life like this is constituted.

[DII, 94 f.]

To Felice, after a silence of over three months, end of October or beginning of November:

As far as I am concerned, Felice, nothing whatever has changed between us in the past 3 months, either for the better, or for the worse. Needless to say, I am ready at your first call, and would have replied without fail and by return to your earlier letter if I had received it. Actually, it had not occurred to me to write to you; the futility of letters and the written word in general had become too apparent at the Askanische Hof; but since my head (even with its aches, above all today) has remained the same, it has not failed to think and dream of you, and the life we lead together in my mind has only occasionally been bitter, most of the time peaceful and happy. As a matter of fact, on one occasion I did mean not actually to write but to send you a message through someone (you will never guess who, it was an exceptional opportunity), a message conceived while falling asleep about 4 in the morning, the habitual hour for my first sleep.

But the main reason why it has not occurred to me to write was that the most important aspect of our relationship really seemed to me to be quite clear. For ages you were mistaken in referring so often to what had been left unsaid. What was lacking was not discussion, but belief.

Because you were unable to believe the things you heard and saw, you thought there were things that had been left unsaid. You were unable to appreciate the immense power my work has over me; you did appreciate it, but by no means fully. As a result you were bound to misinterpret everything that my worries over my work, and only my worries over my work, produced in me in the way of peculiarities which disconcerted you. Moreover, these peculiarities (odious peculiarities, I admit, odious above all to myself) manifested themselves more with you than with anyone else. That was inevitable, and had nothing to do with spite. You see, you were not only the greatest friend, but at the same time the greatest enemy, of my work, at least from the point of view of my work. Thus, though fundamentally it loved you beyond measure, equally it had to resist you with all its might for the sake of self-preservation. It had to do so in every single detail. I thought of it, for instance, when having a meal one evening with your sister consisting almost exclusively of meat. Had you been there, I would probably have ordered almonds.

Nor was my silence at the Askanische Hof due to spite. What you said was so clear I have no wish to repeat it; but it included certain things that ought to be almost impossible for one person to say to another. True, you didn't say them until after I had been silent for some time, or had stammered some inconsequential words. And even then you waited a long time for me to say something. I no longer object to your having brought along Frl. Bl[och]; after all, I had almost discredited you in that letter to her; she had a right to be present. But that you should have allowed your sister [Erna], whom I hardly knew at the time, to come along as well—that I could not understand. However, I was only slightly disconcerted by their presence; had I been capable of saying anything decisive, I might possibly have kept silent out of spite. That is possible, but I had nothing decisive to say. I realized that all was lost; I also realized that even then, at the last moment, I could save the situation by making some startling confession, but I had no startling confession to make. I loved you then as I do now; I knew that though innocent, you had been made to suffer for two years as even the guilty ought not to suffer; but I also realized that you could not understand my position. What ought I to have done? Precisely what I did: join you, keep silent or say something very silly, listen to the story about the funny cab-driver, and gaze at you with the feeling that it was for the last time.

When I say that you could not understand my position, I do not profess to know what you ought to have done. Had I known, I wouldn't have kept it from you. I was continually trying to explain my position to you—and, what's more, you obviously understood it, but couldn't bring yourself to accept it. In me there have always been, and still are, two selves wrestling with each other. One of them is very much as you would wish him to be, and by further development he could achieve the little he lacks in order to fulfill your wishes. None of the things you reproached me with at the Askanische Hof applied to him. The other self, however, thinks of nothing but work, which is his sole concern; it has the effect of making even the meanest thoughts appear quite normal; the death of his dearest friend would seem to be no more than a hindrance—if only a temporary one—to his work; this meanness is compensated for by the fact that he is also capable of suffering for his work. These two selves are locked in combat, but it is no ordinary fight where two pairs of fists strike out at each other. The first self is dependent upon the second; he would never, for inherent reasons never, be able to overpower him; on the contrary, he is delighted when the second succeeds, and if the second appears to be losing, the first will kneel down at his side, oblivious of everything but him. This is how it is, Felice. And yet they are locked in combat, and yet they could both be yours; the trouble is that they cannot be changed unless both were to be destroyed.

What this actually means is that you ought to have accepted it all completely, ought to have realized that whatever was happening here was also happening for you, and that everything the work requires for itself, which looks like obstinacy and moodiness, is nothing but an expedient, necessary partly for its own sake and partly forced on me by the circumstances of my life, so utterly hostile to this work. Imagine the way I live at present. Alone in my eldest sister's apartment. She, because my brother-in-law is in the army, is staying with my parents. Unless certain things interfere, above all the factory, my timetable is as follows: Office until 2:30, followed by lunch at home, followed by 1–2 hours reading newspapers, writing letters, or doing work for the office; then up to my apartment (you know it) to sleep, or just to rest; then at 9 down to my parents for supper (a decent walk), back again by tram at 10, and then to stay awake as long as my strength, or fear of the following morning, fear of headaches at the office, permits. In the course of the last three months this is the second evening I have spent without working; the first was about a month ago, when I was too tired. I also had a fortnight's vacation lately, and during this period of course my timetable was slightly altered insofar as this was possible in the rush of that brief fortnight and the fearful knowledge that the days were passing. On average I sat at my desk until 5 in the morning, once even till 7:30, then I slept; during the last few days of the vacation I managed to sleep properly, until 1 or 2 P.M., and from then on I was really free, and took time off until the evening.

You may be able to accept the kind of life I lead during a vacation, Felice, but not the life I normally lead—at least you haven't been ready to do so as yet. Those hours of the day that I consider to be the only ones lived according to my needs, I spend sitting or lying in these three silent rooms, see no one, not even my friends, except for Max for a few minutes on the way home from the office and—am not happy, certainly not, and yet content at times at the thought that I am doing my duty, as far as the circumstances permit.

I have always admitted to this way of life; it was always the doubtful question as well as the test. While you never said "No" in reply to that question, your "Yes" never encompassed the entire question. But the gap left open by your reply was filled, as far as you were concerned, Felice, with hatred, or, if that's too strong a word, with dislike. It started while you were in Frankfurt; I am not aware of the immediate cause, there may not even have been one; at any rate, it was in your letters from Frankfurt that your dislike first appeared in the way in which you responded to my concern about you, in the way in which you showed your reserve. You yourself probably did not realize it at the time, but later on you must have been aware of it. What, after all, were those fears you kept referring to later in the Tiergarten and which forced you more often into silence than into speech? What were they but dislike of my way of life, as well as indirectly of my intentions, which you could not reconcile with yours, which gave you offense? I can see you with tears in your eyes listening to Dr. W[eiss]—that was fear. That evening (these are a few, perhaps not always appropriate examples!) before I went to see your parents and you were unable to give a definite answer—that was fear. In Prague when you complained of certain things about me—that was fear. Over and over again, fear. I say fear rather than dislike, but the two feelings merged. And the things you finally said at the Askanische Hof, weren't they the eruption of all this? Were you still in doubt when you heard yourself speak? Didn't you even use the expression that you would be bound to lose yourself if you——? And even in today's letter, Felice, I notice passages that could still be due to that fear. You must not misunderstand me, Felice. That dislike was there, yet in the eyes of the whole wide world you had decided to defy it. It might have turned out well in the end, as in happy moments I myself hoped it would. But that's not the point. You want an explanation for my behavior last time, and this explanation lies in the fact that your fears, your dislike, were constantly before my eyes. It was my duty to protect my work, which alone gives me the right to live, and your fears proved, at least made me fear (with far more unbearable fears) that here lay the gravest danger to my work. "I was nervous, I was worn out, I thought I had reached the end of my tether," that's what you write, and that's how it was. Never before had the two selves fought so hard as they did then. And it was then that I wrote that letter to Frl. Bl[och].

But perhaps I have not quite justified the reasons for my fears; after all, your explanations at the Ask. H. [Askanische Hof] were not made until later; I must not make use of them now. One of the clearest examples, however, is the disagreement about the apartment; I was dismayed by every detail of your scheme, though I could not oppose it in any way, and no doubt everyone would have insisted that you were right. It is merely that you yourself ought not to have insisted. What you wanted was perfectly reasonable: a pleasant, pleasantly furnished, family apartment, such as is inhabited by all families of both your and my social standing. Altogether you wanted no more than these people have (they were mentioned again in today's letter, they are the ones into whose "lap things fall"), but what they have, you wanted in its entirety. On one occasion—by which time I was approaching my worst fears—I asked you to cancel the ceremonies in the synagogue; you didn't answer; in my apprehensive state I assumed you had resented my request, and at the A.H. [Askanische Hof] you did in fact mention this request. But your whole idea about the apartment, what does it show? It shows that you agree with the others, not with me; for these others, however, a home, quite legitimately, has an entirely different meaning to the one it would have had for me. These others, when they get married, are very nearly satiated, and marriage to them is but the final, great, delicious mouthful. Not so for me, I am not satiated, I haven't started a business that's expected to expand from one year of marriage to another; I don't need a permanent home from whose bourgeois orderliness I propose to run this business—not only do I not need this kind of home, it actually frightens me. I am so hungry for my work that it makes me feel limp; here, however, the conditions are antagonistic to my work, so if I set up house according to your wishes under these conditions, it would mean—if not in fact, at any rate symbolically—that I am attempting to make these conditions permanent, which is the worst thing that can befall me.

Somehow I should like to narrow down what I have just said, and so define it more clearly. You would be quite justified in asking what kind of proposals I expected of you as regards our home. Actually I can't answer that question. The most apposite and most obvious from the point of view of my work would have been to throw everything away, and to look for an apartment even higher up than the 4th floor, not in Prague, elsewhere; but it appears that neither you nor I are equipped to live in self-appointed misery. Perhaps I am even less equipped to do so than you. Well, so far neither of us has tried it. So could I really expect the suggestion to come from you? Not exactly; though had you suggested it I should have been so happy I wouldn't have known what to do, but I certainly didn't expect it. But certainly a compromise could or rather would have been found. And you would have found it, without so much as looking, quite naturally, if only—yes, if only it had not been for those fears, that dislike, which prevented you from doing the things that were essential to me and to our life together. Indeed, I could have gone on hoping that agreement might yet be reached, but these would have been merely hopes; but at that moment there were signs of the precise opposite which were bound to frighten me, and from which I had to protect myself as long as I wanted you to have a husband who was alive.

Now of course you can turn the whole thing around and say that you, your very nature was as dangerously threatened as mine, and that your fears were as fully justified as mine. I don't believe that this was the case. For I loved you in your true nature, and feared it only when it met my work with hostility. And since I loved you so much I was bound to help you to protect yourself. But even this is not strictly true; you certainly were endangered, but then didn't you want to be endangered at all? Never? Not at all?

What I have said is not new, I may have summarized it in a slightly different way, but it's nothing new. What is new is that it doesn't form part of a regular correspondence, and this, as well as the fact that you asked for this summing-up, gives me hope of receiving a clear-cut answer. I am eager for your reply. You must answer, Felice, no matter how much you may object to my letter. I am extremely impatient for your answer. When I stopped writing this letter yesterday—it was getting late—and went to bed, I slept a while, but when, later on, I woke up and couldn't get to sleep again until the morning, all our sorrows and woes—this really is something we have in common—came over me undiminished, as in the worst days. After all, everything still hangs together, not one of these worries has been resolved, as soon as one allows it all to come a little closer. It tears at one this way and that, as though gripping one by the tongue. There were moments during last night when I thought I had crossed the borderline of madness, and I didn't know how to save myself. So you will answer my letter, and if you want to be especially kind, please notify me by telegram as soon as you receive this.

You mention my correspondence with Erna. I don't know what you mean when you say I should write to you irrespective of this correspondence. It so happens that I shall be writing to Erna tomorrow. So I'll tell her that I have written to you. Erna has been unimaginably kind to me, and to you, too.   [F. 436 ff.]

November 3. Because I had slept very little during the night, did not work any more, partly too because I was afraid to spoil a fair passage I had written yesterday. Since August, the fourth day on which I have written nothing. The letters [to Felice] are the cause of it; I'll try to write

none at all or only very short ones. How embarrassed I now am, and
how it agitates me.   [DII, 96]

*No evidence of a letter to Felice has been found for the period of
the next three months.*

November–December: "Before the Law" (part of The Trial) *written; in December, "The Village Schoolmaster" ["The Giant Mole"].*

November 30. I can't write any more. I've come up against the last
boundary, before which I shall in all likelihood again sit down for
years, and then in all likelihood begin another story all over again
that will again remain unfinished. This fate pursues me. And I have
become cold again, and insensible; nothing is left but a senile love for
unbroken calm. And like some kind of beast at the farthest pole from
man, I shift my neck from side to side again and for the time being
should like to try again to have F. back. I'll really try it, if the nausea I
feel for myself doesn't prevent me.   [DII, 98]

December 2. Afternoon at Werfel's with Max and [Otto] Pick. Read "In
the Penal Colony" aloud; am not entirely dissatisfied, except for its
glaring and ineradicable faults. Werfel read some poems and two acts
of [his] *Esther, Kaiserin von Persien* [*Esther, Empress of Persia*]. The
acts carry one away. But I am easily carried away. The criticisms and
comparisons put forward by Max, who was not entirely satisfied with
the piece, disturb me, and I am no longer so sure of my impression of
the play as a whole as I was while listening to it, when it overwhelmed
me. I remember the Yiddish actors.

The day's conclusion, even before meeting Werfel: Go on working
regardless of everything; a pity I can't work today, for I am tired and
have a headache, already had preliminary twinges in the office this
morning. I'll go on working regardless of everything, it must be possible
in spite of the office or the lack of sleep.   [DII, 98 f.]

*F.K. saw himself as the cause of Felice's father's fatal heart
attack on November 5.*

December 5. A letter from E. [Erna] on the situation in her family. My
relation to her family has a consistent meaning only if I conceive of
myself as its ruin. This is the only natural explanation there is to make
plausible everything that is astonishing in the relation. It is also the
only connection I have at the moment with her family; otherwise I am

completely divorced from it emotionally, although not more effectu-
ally, perhaps, than I am from the whole world. (A picture of my existence apropos of this would portray a useless stake covered with snow
and frost, fixed loosely and slantwise into the ground in a deeply
plowed field on the edge of a great plain on a dark winter's night.) Only
ruin has effect. I have made F. unhappy, weakened the resistance of all
those who need her so much now, contributed to the death of her
father, come between F. and E., and in the end made E. unhappy too, an
unhappiness that gives every indication of growing worse. I am in the
harness and it is my fate to pull the load. The last letter to her that I
tortured out of myself she considers calm; it "breathes so much calm-
ness," as she puts it. It is of course not impossible that she puts it this
way out of delicacy, out of forbearance, out of concern for me. I am
indeed sufficiently punished in general, even my position in my own
family is punishment enough; I have also suffered so much that I shall
never recover from it (my sleep, my memory, my ability to think, my
resistance to the tiniest worries have been weakened past all cure—
strangely enough, the consequences of a long period of imprisonment
are about the same).   [DII, 99 f.]

December 8. Yesterday for the first time in ever so long an indisputable
ability to do good work. And yet wrote only the first page of the
"mother" chapter [a fragment], for I had barely slept at all two nights,
in the morning already had had indications of a headache, and had
been too anxious about the next day. Again I realized that everything
written down bit by bit rather than all at once in the course of the larger
part (or even the whole) of one night is inferior, and that the circumstances of my life condemn me to this inferiority.   [DII, 100 f.]

December 13. Instead of working—I have written only one page (ex-
egesis of the "Legend" ["Before the Law"])—looked through the finished
chapters and found parts of them good. Always conscious that every
feeling of satisfaction and happiness that I have, such, for example, as
the "Legend" in particular inspires in me, must be paid for, and must be
paid for moreover at some future time, in order to deny me all possibility of recovery in the present.

   Recently at Felix's [Felix Weltsch's]. On the way home told Max that
I shall lie very contentedly on my deathbed, provided the pain isn't too
great. I forgot—and later purposely omitted—to add that the best things
I have written have their basis in this capacity of mine to meet death
with contentment. All these fine and very convincing passages always
deal with the fact that someone is dying, that it is hard for him to do,

that it seems unjust to him, or at least harsh, and the reader is moved by this, or at least he should be. But for me, who believe that I shall be able to lie contentedly on my deathbed, such scenes are secretly a game; indeed, in the death enacted I rejoice in my own death, hence calculatingly exploit the attention that the reader concentrates on death, have a much clearer understanding of it than he, of whom I suppose that he will loudly lament on his deathbed, and for these reasons my lament is as perfect as can be, nor does it suddenly break off, as is likely to be the case with a real lament, but dies beautifully and purely away. It is the same thing as my perpetual lamenting to my mother over pains that were not nearly so great as my laments would lead one to believe. With my mother, of course, I did not need to make so great a display of art as with the reader.   [DII, 101 f.]

December 14. My work goes forward at a miserable crawl, in what is perhaps its most important part, where a good night would stand me in such stead.   [DII, 102]

December 15. The joy of lying on the sofa in the silent room without a headache, calmly breathing in a manner befitting a human being.

   The defeats in Serbia, the stupid leadership.   [DII, 103]

December 19. Yesterday wrote "The Village Schoolmaster" [or, "The Giant Mole"] almost without knowing it, but was afraid to go on writing later than a quarter to two; the fear was well founded, I slept hardly at all, merely suffered through perhaps three short dreams and was then in the office in the condition one would expect. Yesterday Father's reproaches on account of the factory: "You talked me into it." Then went home and calmly wrote for three hours in the consciousness that my guilt is beyond question, though not so great as Father pictures it. Today, Saturday, did not come to dinner, partly in fear of Father, partly in order to use the whole night for working; yet I wrote only one page, which wasn't very good.

   The beginning of every story is ridiculous at first. There seems no hope that this newborn thing, still incomplete and tender in every joint, will be able to keep alive in the completed organization of the world, which, like every completed organization, strives to close itself off. However, one should not forget that the story, if it has any justification to exist, bears its complete organization within itself even before it has been fully formed; for this reason despair over the beginning of a story is unwarranted; in a like case parents should have to despair of their suckling infant, for they had no intention of bringing this pathetic and ridiculous being into the world. Of course, one never knows whether the despair one feels is warranted or unwarranted. But reflecting on it can give one a certain support; in the past I have suffered from the lack of this knowledge.   [DII, 103 f.]

December 26. Tonight wrote almost nothing and am in all likelihood no longer capable of going on with "The Village Schoolmaster," which I have been working at for a week now, and which I should certainly have completed in three free nights, perfect and with no external defect; but now, in spite of the fact that I am still virtually at the beginning, it already has two irremediable defects and in addition is stunted.—New schedule from now on! Use the time even better! Do I make my laments here only to find salvation here? It won't come out of this notebook, it will come when I'm in bed and it will put me on my back so that I lie there beautiful and light and bluish-white; no other salvation will come.   [DII, 105]

December 31. Have been working since August, in general not little and not badly, yet neither in the first nor in the second respect to the limit of my ability, as I should have done, especially as there is every indication (insomnia, headaches, weak heart) that my ability won't last much longer. Worked on, but did not finish: *The Trial,* "Memoirs of the Kalda Railroad," "The Village Schoolmaster," "The Assistant Attorney,"[4] and the beginnings of various little things. Finished only: "In the Penal Colony" and a chapter of *The Man Who Disappeared,* both during the two-week vacation. I don't know why I am drawing up this summary, it's not at all like me!   [DII, 106 f.]

1915

From The Trial

The priest had already taken a step or two away from him, but K. cried out in a loud voice, "Please wait a moment." "I am waiting," said the priest. "Don't you want anything more from me?" asked K. "No," said the priest. "You were so friendly to me for a time," said K., "and explained so much to me, and now you let me go as if you cared nothing about me." "But you have to leave now," said the priest. "Well, yes," said K., "you must see that I can't help it." "You must first see who I am," said the priest. "You are the prison chaplain," said K., groping his way nearer to the priest again; his immediate return to the Bank was not so necessary as he had made out, he could quite well stay longer. "That means I belong to the Court," said the priest. "So why should I want anything from you? The Court wants nothing from you. It receives you when you come and it dismisses you when you go."

The Trial, pp. 221 f.

January 4. Great desire to begin another story; didn't yield to it. It is all pointless. If I can't pursue the stories through the nights, they break away and disappear, as with "The Assistant Attorney" now. And tomorrow I go to the factory, shall perhaps have to go there every afternoon after P. joins up. With that, everything is at an end. The thought of the factory is my perpetual Day of Atonement.   [DII, 107]

January 6. For the time being abandoned "Village Schoolmaster" and "The Assistant Attorney." But almost incapable too of going on with The Trial. Thinking of the girl from Lemberg.[1] A promise of some kind of happiness resembles the hope of an eternal life. Seen from a certain distance it holds its ground, and one doesn't venture nearer.   [DII, 107]

January 17. Realized that I have by no means made satisfactory use of the time since August. My constant attempts, by sleeping a great deal in the afternoon, to make it possible for myself to continue working late into the night were absurd; after the first two weeks I could already see that my nerves would not permit me to go to bed after one o'clock, for then I can no longer fall asleep at all, the next day is insupportable and I destroy myself. I lay down too long in the afternoon, though I seldom worked later than one o'clock at night, and always began about eleven o'clock at the earliest. That was a mistake. I must begin at eight or nine o'clock; the night is certainly the best time (vacation!), but beyond my reach.   [DII, 108]

> *Despite the crisis in the relationship with Felice, the two decided to meet again, in Bodenbach, North Bohemia. The meeting took place January 23–24.*

January 17. Saturday I shall see F. If she loves me, I do not deserve it. Today I think I see how narrow my limits are in everything, and consequently in my writing too. If one feels one's limits very intensely, one must burst.   [DII, 108]

January 18. In the factory until half-past six; as usual, worked, read, dictated, listened, wrote without result. The same meaningless satisfaction after it. Headache, slept badly. Incapable of sustained, concentrated work. Also have been in the open air too little. In spite of that began a new story; I was afraid I should spoil the old ones. Four or five stories now stand on their hindlegs in front of me like the horses in front of Schumann, the circus ringmaster, at the beginning of the performance.   [DII, 109]

January 19. I shall not be able to write so long as I have to go to the factory. I think it is a special inability to work that I feel now, similar to what I felt when I was employed by the [Assicurazioni] Generali. Immediate contact with the workaday world deprives me—though inwardly I am as detached as I can be—of the possibility of taking a broad view of matters, just as if I were at the bottom of a ravine, with my head bowed down in addition.   [DII, 109]

January 20. The end of writing. When will it catch me up again? In what a bad state I am going to meet F.! The clumsy thinking that immediately appears when I give up my writing, my inability to prepare for the meeting; whereas last week I could hardly shake off all the ideas it aroused in me. May I enjoy the only conceivable profit I can have from it—better sleep.

[. . .] With what malice and weakness I observe myself. Apparently I cannot force my way into the world, but lie quietly, receive, spread out within me what I have received, and then step calmly forth.   [DII, 111]

January 24. With F. in Bodenbach. I think it is impossible for us ever to unite, but dare say so neither to her nor, at the decisive moment, to myself. Thus I have held out hope to her again, stupidly, for every day makes me older and crustier. My old headaches return when I try to comprehend that she is suffering and is at the same time calm and gay. We shouldn't torment each other again by a lot of writing, it would be best to pass over this meeting as a solitary occurrence; or is it that I believe I shall win freedom here, live by my writing, go abroad or no matter where and live there secretly with F.?

We have found each other quite unchanged in other ways as well. Each of us silently says to himself that the other is immovable and merciless. I yield not a particle of my demand for a fantastic life arranged solely in the interest of my work; she, indifferent to every mute request, wants the average: a comfortable home, an interest on my part in the factory, good food, bed at eleven, central heating; sets my watch—which for the past three months has been an hour and a half fast—right to the minute. And she is right in the end and would continue to be right in the end; she is right when she corrects the bad German I used to the waiter, and I can put nothing right when she speaks of the "personal touch" (it cannot be said any way but gratingly) in the furnishings she intends to have in her home. She calls my two elder sisters "shallow," she doesn't ask after the youngest at all, she asks almost no questions about my work and has no apparent understanding of it. That is one side of the matter.

I am as incompetent and dreary as always and should really have no time to reflect on anything else but the question of how it happens that anyone has the slightest desire even to crook her little finger at me. [. . .] We were alone two hours in the room. Round about me only boredom and despair. We haven't yet had a single good moment together during which I could have breathed freely. With F. I never experienced (except in letters) that sweetness one experiences in a relationship with a woman one loves, such as I had in Zuckmantel and Riva[2]—only unlimited admiration, humility, sympathy, despair, and self-contempt. I also read aloud to her, the sentences proceeded in a disgusting confusion, with no relationship to the listener, who lay on the sofa with closed eyes and silently received them. A lukewarm request to be permitted to take a manuscript along and copy it. During the reading of the doorkeeper story, greater attention and good observation. The significance of the story dawned upon me for the first time; she grasped it rightly too, then of course we barged into it with coarse remarks; I began it.

The difficulties (which other people surely find incredible) I have in speaking to people arise from the fact that my thinking, or rather the content of my consciousness, is entirely nebulous, that I remain undisturbed by this, so far as it concerns only myself, and am even occasionally self-satisfied; yet conversation with people demands pointedness, solidity, and sustained coherence, qualities not to be found in me. No one will want to lie in clouds of mist with me, and even if someone did, *I* couldn't expel the mist from my head; when two people come together it dissolves of itself and is nothing.

F. goes far out of her way to come to Bodenbach, goes to the trouble of getting herself a passport, after a night spent in sitting up must bear with me, must even listen to me read aloud, and all of it senseless. Does she feel it to be the same sort of calamity I do? Certainly not, even assuming the same degree of sensitivity. After all, she has no sense of guilt.

What I said was true and was acknowledged to be true: each loves the other person as he is. But doesn't think it possible to live with him as he is.

The group here: Dr. W. [Ernst Weiss] tries to convince me that F. deserves to be hated, F. tries to convince me that W. deserves to be hated. I believe them both and love them both, or try to.   [DII, 111 ff.]

> *The nature of their correspondence changes after the meeting in Bodenbach; F.K. is more detached and cautious, Felice shows a more active interest in a reunion. Probably in 1915, Grete Bloch becomes the mother of F.K.'s son who died before reaching the age of seven, and of whom F.K. never knew.*

Wrap your cloak, O sublime dream, around the child.   [DF, 210]

> *February: "Blumfeld, an Elderly Bachelor" written. Then follows a period of many months of literary inactivity.*

February 7. Complete standstill. Unending torments.

At a certain point in self-knowledge, when other circumstances favoring self-scrutiny are present, it will invariably follow that you find yourself execrable. Every moral standard—however opinions may differ on it—will seem too high. You will see that you are nothing but a rat's nest of miserable dissimulations. The most trifling of your acts will not be untainted by these dissimulations. These dissimulated intentions are so squalid that in the course of your self-scrutiny you will not want to ponder them closely but will instead be content to gaze at them from afar. These intentions aren't all compounded merely of selfishness, selfishness seems in comparison an ideal of the good and beautiful. The filth you will find exists for its own sake; you will recognize that you came dripping into the world with this burden and will depart unrecognizable again—or only too recognizable—because of it. This filth is the nethermost depth you will find; at the nethermost depth there will be not lava, no, but filth. It is the nethermost and the uppermost, and even the doubts self-scrutiny begets will soon grow weak and self-complacent as the wallowing of a pig in muck. [DII, 114]

February 9. Wrote a little today and yesterday. Dog story.[3]

Just now read the beginning. It is ugly and gives me a headache. In spite of all its truth it is bad, pedantic, mechanical, a fish barely breathing on a sandbank. I write my *Bouvard et Pécuchet* [by Gustave Flaubert] prematurely. If the two elements—most pronounced in "The Stoker" and "In the Penal Colony"—do not combine, I am finished. But is there any prospect of their combining? [DII, 114 f.]

February 10. First evening. My neighbor talks for hours with the landlady. Both speak softly, the landlady almost inaudibly, and therefore so much the worse. My writing, which has been coming along for the past two days, is interrupted, who knows for how long a time? Absolute despair. Is it like this in every house? Does such ridiculous and absolutely killing misery await me with every landlady in every city? [. . .] It is senseless, however, to give way at once to despair; rather seek some means, much as—no, it is not contrary to my character, there is still some tough Jewishness in me, but for the most part it helps the other side. [DII, 115]

February 16. Can't see my way clear. As though everything I possessed had escaped me, and as though it would hardly satisfy me if it all returned.

February 22. Incapable in every respect, and completely so.

February 25. After days of uninterrupted headaches, finally a little easier and more confident. If I were another person observing myself and the course of my life, I should be compelled to say that it must all end unavailingly, be consumed in incessant doubt, creative only in its self-torment. But, an interested party, I go on hoping. [DII, 116]

March 11: Moves to a room in Langegasse.

March 11. How time flies; another ten days and I have achieved nothing. It doesn't come off. A page now and then is successful, but I can't keep it up, the next day I am powerless. [DII, 116 f.]

End of April: Travels with his sister Elli to Hungary to visit Elli's husband, a soldier stationed there.

May 3. Completely indifferent and apathetic. A well gone dry, water at an unattainable depth and no certainty it is there. Nothing, nothing. Don't understand the life in Strindberg's [autobiographical novel] *Separated;* what he calls beautiful, when I relate it to myself, disgusts me. A letter to F., all wrong, impossible to mail it. What is there to tie me to a past or a future? The present is a phantom state for me; I don't sit at the table but hover around it. Nothing, nothing. Emptiness, boredom, no, not boredom, merely emptiness, meaninglessness, weakness.

                                                                [DII, 126]

May 4. In a better state because I read Strindberg *(Separated).* I don't read him to read him, but rather to lie on his breast. He holds me on his left arm like a child. I sit there like a man on a statue. Ten times I almost slip off, but at the eleventh attempt I sit there firmly, feel secure, and have a wide view.

Reflection on other people's relationship to me. Insignificant as I may be, nevertheless there is no one here who wholly understands me. To have someone with this understanding, a woman, for example, would mean to have support from every side, to have God. Ottla understands many things, even a great many; Max, Felix [Weltsch], many things; others, like E. [Erna], understand only details, but with dreadful intensity; F. in all likelihood understands nothing, which, because of our undeniable inner relationship, places her in a very special position. Sometimes I thought she understood me without realizing it; for instance, the time she waited for me at the subway station—I had been longing for her unbearably, and in my passion to reach her as quickly as possible almost ran past her, thinking she would be at the top of the stairs, and she took me quietly by the hand.   [DII, 126]

To Felice, about May 6:
Don't write like that, Felice. You are wrong. There are certain misunderstandings between us which I, at any rate, confidently expect to be cleared up, though not perhaps by letter. I have not changed (alas); the balance—of which I represent the vacillations—has remained the same; the only slight change has been in the distribution of weight; I believe I know more about both of us, and now have a temporary objective. We will discuss it at Whitsun, if we manage to meet. Felice, don't think that the impeding considerations and anxieties are not an almost unbearable and detestable burden to me, that I wouldn't prefer to shed everything, that I wouldn't prefer a straightforward approach, and that I wouldn't rather be happy now and at once in a small intimate circle, and above all give happiness. But this isn't possible, it is a burden I am

forced to bear, I shiver with discontent, and even if my failures stared
me in the face, and not only my failures but also the loss of all hope and
the steady approach of all guilt—I really couldn't behave otherwise.
Incidentally, Felice, why do you think—at least it seems as though you
do at times—that life together here in Prague might be possible? After
all, you used to have grave doubts about it. What has removed them?
This is something I still don't know.   [F, 453]

May 14. Lost all regularity in writing. [. . .] Afraid I am unfit because of
a bad heart.   [DII, 128]

*May 23-24: With Felice and Grete Bloch for the Whitsun holiday
in Bohemian Switzerland. A happy meeting.*

May 27. A great deal of unhappiness in the last entry. Going to pieces.
To go to pieces so pointlessly and unnecessarily.   [DII, 128]

*No further diary entry until September 13. June: Meeting with
Felice in Karlsbad; things went wrong. July 20-31: In a sanatorium in Rumberg (Northern Bohemia). From August 9 to December 5: No letters to Felice.*

September 13. Eve of Father's birthday, new diary. I don't need it as
much as I used to, I mustn't upset myself, I'm upset enough, but to what
purpose, when will it come, how can one heart, one heart not entirely
sound, bear so much discontent and the incessant tugging of so much
desire?

   Distractedness, weak memory, stupidity!   [DII, 128]

September 14. With Max and Langer[4] at the wonder-rabbi's on
Saturday [in a suburb of Prague]. A lot of children on the sidewalk and
stairs. An inn. Completely dark upstairs, groped blindly along with my
hands for a few steps. A pale, dim room, whitish-gray walls, several
small women and girls standing around, white kerchiefs on their heads,
pale faces, slight movements. An impression of lifelessness. Next room.
Quite dark, full of men and young people. Loud praying. We squeezed
into a corner. We had barely looked around a bit when the prayer was
over, the room emptied. A corner room, windows on both sides, two
windows each. We were pushed toward a table on the rabbi's right. We
held back. "You're Jews too, aren't you?" A nature as strongly paternal
as possible makes a rabbi. All rabbis look like savages, Langer said. This
one was in a silk caftan, trousers visible under it. Hair on the bridge of

his nose. Furred cap which he kept tugging back and forth. Dirty and pure, a characteristic of people who think intensely. Scratched in his beard, blew his nose through his fingers, reached into the food with his fingers; but when his hand rested on the table for a moment you saw the whiteness of his skin, a whiteness such as you remembered having seen before only in your childhood imaginings—when one's parents too were pure.   [DII, 128 f.]

September 16. The Polish Jews going to Kol Nidre.⁵ The little boy with prayer shawls under both arms, running along at his father's side. Suicidal not to go to temple.

Opened the Bible. The unjust Judges. Confirmed in my own opinion, or at least in an opinion that I have already encountered in myself. But otherwise there is no significance to this, I am never visibly guided in such things, the pages of the Bible don't flutter in my presence.   [DII, 130]

September 28. Why is it meaningless to ask questions? To complain means to put a question and wait for the answer. But questions that don't answer themselves at the very moment of their asking are never answered. No distance divides the interrogator from the one who answers him. There is no distance to overcome. Hence meaningless to ask and wait.   [DII, 130 f.]

September 29. At one time I used to think: Nothing will destroy you, not this tough, clear, really empty head; you will never, either unwittingly or in pain, screw up your eyes, wrinkle your brow, twitch your hands, you will never be able to do more than act such a role.

How could Fortinbras say that Hamlet had prov'd most royally?

In the afternoon I couldn't keep myself from reading what I had written yesterday, "yesterday's filth"; didn't do any harm, though.

[DII, 131 f.]

September 30. Rossmann [in *Amerika*] and K. [in *The Trial*], the innocent and the guilty, both executed without distinction in the end, the guilty one with a gentler hand, more pushed aside than struck down.

[DII, 132]

> *To Verlag Kurt Wolff, October 25, regarding a projected illustration of the title page of* The Metamorphosis *by the artist Ottomar Starke:*
It occurs to me in this connection [. . .] that he might be proposing to

draw the actual insect. Don't let him, please don't let him! I have no wish to encroach on his domain, but since I naturally know the story so much better, I would like to make a request. The actual insect cannot be drawn. It cannot even be shown from a distance. If he has no such intertion, and if, therefore, my request proves fatuous—so much the better. Meanwhile, however, I would be very grateful if you would endorse my request and pass it on. If I might be allowed to make suggestions for an illustration, I would choose scenes such as: the parents and the head clerk in front of the closed door; or, better still, the parents and the sister in the illuminated room with the door leading to the adjoining darkened room standing open. [Br, 136]

October–November: Publication of The Metamorphosis. *Gustav Janouch (see entry end of March 1920) suggested that Samsa in* The Metamorphosis *might be a cryptogram for Kafka. F.K. replies:*

It is not a cryptogram. Samsa is not merely Kafka, and nothing else. *The Metamorphosis* is not a confession, although it is—in a certain sense —an indiscretion. [J, 35]

November 4. I remember [. . .] a church in Verona I forlornly and reluctantly went into, only because of the slight compulsion of duty that a tourist feels, and the heavy compulsion of a man expiring of futility; saw an overgrown dwarf stooped under the holy water font, walked around a bit, sat down; and as reluctantly went out again, as if just such a church as this one, built door to door with it, awaited me outside. [DII, 141]

On Abraham Grünberg, a refugee from Warsaw, whom F.K. met frequently. Grünberg died of tuberculosis during the war.
November 6. Is there anyone, by the way, to whom I don't bow down? Take Grünberg, for instance, who in my opinion is a very remarkable person and almost universally depreciated for reasons that are beyond me—if it were a question, let's say, of which of the two of us should have to die immediately (no great improbability in his case, for they say he is in an advanced stage of tuberculosis), and the decision lay with me as to which it should be, then I should find the question a preposterous one, so long as it was looked at merely theoretically; for as a matter of course Grünberg, a far more valuable person than I, should have to be spared. Grünberg too would agree with me. But in the final desperate moment I should, as everyone else would have done long before, invent arguments in my favor, arguments that at any other time, because of their crudity, nakedness, and falsity, would have made me

vomit. And these final moments I am surely undergoing now, though no
one is forcing a choice upon me; they are those moments when I put off
all external distracting influences and try really to look into myself.

[DII, 142 f.]

November 19. In the Altneu Synagogue at the Mishnah lecture. Home
with [talmudic scholar] Dr. Jeiteles. Greatly interested in certain con-
troversial issues.   [DII, 143 f.]

*To Martin Buber, who apparently invited F.K. to contribute to
the journal* Der Jude, *November 29:*
I feel greatly honored by your kind invitation, but I fear I am unable to
accept it; I am—somewhere within me a hopeful voice naturally mur-
murs "as yet"—far too burdened and insecure to think of expressing
myself, however modestly, in such company.

But please allow me, my dear Dr. Buber, to take this opportunity of
thanking you for the afternoon I spent in your company nearly two
years ago. My thanks are belated, but perhaps not too belated, since for
me that meeting has remained an ever-present memory. It is in every
way my purest recollection of Berlin, and has often afforded me a kind
of sanctuary, which was all the more secure since I had not thanked
you and so nobody knew of this possession.   [Martin Buber, Briefwechsel I. 409]

December 25. Open the diary only in order to lull myself to sleep. But
see what happens to be the last entry and could conceive of thousands
of identical ones I might have entered over the past three or four years.
I wear myself out to no purpose, should be happy if I could write, but
don't. Haven't been able to get rid of my headaches lately. I have really
wasted my strength away.

Yesterday spoke frankly to my boss; my decision to speak up and my
vow not to shrink from it had made it possible for me to enjoy two—if
restless—hours of sleep the night before last. Put four possibilities to
him: (1) Let everything go on as it has been going this last tortured week,
the worst I've undergone, and end up with brain fever, insanity, or
something of the like; (2) out of some kind of sense of duty I don't want
to take a vacation, nor would it help; (3) I can't give notice now because
of my parents and the factory; (4) only military service remains.
Answer: One week's vacation and hematogen treatment, which my
boss intends to take with me. He himself is apparently very sick. If I
went too, the department would be deserted.

Relief to have spoken frankly. For the first time, almost caused an official convulsion in the atmosphere of the office with the word "notice."

Nevertheless, hardly slept at all today.

[DII, 144 f.]

No further diary entry until April 19, 1916. December: Publication of "Before the Law."

1916

From "A Country Doctor"

A false alarm on the night bell once answered—it cannot be made good, not ever.
The Penal Colony, p. 143

To Felice, January 18:
I shall be coming to Berlin after the war. My first task will be to crawl into some hole and examine myself. What will be the outcome? Needless to say, the living man in me is hopeful, which is not surprising. The thinking man, however, is not. Yet even the thinking man maintains that though in the end I do away with myself in that hole, I shall have done the best I could do at the time. But you, Felice? I have no right to you, not until I emerge from that hole, emerge from it somehow. So until then you too will not see me for what I am, because to you, and quite rightly so, I am at present—whether in the Askanische Hof, in Karlsbad, or in the Tiergarten—a naughty child, a madman, or something of the kind; a naughty child whom you treat with undeserved kindness, when it ought to be deserved. [F, 460 f.]

To Felice, January 24:
I would like to open a trap door under my feet, and allow myself to disappear to a place where the wretched remnants of my remaining powers could be preserved for some future freedom. That's all I know.
[F, 461]

May 13–15: On business to Karlsbad and Marienbad.

To Felice from Marienbad, mid-May, in a new attempt to win her favor:
Karlsbad is rather pleasant, but Marienbad is unbelievably beautiful. A long time ago I ought to have followed my instinct which tells me that the fattest are also the wisest. After all, one can diet anywhere, no need to pay homage to mineral springs, but only here can one wander about in woods such as these. Just now in fact the beauty is enhanced by the peace and solitude as well as by the eager receptivity of all things animate and inanimate; while it is hardly affected by the overcast and

windy weather. I imagine if I were a Chinese and were about to go home (indeed I am a Chinese and am going home), I would make sure of returning soon, and at any price. How you would love it! [F, 468]

F.K. and Felice plan to spend some time in the summer in Marienbad.

June 2. What a muddle I've been in with girls, in spite of all my headaches, insomnia, gray hair, despair. Let me count them: there have been at least six since the summer. I can't resist, my tongue is fairly torn from my mouth if I don't give in and admire anyone who is admirable and love her until admiration is exhausted. With all six my guilt is almost wholly inward, though one of the six did complain of me to someone. [DII, 154 f.]

June 19. Forget everything. Open the windows. Clear the room. The wind blows through it. You see only its emptiness, you search in every corner and don't find yourself. [DII, 155]

July 3–13: With Felice in Marienbad, Hotel Balmoral & Osborne.

July 3. First day in Marienbad with F. Door to door, keys on either side. [DII, 156]

July 5. The hardship of living together. Forced upon us by strangeness, pity, lust, cowardice, vanity, and only deep down, perhaps, a thin trickle of a brook worthy of the name of love, not to be found when you look for it, but suddenly shining forth in the twinkling of an eye. [DII, 157]

July 6. Unhappy night. Impossible to live with F. Intolerable living with anyone. I don't regret this; I regret the impossibility for me of not living alone. And yet how absurd it is for me to regret this, to give in, and then finally to understand. Get up from the ground. Hold to the book. But then I have it all back again: insomnia; headaches; jump out of the high window but onto the rain-soaked ground where the fall won't be fatal. Endless tossing with eyes closed, exposed to any random glance.

Receive me into your arms, they are the depths, receive me into the depths; if you refuse me now, then later.

Take me, take me, web of folly and pain. [DII, 157, 159]

F.K. and Felice to Anna Bauer, Felice's mother, from Marienbad,
July 10:
Dear Mother, my right to this mode of address lies not in the past, but in
the present. Felice and I have met (such things do happen) here in
Marienbad and discovered that years ago we tackled things in the
wrong way. Nor was this very difficult to see. Good things, however,
are not accomplished at the first attempt, nor at the second, but perhaps
at the ten-thousandth, and this is where we now are. And where we
mean to stay, and I believe I can be sure of your maternal consent
dating from the days when you followed my last walk down Momm-
senstrasse with a friendly wave from your balcony. Many things have
changed since then, few for the better, this I do know; but one of the
few is the relationship between Felice and me and its assurance for the
future.   [F, 473]

July 13: With Felice in Franzensbad to meet F.K.'s mother and his
sister Valli. Felice returns to Berlin; F.K. spends ten more days in
Marienbad.

July 13. Then open yourself. Let the human person come forth. Breathe
in the air and the silence.   [DII, 159]

Only one word. Only one plea. Only one stirring of the air. Only one
proof that you are still alive and waiting. No, no plea, only a breathing,
no breathing, only a readiness, no readiness, only a thought, no
thought, only quiet sleep.   [DF, 296]

July 20. Have mercy on me, I am sinful in every corner of my being. But
my talents were not entirely contemptible; I had some small capa-
bilities, squandered them, ill-advised creature that I was, am now near
my end just at a time when outwardly everything might at last turn out
well for me. Don't thrust me in among the lost souls. I know it is my
ridiculous love of self that speaks here, ridiculous whether looked at
from a distance or close at hand; but, as I am alive, I also have life's love
of self, and if life is not ridiculous its necessary manifestations can't be
either.—Poor dialectic!
    If I am condemned, then I am not only condemned to die, but also
condemned to struggle till I die.

    Sunday morning, shortly before I left, you seemed to want to help
me. I hoped. Until today a vain hope.
    And no matter what my complaint, it is without conviction, even

without real suffering; like the anchor of a lost ship, it swings far above the bottom in which it could catch hold.

Let me only have rest at night—childish complaint.   [DII, 161]

On the eve of Felice's departure from Marienbad (July 13) F.K. started to write a letter to Brod, completed after her departure: Since the situation could not get any worse, it had to get better. The ropes that bound me slackened a little, I was able to find my bearings to some extent; she, who constantly reached out into that endless void to offer a helping hand, helped yet again, with the result that we were able to establish a relationship from person to person, such as I had never known before, one that compared in terms of human value with the relationship we had during that splendid period when we corresponded with one another. Previously, I had never known what it was to be intimate with a woman, save in Zuckmantel (where she had been a woman and I a boy) and Riva (where she had still been half a child and I totally confused and sick in every corner of my mind).[1] But now I saw a woman look at me with trust, and I was unable to shut myself off. Much will be opened up that I had intended to keep to myself forever (I do not mean single details but a whole complex), and through this opening—of that I am certain—enough misery will emerge for more than one life; but it will be a misery that is imposed from without, not conjured up from within. I have no right to resist it, especially since, if this process had not been initiated, I would have initiated it of my own free will just to receive that look of trust. I simply did not know her; I had other misgivings, it is true, but what really inhibited me at the time was the fear of meeting my correspondent as a real person; when she came toward me in the large room to accept my kiss and so seal the engagement, a shudder passed through me; that engagement expedition with my parents was systematic torture for me; nothing terrified me as much as being alone with F. before the wedding. Now things have changed, and changed for the better. Briefly, we have agreed to marry once the war is over, we will take two or three rooms in a Berlin suburb, and continue to support ourselves as before. F. will go on working, and I, well, I cannot say as yet what I shall be doing.

And so, as far as Wolff is concerned, I will not be writing for the time being. In any case, it is not such a good idea to approach him with a collection of three stories, two of which have already appeared in print. I would do better to remain silent until I can submit an entirely new collection. And if I cannot do that, then I may as well remain silent forever.   [Br, 139 f.]

After the Marienbad meeting, F.K.'s letters to Felice become more open, friendly, free of anxiety. They discuss Felice's participation in the educational and recreational work of the Jewish People's Home, which cared for Jewish war refugees and refugee children.

To Felice, July 30:

Dearest—I am re-reading yesterday's postcard. What are you going to say to Dr. [Siegfried] Lehmann [head of the Jewish People's Home]? In any case, put yourself at his disposal. With the exception of walking and gymnastics, there is no better way of spending the little free time you have than with him; it is a hundred times more important than the theater, than Klabund, Gerson, or whoever else there may be. Besides, it is one of the most self-interested of occupations. One is not helping, but seeking help; more honey can be gathered from these exertions than from all the flowers in all the Marienbad woods. I don't know how you got the idea that only students are wanted. Needless to say, it was students (of both sexes)—commonly the least selfish, most determined, most restless and exacting, keenest, most independent and farsighted of people—who started the venture and run it; but everyone alive has as much right to be part of it.   [F, 481]

To Verlag Kurt Wolff, August 10:

From the remark you made about me in a letter to Max Brod I gather that you too are moving away from the idea of publishing my short stories in a single volume. The way things are at present, you are, of course, entirely right, for it seems most improbable that such a book would bring you the ready sale that you desire. On the other hand, I would be very happy if the "Penal Colony" were to be published in the *Jüngste Tag*, and not only the "Penal Colony" but the "Judgment" from *Arkadia* as well, so that each of these stories appeared in its own small volume. For me, the advantage of this kind of publication, by comparison with a single edition, is that each story could be considered, and would function, individually. If you agree, then I would ask that the "Judgment," to which I attach greater importance, should appear first; the "Penal Colony" could follow at any suitable time.   [Br, 147 f.]

August 20: A list of reasons for and against marriage:

Remaining pure	Being married
bachelor	Married man
I remain pure	Pure?
I hold all my vigor together	You remain outside the context, become a fool, fly to all four quarters of the sky, but you don't get any further, I draw all strength that is at all available to me out of the bloodstream of human life.
Only responsible for myself	All the more infatuated for (with) you. (Grillparzer, Flaubert)
No worry. Concentration on work.	Since I grow in vigor, I carry more. Here is nevertheless a certain truth.

[DF, 211]

To Felice, September 12, on the Jewish People's Home, which became an important subject in F.K.'s letters to her:
That's why I was so pleased in Marienbad when, without my having expected or intended it, you tackled the idea of the Home[2] quite independently and very well, and now intend to let it lead you on. Only the reality of the Home can teach you anything of importance—any reality, however small. Don't be prejudiced in favor or against, nor let the thought of me affect your open mind. You will see those in need of help, and opportunities of giving help judiciously, and in yourself the power to help—so help. It is very simple, yet more profound than any fundamental ideas. Everything else you ask about will, if you go through with it, follow quite naturally from this one simple fact. As far as I am concerned, please consider that this work removes you to some extent from me, since—in any case at present, and I am not thinking of my state of health in this connection—I wouldn't be capable of doing this kind of work; I would lack the necessary dedication. However, this is only to some extent. On the whole I can think of no closer spiritual bond between us than that created by this work. I shall live on every small thing you do, on every difficulty you shoulder (though it must not be detrimental to your health); I shall live on every one of these things, as on your last letter.

As far as I can see, it is positively the only path, or threshold to it, that can lead to spiritual liberation. The helpers, moreover, will attain that goal earlier than those who are being helped. Beware of the arrogance of believing the opposite, this is most important. What form will the help in the Home take? Since people are sewn into their skins for life and cannot alter any of the seams, at least not with their own hands and not directly, one will try to imbue the children—at best respecting their individual characters—with the spirit and more indirectly the mode of life of their helpers. In other words one will try to raise them to the standard of the contemporary, educated, West European Jew, Berlin version, which admittedly may be the best type of its kind. With that, not much would be achieved.

If, for instance, I had to choose between the Berlin Home and another where the pupils were the Berlin helpers (dearest, even with you among them, and with me, no doubt, at the head), and the helpers simple East European Jews from Kolomea or Stanislaw, I would give unconditional preference to the latter Home—with a great sigh of relief and without a moment's hesitation. But I don't think this choice exists; no one has it; the quality corresponding to the value of the East European Jew is something that cannot be imparted in a Home; on this point even family education has recently been increasingly unsuccessful; these are things that cannot be imparted, but perhaps, and here lies the hope, they can be acquired, earned. And the helpers in the Home have, I imagine, a chance to acquire them. They will accomplish little, for they know little and are not very bright, yet once they grasp the meaning of it, they will accomplish all they can with all their hearts, which on the other hand is a lot, this alone is a lot.

The connection between all this and Zionism (valid for me, not necessarily for you) lies in the fact that the work in the Home derives from Zionism a youthful vigorous method, youthful vigor generally, and that where other means might fail it kindles national aspirations by invoking the ancient prodigious past—admittedly with the limitations without which Zionism could not exist. How you come to terms with Zionism is your affair; any coming to terms with it (indifference is out of the question) will give me pleasure. It is too soon to discuss it now, but should you one day feel yourself to be a Zionist (you flirted with it once, but these were mere flirtations, not a coming to terms), and subsequently realize that I am not a Zionist—which would probably emerge from an examination—it wouldn't worry me, nor need it worry you; Zionism is not something that separates well-meaning people.   [F. 500 f.]

To Felice, September 16:
Dearest, again just a few words, but intimate ones. It is the Home that brings us so close. Don't be afraid of the girls' questions, or rather, be afraid of them, and regard this fear as the most beneficial part of the

Home. Actually, it's not the questioning you fear, it is also the unasked questions that you will sometimes find frustrating; nor is it merely the questions asked by these girls, but also those asked by the menacing or benevolent "useful people" of whom you wrote so kindly and devotedly. On the whole it will be up to you to get them to trust you in other than religious matters and, where the sharing of religious experience is needed, to let the dark complexity of Judaism, which contains so many impenetrable features, do its work. Nothing of course should be blurred in this way, as people are inclined to do here. In my opinion this would be entirely wrong. I wouldn't think of going to the synagogue. The synagogue is not a place one can sneak up to. One can do this today no more than one could as a child; I still remember how as a boy I almost suffocated from the terrible boredom and pointlessness of the hours in the synagogue; these were the rehearsals staged by hell for my later office life. Those who throng to the synagogue simply because they are Zionists seem to me like people trying to force their way into the synagogue under cover of the Ark of the Law, rather than entering calmly through the main door.

But as far as I can see, it is quite different for you than it is for me. While I should have to tell the children (it is unwise, of course, to encourage such conversations, and on their own they would arise but rarely, for town-bred children have sufficient experience of the world and, if they are East European Jews, know how to protect themselves and at the same time to accept the other person) that owing to my origin, my education, disposition, and environment I have nothing tangible in common with their faith (keeping the Commandments is not an outward thing; on the contrary, it is the very essence of the Jewish faith)—thus, while I would somehow have to admit it to them (and I would do so candidly, for without candor everything would be quite pointless in this case), you on the other hand may not be altogether lacking in tangible connections with the faith. They may of course be merely half-forgotten memories buried beneath the clamor of the city, of business life, and of the tangled mass of discussions and ideas assimilated over the years. I don't mean to say that you are still standing on the threshold of the door, but perhaps somewhere in the distance you can just see the gleam of the door handle. I mean that in reply to their questions you might be able to give the children at least a sad answer; I could not do even that. But this would be enough to gain their trust in every case. And now, dear teacher, when are you to start?

[F, 502 f.]

To Felice, September 23:
I keep meaning to tell you about the following: Do you remember the

short piece of prose that was supposed to have appeared in *Der Jude* as a postscript to an article of Max's? The consignment was first lost, then sent again at a later date, and finally [Martin] Buber accepted Max's article with some reservations (which I too considered the only sensible thing to do), but rejected my "Dream," though in a letter more complimentary than any ordinary letter of acceptance could have been. I mention this for two reasons: firstly because the letter gave me pleasure, and secondly, by this trivial example to show you, with an official's typical apprehension, the precariousness of my financial and intellectual existence. And even supposing I do one day accomplish something (my restlessness won't let me write a line), it is quite possible that even people who are well disposed toward me will turn me down, and the others of course all the more so.   [F, 506]

To Felice, September 26:
Dearest, no news the day before yesterday, yesterday, or today; rather a long time, isn't it? Though I do understand it: on Saturday and Sunday you simply hadn't the time. But today is a bad day anyway. Though yesterday was all the better; the weather was lovely and I went on an excursion all by myself to that plateau with the wide panoramic view I told you about once before. It was like being in the brighter Beyond. By the way, do you know the joys of being alone, walking alone, lying in the sun alone? Which doesn't mean I have anything against doing things in twos, and not much against doing them in threes. But what a joy it is for the tormented, for heart and head! Do you know what I mean? Have you ever walked a long way by yourself? The ability to enjoy it presupposes a great deal of past misery as well as past joys. As a boy I was alone a lot, but it was more from force of circumstance, rarely from choice. Now, however, I rush toward being alone as rivers rush toward the sea.   [F, 510]

To Felice, October 7:
And incidentally, won't you tell me what I really am: in the last *Neue Rundschau*, *Metamorphosis* is mentioned and rejected on sensible grounds, and then says the writer: "There is something fundamentally German about K's narrative art." In Max's article on the other hand: "K's stories are among the most typically Jewish documents of our time."
    A difficult case. Am I a circus rider on 2 horses? Alas, I am no rider, but lie prostrate on the ground.   [F, 517]

To Felice, October 19:
Roughly—hence with rather more ruthlessness than the truth would

warrant—I can describe my position as follows: Having as a rule depended on others, I have an infinite longing for independence,
self-reliance, freedom in all directions; I would rather wear blinkers
and go my own way to the bitter end, than have my vision distorted by
being in the midst of frenzied family life. That's why every word I say
to my parents, or they to me, so easily turns into a stumbling block
under my feet. Any relationship not created by myself, even though it
be opposed to parts of my own nature, is worthless; it hinders my
movements, I hate it, or come near to hating it. The road is long, one's
resources few, there is reason in plenty for this hatred. Yet, I am my
parents' progeny, am bound to them and to my sisters by blood; in my
daily life, and because of the necessary obsession with my particular
objectives, I am not conscious of this, yet fundamentally I respect it
more than I know. Sometimes this too becomes the object of my hatred;
at home the sight of the double bed, of sheets that have been slept in, of
nightshirts carefully laid out, can bring me to the point of retching, can
turn my stomach inside out; it is as though my birth had not been final,
as though from this fusty life I keep being born again and again in this
fusty room; as though I had to return there for confirmation, being—if
not quite, at least in part—indissolubly connected with these distasteful
things; something still clings to the feet as they try to break free, held
fast as they are in the primeval slime. That is sometimes. At other times
I know that after all they are my parents, are essential, strength-giving
elements of my own self, belonging to me, not merely as obstacles but
as human beings. At such times I want them as one wants perfection;
since from way back and despite all my nastiness, rudeness, selfishness, and unkindness I have always trembled before them—and do so to
this day, for in fact one never stops; and since they, Father on
the one hand and Mother on the other, have—again quite naturally
—almost broken my will, I want them to be worthy of their actions.
(Now and again I think that Ottla would be the kind of mother I should
like in the background: pure, truthful, honest, consistent—with humility and pride, receptiveness and reticence, devotion and self-reliance,
timidity and courage, in unerring equilibrium. I mention Ottla because
my mother after all is also part of her, though altogether unrecognizable.) So I want them to be worthy of their actions. In consequence, for
me, they are a hundred times more unclean than they may be in reality,
which doesn't really worry me; their foolishness is a hundred times
greater, their absurdity a hundred times greater, their coarseness a
hundred times greater. On the other hand their good qualities seem a
hundred thousand times smaller than they are in reality. Thus they
deceive me, and yet I cannot rebel against the laws of nature without
going mad. So again there is hatred, and almost nothing but hatred. But

you belong to me, I have made you mine; I do not believe that the battle for any woman in any fairy tale has been fought harder and more desperately than the battle for you within myself—from the beginning, over and over again, and perhaps forever. So you belong to me. [F, 524 f.]

To Felice, October 30:
My life is made up of two parts, the one feeds on your life with bulging cheeks and could in itself be happy and a great man; but the other part is like a cobweb come adrift; being free of tension, free of headaches is its supreme though not too frequent joy. What can we do about this second part? Soon it will be two years since it did any work, and yet it consists of nothing but the capacity and longing for this work.   [F, 531]

To Felice, October 31:
Schaffstein's green books, my favorites, are best, but I didn't want to send them all at once, so I will let you have these later. Among them, for example, is one book that affects me so deeply that I feel it is about myself, or as if it were the book of rules for my life, rules I avoid, or have avoided (a feeling I often have, by the way); the book is called *The Sugar Baron*, and its final chapter is the most important.[3] Actually, it is very difficult to decide between one children's book and another. If I were asked to name the best children's books from my own experience, I would probably choose the little volumes by Hoffmann,[4] obvious trash. How beautiful the books we're reading now will seem in the next world!
[F, 532]

November 10–12: In Munich with Felice. November 10, F.K. reads "In the Penal Colony" ("Evenings for New Writing"). The critics considered the reading a failure; the meetings with Felice were unhappy.

To Felice, December 20:
Dearest, now don't be sad if you don't hear from me. This is truly not as I would want it, it worries me, and at the moment I am so vulnerable. This is pure selfishness which transmits itself to the other soul. All the same, please don't be sad. The absence of news is at least no worse than the accumulation of letters.—My life is monotonous and proceeds within the prison of my innate, as it were threefold misfortune. When I am unproductive I am unhappy; when I am productive there isn't enough time; and when I count on the future then at once there is the fear, a variety of fears, that I shall be more than ever unable to work. An exquisitely calculated hell. Yet—and this is the main point—not without its good moments.   [F, 538]

The relationship between F.K. and Felice had again reached a low point. Bothered by noise, he moves to Alchemists' Lane (on the Hradshin); there, in early December, his sister Ottla found a cottage where he could write. Here he began writing the eight octavo notebooks, which were continued until February 1919. Winter 1916-17: "The Warden of the Tomb," "A Country Doctor," and a few shorter stories. He declined to see Felice at Christmas 1916.

1917

From "The Hunter Gracchus"

"Extraordinary," said the Burgomaster, "extraordinary. And now do you think of staying here in Riva with us?"

"I think not," said the Hunter with a smile, and, to excuse himself, he laid his hand on the Burgomaster's knee. "I am here, more than that I do not know, further than that I cannot go. My ship has no rudder, and it is driven by the wind that blows in the undermost regions of death."   *The Great Wall of China, p. 214*

First half of 1917: "The Hunter Gracchus." Studying the Hebrew language. Early March: Moves to an apartment in the Schönborn Palace, in preparation for marriage with Felice. Writes "The Great Wall of China," "An Imperial Message," and "A Report to an Academy." There are no diary entries from October 20, 1916, to April 6, 1917.

Martin Buber invited F.K. to submit some of his stories to Der Jude. F.K. sent in twelve stories, of which Buber selected "Jackals and Arabs" and "A Report to an Academy."

To Martin Buber, April 22:
It has taken me a few days to reply to your letter because I have had to have the things copied. I am sending you 12 pieces. *Marsyas* has two of them—"The New Advocate" and "A Country Doctor"—but if you think they can be used I will get them back; that should not be too difficult. At some later date I hope that all of these pieces will appear, together with a number of others, in a single volume under the general title *Responsibility.*   [Martin Buber, *Briefwechsel* I, 491 f.]

To Martin Buber, May 12:
Many thanks for your friendly letter. So I shall be appearing in *Der Jude* after all, a thing I would never have dreamed possible. But please do not call my two pieces parables, because they are not really parables; if a general title is needed, perhaps "Two Animal Stories" would be the best solution.   [Martin Buber, *Briefwechsel* I, 494]

The stories appeared in Der Jude, II (1917–18), 488 ff. and 559–65.

To Kurt Wolff, from Prague, July 7:
I was terribly pleased to hear from you again. During this winter, which has of course also passed, I felt a little less troubled. I am sending you a few of the more serviceable things I wrote during this period: thirteen pieces of prose. They are far removed from what I really want. [Br, 156]
The stories appeared, end of 1919, in the volume A Country Doctor.

To Kurt Wolff, July 27:
Your favorable reaction to the manuscripts has made me feel rather more sure of myself. If you think the time is right for an edition of these small prose works (which would have to include at least two other short pieces: "Before the Law," which has already appeared on your list, and "The Dream," which I am enclosing), I would gladly give my approval; as far as the type of edition is concerned, I place myself entirely in your hands; and I am not interested in making a profit at the moment. Things will be very different in this latter respect after the war. I shall give up my post (of all my hopes that of giving up my post is by far the strongest), I shall marry and move away from Prague, possibly to Berlin. And although, as things stand at present, I shall not be entirely dependent on the income from my literary work, I or the civil servant lurking within me, which amounts to the same thing, am nonetheless oppressed and fearful at the thought of that period; I only hope, my dear Herr Wolff, that, always provided I show some sort of merit, you will not completely forsake me when the time comes. A word from you now in this respect would mean a great deal to me, it would carry me over all the insecurity of the present and future.
[Br, 157 f.]

Early July: Felice comes to Prague; second engagement. Official engagement visits. Second half of July: Journey with Felice to her sister in Arad, Hungary; presumably, an unhappy encounter. F.K. returns alone via Vienna.

August 3. The alarm trumpets of nothingness. [DII, 175]

Nothing, only an image, nothing else, utter oblivion. [DF, 313]

August 5. The afternoon in Radešovice with Oskar [Baum]. Sad, weak, made frequent efforts to keep track of the main question. [DII, 175]

August 9-10: Lung hemorrhage. Feeling of relief. September 4:
Diagnosis of tuberculosis.

Brod relates in his diary:
September 4. In the afternoon went with Kafka to Professor Friedl
Pick. It has taken all that time to carry it through.
Catarrh in the lungs diagnosed. Must have three months' leave.
There is a danger of T.B. My God! Nothing so horrible can happen.
Then the Sophie Island. Swimming pool with Franz. He feels himself
released and beaten at the same time. There is a part in him that
resists, and considers marriage as a distraction from the one direction
of his gaze—toward the absolute. Another part fights for marriage as in
accordance with nature. This struggle has worn him out. He considers
his illness as a punishment, because he has often wished for a violent
solution. But this solution is too drastic for him. He quotes against God,
from the Meistersinger, "I should have taken him for more of a gentle-
man."   [B, 162 f.]

To Kurt Wolff, September 4:
I could not have wished for a more attractive suggestion for the
"Country Doctor." If it had been left to me I am quite sure that, out of
deference for myself, for you, and for the project, I simply would not
have dared to chose that form of lettering; but since you yourself have
offered it to me, I gladly accept. I assume that you will also be using the
Meditation format, which I find so attractive?

With regard to the "Penal Colony," there may have been a misunderstanding here. I have never been really wholehearted in my desire
to have this story published. There are two or three pages shortly
before the end that are contrived, and their presence points to a deeper
defect; somewhere a worm is at work, devouring the very substance of
the story. By offering to publish this work in the same way as the
"Country Doctor," you are, of course, making me a very tempting
proposition, one that is so enticing as to be almost irresistible—nonetheless, I must ask you, at least for the time being, not to publish the
"Penal Colony." If you were in my position, and the story were looking
at you as it is looking at me, you would find nothing particularly
resolute in my request. Incidentally, if my strength holds out to any
extent at all, you will receive better works from me than the "Penal
Colony."

The illness that I have been inducing for years with my headaches
and insomnia has now suddenly erupted. It is almost a relief. I shall
make a long trip to the country, or rather I shall have to.   [Br, 159]

To Brod and Felix Weltsch, on his illness, September 5:
Providing an initial explanation for my mother was surprisingly easy. I simply told her in passing that for the time being I would probably not be renting an apartment because I was not feeling well, because I was rather nervous, and that I proposed instead to ask for an extended leave, and then to visit O [Ottla]. Since she is prepared to grant me leave at the drop of a hat (if it only depended on her), she found nothing at all suspicious about my statement, and, for the time being at least, is unlikely to do so; the same applies to my father. So if you should discuss this matter with anybody (in actual fact, of course, there is nothing secret about it; on the one hand my earthly possessions have been increased through the acquisition of tuberculosis while on the other hand they have, admittedly, been somewhat depleted), or if you should already have done so, please ask him not to discuss it with my parents, even if they should try to sound him out in the course of conversation. When it is so easy to relieve one's parents of a burden for a while, one should certainly try to do so.   [Br, 160]

To Felice, September 9:
Dearest, no evasions and gradual revelations, least of all with you. The only evasion is my not writing until today. I did not keep silent on account of your silence. Your silence was not surprising, what does surprise me is your kind reply. My last 2 letters, though characteristic, were nevertheless monstrous; there was no way of answering them, directly or evasively, and this I knew: I am asleep while writing; I wake up quick enough afterwards, but then it's too late. This, by the way, is not my worst attribute. Here is the reason for my silence: 2 days after my last letter, precisely 4 weeks ago, at about 5 A.M., I had a hemorrhage of the lung. Fairly severe; for 10 minutes or more it gushed out of my throat; I thought it would never stop. The next day I went to see a doctor, who on this and several subsequent occasions examined and X-rayed me; and then, at Max's insistence, I went to see a specialist. Without going into all the medical details, the outcome is that I have tuberculosis in both lungs. That I should suddenly develop some disease did not surprise me; nor did the sight of blood; for years my insomnia and headaches have invited a serious illness, and ultimately my maltreated blood had to burst forth; but that it should be of all things tuberculosis, that at the age of 34 I should be struck down overnight, with not a single predecessor anywhere in the family—this does surprise me. Well, I have to accept it; actually, my headaches seem to have been washed away with the flow of blood. Its course at present cannot be foreseen; its future development remains its secret; my age

may possibly help to retard it. Next week I am going to the country for at least 3 months, to Ottla in Zürau (Post Office Flöhau); I wanted to retire, but for my own good they think it would be best not to let me; the somewhat sentimental farewell scenes which, from force of habit, I am unable to deny myself even now, do rather counteract my request, so I remain a regular employee, and am granted leave of absence. Although of course I am not treating the whole affair as a secret, I am withholding it from my parents. This never occurred to me at first. But when, simply as an experiment, I told my mother casually that I was feeling nervous and was going to ask for a long leave, and she took it all as a matter of course and was not in the least suspicious (for her part she is always perfectly ready at the slightest suggestion to give me a leave for all eternity), I simply left it at that, and this is how it stands for the time being with regard to my father as well.

So this is what I have been keeping secret for 4 weeks, or actually for only one week (the precise diagnosis being not much older than that). "Poor dear Felice"—were the last words I wrote; is this to be the closing phrase to all my letters? It's not a knife that stabs only forward but one that wheels around and stabs back as well.

In conclusion, and so as not to give you the idea that I am feeling especially ill at this moment: I am not; on the contrary. True, I have been coughing since that night, but not badly; sometimes I run a slight temperature, sometimes at night I sweat a little, am rather short of breath, but otherwise I am positively better than I have been these last few years. The headaches have left me, and since 5 o'clock that morning I have been sleeping almost better than before. And until then, after all, what I suffered from most were headaches and insomnia.   [F, 543 f.]

> *September 12: Leave of absence from the office. Stays with his sister Ottla in Zürau, a village in Northwest Bohemia; she managed a farm that belonged to Karl Hermann, her brother-in-law. Before going to Zürau, F.K. decided again to break off his engagement to Felice.*

> *Entry in Brod's diary, September 12:*
> Said goodbye to Kafka. It hurts me. I have not been without him for such a long time for years. He now thinks he can't marry F. because of his illness. Despairing letter from her, although she knows nothing about it yet. Two people come from the shop with handcarts to take his luggage. He says, "They are coming for the coffin."   [B, 164]

September 15. You have the chance, as far as it is at all possible, to make a new beginning. Don't throw it away. If you insist on digging into yourself, you won't be able to avoid the muck that will well up. But don't wallow in it. If the infection in your lungs is only a symbol, as you say, a symbol of the wound whose inflammation is called F. and whose depth is its justification; if this is so then the medical advice (light, air, sun, rest) is also a symbol. Lay hold of this symbol.

O wonderful moment, masterful version, garden gone to seed. You turn the corner as you leave the house and the goddess of luck rushes toward you down the garden path.

Majestic presence, prince of the realm.   [DII, 182]

September 18. Tear everything up.   [DII, 182]

> *To Brod, from Zürau, mid-September:*
> F. [Felice] has sent a few lines announcing her arrival. I do not understand her, she is quite extraordinary, or rather, I understand her but I cannot grasp her. I run around her barking like a nervous dog around a statue or—to use a contrary but equally valid simile—I look at her as a stuffed animal looks at a person living quietly in his room. Half-truths, thousandth-truths! The only really true thing is that F. is probably coming.
> There is so much that harasses me, I can find no way out. Am I subscribing to a false hope, am I deluding myself, by thinking that I always wanted to stay here, I mean here in the country, far from the railway, close to the indissoluble evening, which descends without invoking the slightest resistance from anybody or anything? If it is a delusion, then my blood is using it to induce me to create a new incarnation of my uncle [Siegfried Löwy], the country doctor, whom I (with great, indeed the greatest, sympathy) sometimes call the "twitterer" on account of his unbelievably thin, birdlike, bachelor's wit, which erupts from his cramped throat, and which never deserts him. And he lives like this in the country, ineradicable and contented, for contentment can come from the gentle sighing of madness, when the listener mistakes it for the melody of life. On the other hand, if this longing for the countryside is not a delusion, it must be something good. But have I any right to expect that, at thirty-four years of age, with a highly suspect lung and even more suspect human relationships? The country doctor is the more likely version; and if you want confirmation, then remember the father's curse; a fine nocturnal sight, when hope struggles with the father.   [Br, 164]

> *Oscar Baum spent a week in Zürau as F.K.'s guest. Baum in his Memoirs:*
> *In the long nights we talked right through till the morning, I got to*

know more about him than in the ten previous years, and the five that
followed.   [B. 165]

To Brod, from Zürau, mid-September:
Ottla really is carrying me on her wings through this difficult world; the
room (although facing northeast) is excellent, airy and warm, and, as if
that were not enough, the house is almost entirely still; all the different
foods that I am supposed to eat have been provided in generous abundance (only my lips are sealed from aversion, but then that invariably
happens during the first few days in any new place); and then there is
the freedom, above all there is the freedom.

At all events, I now cling to my tuberculosis as a child clings to its
mother's apron strings. If the illness stems from my mother, then the
simile is even more apt, and it would seem that in her boundless
solicitude my mother will unwittingly have performed this service for
me as well. I am constantly seeking an explanation of this illness, for I
have certainly not flushed it out by my own efforts. Sometimes it seems
to me as if my brain and my lung had come to an agreement without my
knowledge. "Things can't go on like this," my brain said, and five years
later my lung agreed to help.

But in another sense this version is entirely false. Recognition of the
first step. The first step on the stairs leading to the room where a
marriage bed is quietly being assembled as the goal and meaning of my
human (and in this context virtually Napoleonic) existence. It will not
be assembled, and I, it has now been decided, will not be leaving Cor-
sica.   [Br, 161]

To Brod, from Zürau, mid-September:
The strange thing, one that could well engage my attention now, is that
all the people I know, from what I regard as the most humble to the
most mighty, are inordinately friendly to me and would, if I let them,
devote themselves to my welfare without a moment's hesitation. I have
drawn general conclusions about human nature from this personal
experience, and felt even more depressed as a result. However, it is
probably untrue that people are consistently friendly only to those
who cannot be helped. Certainly, they have a sixth sense for such
cases. But many (not all) people arc friendly and devoted to you, Max,
and you constantly repay the world for such kindness, in fact you have
developed a regular commercial traffic (that is why you are able to
strike a balance, in human terms, between things I scarcely dare touch),
whereas I repay nothing, or at least nothing to people.   [Br, 166 f.]

September 19. Have never understood how it is possible for almost everyone who writes to objectify his sufferings in the very midst of undergoing them; thus I, for example, in the midst of my unhappiness, in all likelihood with my head still smarting from unhappiness, sit down and write to someone: I am unhappy. Yes, I can even go beyond that and with as many flourishes as I have the talent for, all of which seem to have nothing to do with my unhappiness, ring simple, or contrapuntal, or a whole orchestration of changes on my theme. And it is not a lie, and it does not still my pain; it is simply a merciful surplus of strength at a moment when suffering has raked me to the bottom of my being and plainly exhausted all my strength. But then what kind of surplus is it?

In peacetime you don't get anywhere, in wartime you bleed to death.

[DII, 183 f.]

September 20–21: Felice visits F.K. in Zürau.

September 21. F. was here; traveled thirty hours to see me; I should have prevented her. As I see it, she is suffering the utmost unhappiness, essentially through my fault. I myself am unable to take hold of myself, am as helpless as I am unfeeling, think of the disturbance of a few of my comforts, and, as my only concession, condescend to act my part. In small details she is wrong, wrong in defending what she calls—or what are really—her rights, but on the whole she is an innocent person condemned to be severely tortured. I am guilty of the wrong for which she is being tortured, and am in addition the torturer.   [DII, 184 f.]

September 22. Nothing.   [DII, 186]

September 25. I can still have passing satisfaction from works like "A Country Doctor," provided I can still write such things at all (very improbable). But happiness only if I can raise the world into the pure, the true, and the immutable.   [DII, 187]

To Brod, from Zürau, end of September:
You think I assess the future course of this illness too seriously? No, how could I, since I feel its present course to be so light, and since feeling is the principal yardstick in this matter. If I occasionally say such things, it is pure affectation, with which I am always richly endowed in poor times; or else the illness is speaking for me because I have asked it to do so. The only certainty is that there is nothing to which I could surrender myself up with more perfect confidence than death.   [Br, 171]

To Brod, from Zürau, end of September:
It would have been particularly sad if the last consignment had been
lost; the hasidic stories in the [journal] *Jüdisches Echo* are perhaps not
the best of their kind, but such stories—I cannot think why—are the
only Jewish genre in which I invariably and immediately feel at home,
irrespective of my mood; my reaction to other Jewish works is almost
entirely fortuitous: I am wafted toward them on one current of air only
to be carried away again on another. I will keep the stories here for the
time being if you have no objection.   [Br, 172 f.]

September 28. Outline of my conversations with F.
I: This, then, is what I have come to.
F.: This is what *I* have come to.
I: This is what I have brought you to.
F.: True.

I would put myself in death's hands, though. Remnant of a faith.
Return to a father. Great Day of Atonement.   [DII, 187 f.]

To Felice, from Zürau, September 30 or October 1, on the se-
riousness of his situation, and in a studied preparation for the
end of the relationship between them:
As you know, there are two combatants at war within me. During the
past few days I have had fewer doubts than ever that the better of the
two belongs to you. By word and silence, and a combination of both,
you have been kept informed about the progress of the war for 5 years,
and most of that time it has caused you suffering. Were you to ask if I
have always been truthful, I could only say that with no one else have I
suppressed deliberate lies as strenuously, or—to be more precise—more
strenuously than I have with you. Subterfuges there have been, lies
very few, assuming that it's possible to tell "very few" lies. I am a
mendacious creature; for me it is the only way to maintain an even keel,
my boat is fragile. When I examine my ultimate aim it shows that I do
not actually strive to be good, to answer to a supreme tribunal. Very
much the opposite. I strive to know the entire human and animal
community, to recognize their fundamental preferences, desires, and
moral ideals, to reduce them to simple rules, and as quickly as possible
to adopt these rules so as to be pleasing to everyone, indeed (here
comes the inconsistency) to become so pleasing that in the end I might
openly act out my inherent baseness before the eyes of the world
without forfeiting its love—the only sinner not to be roasted. In short,
my only concern is the human tribunal, and I would like to deceive
even this, and what's more without actual deception.
    Apply this to our own case, which is not just an arbitrary one, but

altogether the one most truly representative of me. You are my human tribunal. Of the two who are at war within me, or rather whose war I consist of—excepting one small tormented remnant—the one is good, the other evil. From time to time they reverse their roles, which adds to the confusion of their war, already so confused. Until very recently, however, despite reverses, it was possible for me to imagine that the most improbable would happen (the most probable would be eternal war), which always seemed like the radiant goal, and I, grown pitiful and wretched over the years, would at last be allowed to have you.

Suddenly it appears that the loss of blood was too great. The blood shed by the good one (the one that now seems good to us) in order to win you, serves the evil one. Where the evil one on his own would probably or possibly not have found a decisive new weapon for his defense, the good one offers him just that. For secretly I don't believe this illness to be tuberculosis, at least not primarily tuberculosis, but rather a sign of my general bankruptcy. I had thought the war could last longer, but it can't. The blood issues not from the lung, but from a decisive stab delivered by one of the combatants.

From my tuberculosis this one now derives the kind of immense support a child gets from clinging to its mother's skirts. What more can the other one hope for? Has not the war been most splendidly concluded? It is tuberculosis, and that is the end. Weak and weary, almost invisible to you when in this state, what can the other one do but lean on your shoulder here in Zürau, and with you, the purest of the pure, stare in amazement, bewildered and hopeless, at the great man who—now that he feels sure of universal love, or of that of its female representative assigned to him—begins to display his atrocious baseness. It is a distortion of my striving, which in itself is already a distortion.

Please don't ask why I put up a barrier. Don't humiliate me in this way. One word like this from you and I would be at your feet again. But at once my actual, or rather, long before that, my alleged tuberculosis would stab me in the face, and I would have to give up. It is a weapon compared to which the countless others used earlier, ranging from "physical incapacity" up to my "work" and down to my "parsimony," look expedient and primitive.

And now I am going to tell you a secret which at the moment I don't even believe myself (although the distant darkness that falls about me at each attempt to work, or think, might possibly convince me), but which is bound to be true: I will never be well again. Simply because it is not the kind of tuberculosis that can be laid in a deckchair and nursed back to health, but a weapon that continues to be of supreme necessity as long as I remain alive. And both cannot remain alive.

[F, 544 ff.]

*F.K.'s last letter to Felice was that of October 16, 1917; it dealt
with Brod's theory of "happiness within unhappiness."*

October 8. General impression given one by peasants: noblemen who
have escaped into agriculture, where they have arranged their work so
wisely and humbly that it fits perfectly into everything and they are
protected against all insecurity and worry until their blissful death.
True dwellers on this earth.   [DII, 188]

To Elsa and Max Brod, from Zürau, early October:
I feel quite well here among all the animals. This afternoon I fed the
goats. Where I sit there are a few bushes, whose most succulent leaves
are too high for the goats to reach, and so I held the branches down for
them. In their external appearance, these goats are pure Jewish types;
most of them are doctors, but there are some who look as if they could
be lawyers, and you also find a few Polish Jews, and here and there a
young girl. Dr. W, the physician who is treating me, is well represented
among the goat population. The three-man council of Jewish doctors
that I fed today was so pleased with me that when milking time came
around this evening it practically refused to be driven off to the parlor.
And so our days, theirs and mine, draw to a peaceful close.   [Br, 176]

To Felix Weltsch, from Zürau, early October:
The principal prerequisite for recovery—in this you are, of course,
quite right—is the will to recover. I have that will, but—if I can say this
without affectation—I also have an antithetical will. It is a special
illness, one that is, so to speak, conferred on the patient, and is quite
different from any illness I have ever known before. I am reminded of
the happy lover who declares: "All my earlier love affairs were false,
but this is true love."   [Br, 180]

To Brod, from Zürau, October 12:
I have never been able to understand why you should think that I, and
others, seek our "happiness in unhappiness" or why, when you speak
about it, instead of making a simple statement or expressing your regret
or, if you feel you must, issuing a warning, you actually reproach us.
Can it be that you do not know what this expression means? When the
mark was set upon Cain, it was done with this idea in mind, which
naturally embraces the antithetical conception of seeking "unhappiness in happiness." But if somebody seeks "happiness in unhappiness"
it means, in the first place, that he has fallen out of step with the world,
and over and above this it means that his whole life has disintegrated,
or is in the process of disintegrating, with the result that no voice can

reach him without breaking, and he is unable to make a genuine response. Things are not quite that bad with me, or at least they have not
been up till now; I have had my fill of happiness and unhappiness,
although as far as my general composure is concerned, there you are
largely in the right, even in respect of the present period, only you must
learn to express your views in a different form.

Your justification of the need for recovery is attractive but Utopian.
The task you have set me might perhaps have been achieved by an
angel hovering above my parents' marriage bed, or better still, above
the marriage bed of my nation, always assuming that I have one.

[Br, 181 ff.]

To Oskar Baum, from Zürau, October–November:
Kierkegaard is a star, but he shines over a district that is virtually
inaccessible to me; I am glad you are going to read him; I only know
Fear and Trembling.[1]   [Br, 190]

November 6. Sheer incapacity.

November 10. I haven't yet written down the decisive thing, I am still
going in two directions. The work awaiting me is enormous.   [DII, 190]

*Diary entries break off. There are no entries for 1918. The next
note is that of June 27, 1919.*

*In early November Brod recorded a conversation with F.K. hav-
ing to do with Brod's conflict with himself:*
He: That's the way it is always. The fault lies just in the fact that we
think things over.
I: Well, should one do things without thinking them over?
He: That is, of course, not a law. But it is written: Thou shalt not be
able to think things over. You can't do it by force. Thinking things over
is the advice of the serpent. But it is also good and human. Without it
one is lost.   [B, 165]

To Brod, from Zürau, mid-November:
What I am doing is both simple and logical: in the city, in my family, in
my profession, in society, in my love affairs (you may, if you wish,
place these at the head of the list), in the national community, both in
its present form and in the future form that has yet to be achieved—in
all of these things I have failed to prove my worth, and failed in a way
in which nobody with whom I have come into contact—and I have
taken very careful stock—has ever failed. Essentially, this is the kind of

attitude adopted by a young child ("nobody is as nasty as I am"), but in this particular instance (I am no longer talking in terms of nastiness or self-reproach but of the manifest psychological fact of failing to prove one's worth) this attitude has been, and continues to be, maintained.

Far be it from me to boast about the suffering that was a concomitant of this unlived life; and anyway, looking back (from every minor halt along the line), this suffering appears quite trivial by comparison to the facts whose pressure it had to resist; although it was too great or, if not too great, then certainly too meaningless for it to be endured any longer. (In such troughs it is perhaps permissible to consider the question of meaning.)

The first solution to offer itself—which may well have been present from childhood onward—was not suicide, but the idea of suicide. In my case there is no need to embark on a special analysis of cowardice, for it was not cowardice that stopped me from committing suicide but a simplistic and ultimately senseless argument: "So you, who are incapable of doing anything, want to do this thing? How can you even entertain the idea? If you are able to murder yourself, then surely you no longer need to do so? Etc." Subsequently, as I gradually acquired other insights, I stopped thinking about suicide altogether. What I had to look forward to then—on the rare occasions when the idea of staying alive enabled me to transcend my confused hopes, my isolated states of happiness, and my puffed-up vanities—was: a wretched life and a wretched death. "It was as if the shame of it must outlive him" is the final remark in The Trial.

I now see another solution, one that is far more complete than I would previously have thought possible and which I would never have found on my own initiative (unless the tuberculosis is part of "my initiative"). But although I can see, or believe I can see, it, I have yet to adopt it. It consists, or rather would consist, of acknowledging—not only in private, not only in asides, but openly, through my personal behavior—that I am unable to prove my worth in this world. To achieve this end, all I need do is ink in the outline of my earlier life with a firm hand. I would then be able to take a grip on myself, I would not fritter my energy away on meaningless activities. I would have an unimpeded view.   [Br, 194 ff.]

To Felix Weltsch, from Zürau, mid-November:
Zürau's first great defect: a night of mice, a terrible experience. I came through it all unscathed, and my hair is no whiter than it was yesterday, but it was the most horrible thing in the world. On previous occasions I had already heard here and there (I keep on having to break off from my letter, you will learn why later) here and there a gentle

nibbling at night; once I even rose trembling from my bed to investi-
gate, but the noise stopped immediately—on this occasion, however,
there was uproar. What a terrible, dumb, blustering race they are. At
two o'clock I was awoken by a rustling sound at the side of my bed, and
from then onward it did not stop until morning. They jumped up on the
coalbin, they jumped down from the coalbin, they ran from one corner
of the room to the other, they described circles, they gnawed at the
woodwork, and even when they rested from their labors they whistled
softly to one another; yet all the time there was a great sense of stillness,
it was as if some oppressed proletarian people, true creatures of the
night, were engaged in clandestine operations. I found a refuge for my
thoughts by identifying the area around the stove, from which I was
separated by the whole length of the room, as the principal source of
noise, but in fact it was everywhere, and the worst of all was when a
whole crowd of them jumped down *en masse* from some piece of
furniture or other.

I was completely helpless, in my whole being I could find nothing to
hold on to, I did not dare get up and switch on the light, all I was able to
do was to cry out a few times in the hope that this would intimidate
them. And so the night passed; in the morning I felt so depressed and so
revolted that I could not get out of bed, I lay there until one o'clock, and
strained my ears all morning trying to make out what one indefatiga-
ble creature, who was either winding up the previous night's activities
or preparing for the next, was doing in the coalbin. I have now brought
the cat, which I have always secretly hated, into my room; time and
again I have to chase her away because she tries to jump on my lap (you
see now why I have to keep breaking off); if she is dirty, I have to fetch
the maid from the ground floor; if she is good (the cat), and lies by the
stove, then some mouse, which has woken too early, begins to scratch
over by the window; the sound is unmistakable. Today everything has
turned sour on me. Even the good, moist taste and smell of the home-
made bread is mousy.   [Br. 197 f.]

To Brod, from Zürau, November 24:
Ottla is in Prague, perhaps she will be able to tell me more about the
Viennese evening when she returns. You could not have wished for
anything better than an audience of young people. I have the same faith
in them as you, and yet I had none in my own youth, although by the
mere fact of being a young person, with no thought for the future, with
no thought for anything but being a young person (and a young young
person at that), I surely deserved to have it. How pleasant it must be to
be able to show such faith.   [Br. 201]

To Felix Weltsch, from Zürau, early December:
If you know of an edition of Augustine's *Confessions* (that is the correct
title, isn't it), one that is well printed and inexpensive, I would be
grateful if you would tell me, for I would very much like to order a
copy. Who was Pelagius? I have read so much about Pelagianism, and
have not remembered a thing—was it some sort of Catholic heresy? If
you are reading Maimonides, *Salomon Maimons Lebensgeschichte* (by
[J.] Fromer, published by Georg Müller) might be helpful; it is also a
good book in its own right, an extremely vivid autobiography of a man
who moves backward and forward like some strange phantom
between East European and West European Judaism. He also gives an
outline of the doctrine evolved by Maimonides, whose spiritual de-
scendant he felt himself to be. But you probably know the book better
than I.

You are surprised to find yourself gravitating toward religion? When
you started to build your ethic—this is the one thing that I think I can
claim to know about it with certainty—you built without foundations,
and now you are perhaps beginning to realize that it has foundations
after all. Would that be so strange?   [Br, 203]

To Brod, from Zürau, early December:
What I feel about the mice is downright fear. Tracing the source of that
fear would be a matter for a psychoanalyst, and I am no psychoanalyst.
Like my fear of vermin, it is no doubt connected with the unexpected,
uninvited, unavoidable appearance of these obsessive, secretive, and
in a sense silent animals, with the feeling that they have dug a hundred
holes in the walls of the house and lurk inside them, that because of
their nocturnal habit and their tiny stature they are so far removed
from us and consequently even less vulnerable. Their smallness is a
particularly important facet of their ability to engender fear. Just imagine an animal that looked like a pig and ought, therefore, to be a rather
amusing creature, but that was as small as a rat and emerged snorting
from a hole in the floor—that is a terrifying idea.

A few days ago I discovered quite an effective, albeit purely pro-
visional, solution. During the night I leave the cat in the empty room
next door, and in this way I prevent her from making a mess in my
room (it is difficult to reach an understanding with an animal in this
respect. It would all seem to be due to a misunderstanding, for the cat
knows from being beaten, and from various other forms of enlightenment, that the relief of nature is an unpleasant business and that
consequently the place used for this purpose must be carefully chosen.
So how does she set about it? She chooses a place that is dark, one that
also demonstrates her attachment to me, and that she herself finds

pleasant. Seen in human terms, this place turns out to be the inside of my slipper. A simple misunderstanding, but one that is repeated every night and every time the cat feels the need) and I also preclude the possibility of her jumping on my bed, while at the same time having the comforting feeling that I can always let the cat in if things should get too bad. In fact, the past few nights have been quiet, at least there were no incontrovertible signs of mice. Of course, it is not conducive to sleep if you undertake part of the cat's duties yourself by leaning forward or sitting bolt upright in bed with burning eyes and ears pricked; but that happened only during the first night, and things are better now.

I remember your telling me on various occasions about special traps, but I believe they are unobtainable at present, and in any case I don't think I want them. Traps actually attract mice, and they only eliminate the ones they kill. Cats, on the other hand, banish mice simply by their presence, perhaps simply by their deposits, which means, of course, that these deposits are not to be completely despised. It was particularly noticeable in the first night of the cat, which followed the great night of the mice. True, it was not "as quiet as a mouse," but no mouse ran around the room. The cat, disconcerted by her enforced change of locale, sat in the corner and did not stir; but it was enough, the teacher was in attendance, the mice stayed in their holes and just chattered to one another from time to time.

You have told me so little about yourself that I am punishing you with the saga of the mice.

You write: "I am waiting for redemption." Fortunately, you do not act in strict accordance with your precepts. Who does not feel "ill, guilty, and impotent" when he is striving to fulfill his life's task, or rather when he realizes that he himself is a task that is resolving itself? Who can resolve a thing without being resolved? [. . .]

And I would have told that story from the Talmud² quite differently: the just men weep because they thought they had overcome so much suffering and then realized that it was nothing by comparison with what they have become. As for the unjust men—are there any?   [Br, 205 f.]

To Brod, from Zürau, December 10:
All that I meant by my "burning eyes" was that I had tried unsuccessfully to probe the mousy darkness by staring like a cat. And now, for the time being at least, that has all become quite superfluous, for what had previously been distributed by the cat over the rugs and sofa is now very largely accommodated by a single box of sand. Coming to terms with an animal is a wonderful thing. In the evenings, after she has had her milk, she goes to the box like a well-trained child, climbs in,

arches her back because the box is too small, and does what she has to
do. So, at the moment, I have no worries in this respect.   [Br, 207]

> December 25–27: Felice in Prague; the final act of separation.
> Brod's note, December 26:

Yesterday he told F. everything quite clearly. We spoke about everything but that. Kafka on Tolstoy's Resurrection: "You cannot write
about salvation, you can only live it." In the afternoon, an excursion
with Baum and Weltsch. So three married couples, alongside Kafka and
F. Kafka unhappy. He said to me, "What I have to do, I can do only
alone. Become clear about the ultimate things. The West European
Jew is not clear about them, and therefore has no right to marry. There
are no marriages for them. Unless he is the kind that is not interested in
such things—businessmen, for example."

The next morning Franz came to my office to see me. To rest for one
moment, he said. He had just been to the station to see F. off. His face
was pale, hard, and severe. But suddenly he began to cry. It was the
only time I saw him cry. I shall never forget the scene, it is one of the
most terrible I have ever experienced. [. . .]

Kafka had come straight into the room I worked in, to see me, in the
middle of all the office work, sat near my desk on a small chair which
stood there ready for bearers of petitions, pensioners, and debtors. And
in this place he was crying, in this place he said between his sobs: "Is it
not terrible that such a thing must happen?" The tears were streaming
down his cheeks. I have never except this once seen him upset quite
without control of himself.   [B, 166 f.]

> To Brod, from Prague, end of December:

Here are the manuscripts for your wife (the only ones I have); do not
show them to anybody. Perhaps you could have copies made at my
expense of the "Bucket Rider" and the "Old Manuscript," and then
send them to me, I need them for [Paul] Kornfeld.

I am not sending you the novels. Why revive these old endeavors?
Simply because I have not burned them? Next time [. . .], when I come,
I hope this will be done. What is the point of keeping such works,
which are a failure "even" in artistic terms? Is it because people cherish
the hope that my whole being can be reconstituted, as if they were
some court of appeal to which I would be able to turn when I am in
need? I know that is not possible, that no help will come from that
quarter. So what am I to do with these things? Should those who
cannot help me be allowed to harm me, for I know that would be the
outcome.   [Br, 216 f.]

October 1917 to February 1918, while in Zürau, F.K. wrote a series of aphorisms and reflections "on sin, suffering, hope, and the true way" (as Brod called them), interspersed with other entries in the octavo notebooks. At a later point, F.K. excerpted the aphorisms on separate slips of paper and numbered them (GW, 162–84).

Prometheus

There are four legends concerning Prometheus:

According to the first he was clamped to a rock in the Caucasus for betraying the secrets of the gods to men, and the gods sent eagles to feed on his liver, which was perpetually renewed.

According to the second Prometheus, goaded by the pain of the tearing beaks, pressed himself deeper and deeper into the rock until he became one with it.

According to the third his treachery was forgotten in the course of thousands of years, forgotten by the gods, the eagles, forgotten by himself.

According to the fourth everyone grew weary of the meaningless affair. The gods grew weary, the eagles grew weary, the wound closed wearily.

There remained the inexplicable mass of rock. The legend tried to explain the inexplicable. As it came out of a substratum of truth it had in turn to end in the inexplicable.

The Great Wall of China, pp. 251 f.

To Kurt Wolff, from Zürau, January 27, regarding the volume A Country Doctor:

I enclose the proofs herewith and would be grateful if you would take note of the following points: The book is to consist of 15 short stories which are to appear in the sequence given in my recent letter. I cannot remember the entire sequence at this moment, but I do know that "A Country Doctor" is the second story and not the first; the first is "The New Advocate." At all events, I would request that you arrange the book according to the sequence I gave you. I would also like to request a dedication page at the front of the book bearing the inscription "To My Father." The proof for the title, which should read

A Country Doctor
Short Stories,

has not yet arrived. [Br, 228]

*The fourth octavo notebook (January 29 to the end of February)
contains the following sketch of a program:*

GUILD OF WORKERS WITHOUT POSSESSIONS

DUTIES: to possess no money, no valuables, and not to accept any. Only the following possessions are permitted: the most simple dress (to be defined in detail), whatever is necessary for work, books, food for one's own needs. Everything else belongs to the poor.

To get one's living only by working for it. Not to shrink from any work that one's strength suffices to perform without damaging one's health. Either to choose the work oneself or, in the event of this not being possible, to fall in with the arrangements made by the Labor Council, which is responsible to the government.

To work for no wages other than what is necessary to support life (to be defined in detail according to the various districts) for two days.

Life to be of the utmost moderation. To eat only what is absolutely necessary, for instance as a minimum wage, which is in a certain sense also a maximum wage: bread, water, dates. Food as eaten by the poorest, shelter like that of the poorest.

The relationship to the employer to be treated as a relation of mutual trust. The intervention of the courts never to be invoked. Each job taken on to be completed, in all circumstances, except for grave reasons of health.

RIGHTS: maximum working time six hours, for manual work four to five hours.

In sickness and in the incapacity of old age reception into a state home for the aged and into hospitals.

Working life as a matter of conscience and a matter of faith in one's fellow men.

Inherited possessions to be presented to the state for the erection of hospitals and homes.

Provisionally, at least, exclusion of independent persons, married persons, and women.

Council (grave duty) negotiates with the government.

Also in capitalist enterprises [two words illegible].

In places where one can help, in abandoned districts, almshouses, [as] teacher.

Five hundred men upper limit.

One year's novitiate.

[DF, 103 ff.]

To Brod, from Zürau, early March:

My silence is also part of the countryside, both when I come here straight from Prague (after my last journey I arrived as if downright intoxicated; it seemed to me as if I come to Zürau simply in order to sober up, and then, when I am still only partially sober, promptly return to Prague to intoxicate myself once again), and also when I have been here for some time, in fact always. It goes without saying that my world is becoming more and more impoverished by the stillness; I have always regarded it as my special misfortune that I (the embodiment of symbols!) simply did not have enough power in my lungs to inspire the world with diversity for myself, although it undoubtedly possesses diversity, as I can clearly see; now I have stopped trying, this particular endeavor has been dropped from my timetable, and my days are none the gloomier for it. But I now have even less to say than I had then, and what I say is said almost against my will.   [Br, 234 f.]

To Brod, from Zürau, end of March:
Thank you for mediating with Wolff. Now that I have decided to dedicate the book to my father, I would like to see it published as soon as possible. Not that this could ever reconcile my father, our hostility is ineradicable; but it would mean that I had done something, that even if I had not settled in Palestine, I had at least traced out the route on the map with my finger. And since Wolff has shut himself off, since he does not reply to my letters and sends me nothing, and since this will probably be my last book, I thought of sending the manuscripts to Reiss,[1] who was good enough to make me an offer. I then sent an ultimatum to Wolff, which has also remained unanswered; but meanwhile, about ten days ago, I received a new batch of proofs, and decided not to approach Reiss after all. Do you think I should send the manuscripts to another publisher? I have also had an invitation to visit Paul Cassirer.[2] Do you happen to know how he obtained my Zürau address?   [Br, 237]

To Oskar Baum, from Zürau, June:
I would have written to you long ago if there had been anything particularly good to write about my recovery. But from the medical point of view—and I am being serious as well as flippant—it is a hopeless case. Would you like to hear a layman's diagnosis? My physical illness is simply an inundation of my mental illness; and my mind naturally resists any attempt to force it back within its banks; after all, it has just produced this tuberculosis to alleviate its own distress, and now people want to make it reabsorb this illness at the very moment when it would dearly like to produce other illnesses as well. And to start with my mind, and heal that, would require the stamina of a

furniture mover, which I could never hope to acquire for the reason I
have just given. So nothing has changed. In my early years of self-
diagnosis I was of the opinion—a stupid opinion but understandable in
a novice—that the fact that I was never able to make a full recovery
from a specific illness was due to some purely contingent factor, but
now I know that I always carry this negative factor around with me.

Otherwise, it is very beautiful here, even though the June sunshine is
interspersed with rain; the soft-scented air caresses me constantly,
asking in its innocence to be forgiven for its inability to effect a cure.

[Br, 242]

Summer and fall: Prague.

A note by Brod on F.K.'s views:
Country as opposed to town. And yet he feels better in Prague, because
in Zürau he was lying about doing nothing. Here he studies Hebrew
and gardening. The positive things in his life. Wants to keep these quite
pure—they are the "country things." Would like to withdraw from
everything else.   [B, 168 f.]

To Felix Weltsch, presumably fall:
One good thing has come out of this summer, Felix; I will never again
set foot in a sanatorium. Now that I am becoming really ill, I will never
again set foot in any sanatorium. Everything is wrong.   [Br, 243]

To Kurt Wolff, October 1, regarding A Country Doctor:
Many thanks for your letters. If I understand your reference to the
printing schedule correctly, it would seem that I am to receive no page
proofs; that would be a pity. The sequence of the stories as listed in
your letter is correct apart from one error which must be rectified at all
costs: the book should begin with "The New Advocate," and the story
you have put at the beginning and which you wrongly call "A Murder"
should be discarded since it is identical in all essential respects with a
later story which you have rightly called "A Fratricide." Please do not
forget the dedication "To My Father" on the flyleaf. I am enclosing the
manuscript of "A Dream."   [Br, 245]

To Kurt Wolff, November 11, regarding The Penal Colony:
After a long period of bed rest I hasten to thank you most warmly for
your kind letter. As far as the publication of the *Penal Colony* is
concerned, I gladly agree to all your proposals. I have received the

manuscript, and deleted one short passage, and I will return it to your
publishing house today.   [Br, 245]

*November: Schelesen, Pension Stüdl. Meets Julie Wohryzek,
daughter of a synagogue custodian and shoemaker, and enters
into an intimate friendship with her. His letters to her are no
longer extant.*

1919

From Letter to His Father

You had worked your way up so far by your own energies alone, and as a result you had unbounded confidence in your opinion. That was not yet so dazzling for me as a child as later for the boy growing up. From your armchair you ruled the world. Your opinion was correct, every other was mad, wild, *meshugge*, not normal. Your self-confidence indeed was so great that you had no need to be consistent at all and yet never ceased to be in the right.

Letter to His Father, p. 21

To Brod, from Schelesen, February 6, on Julie Wohryzek:
The Jewish element is a young girl, I hope she is not seriously ill. An ordinary and an astonishing person. Not Jewish and not un-Jewish, not German and not un-German; in love with the cinema, operettas, and comedies, with powder and veils; a person with an inexhaustible and irresistible fund of the cheekiest Yiddish expressions at her command, on the whole uneducated, merry rather than sad—that is how I would describe her. As for her nationality, if I am to be accurate, I can only say that she owes her allegiance to the great nation of office workers. And she is honest and courageous at heart, and is quite selfless—such great qualities in a creature who, although physically by no means unattractive, is as fragile as the mosquito that flies into the light of my lamp. In this, as in other respects, she resembles Fräulein Bl. [Bloch], whom you may well remember with distaste. Could you lend me a copy of [your] *Die dritte Phase des Zionismus* for her, or some other work that you consider appropriate? She will not understand it, it will not interest her, and I will not force it on her—but nonetheless. [Br. 252]

Spring: Engagement to Julie Wohryzek. Felice marries.

To Brod, spring (?):
As of today I will not allow myself to be dissuaded or diverted in any way: a bullet would be the best solution. I shall simply shoot myself and vacate this spot where I fail to exist. Granted, it would be

cowardly; and cowardice is cowardice, even in those cases where it is the only possible solution. This is such a case, this is a situation that must be eliminated at all costs; and nobody, only cowardice, can eliminate it, courage simply reduces it to a grim struggle. But have no fear, the grim struggle will continue.　　　　　　　　　　　　　　[Br, 254 f.]

I have spent my life resisting the desire to end it.　　　　　　[DF, 303]

> May: Publication of The Penal Colony. June 27: Resumption, on a limited scale, of entries in the diary. The volume Briefe contains only eight letters from 1919.

June 30. Was in Rieger Park. Walked up and down with J. [Julie Wohryzek] beside the jasmine bushes. False and sincere, false in my sighs, sincere in my feeling of closeness to her, in my trustfulness, in my feeling of security. Uneasy heart.　　　　　　　　　　　　　[DII, 191]

July 6. The same thought continually, desire, anxiety. Yet calmer than usual, as if some great development were going forward the distant tremor of which I feel. Too much said.　　　　　　　　　　　[DII, 191]

> Fall: Publication of A Country Doctor, dedicated to his father.

> From a letter to a sister of Julie Wohryzek's, November 24, on the crisis in his relationship with Julie:

There now appear to be only two possibilities.

One would be for us to separate. From what I have been told, you would doubtless find this the most desirable solution. And although I cannot imagine any kind of future for myself without J., I too would opt for separation on two conditions, namely, if there were a reasonably reliable and not too distant prospect of J.'s marrying some good man, of whom she approved, and with whom she could have children and live as cleanly and decently as is possible for the average person in our circumstances. There would, of course, be no comparison between the happiness provided by such a marriage and what I am able to offer at the present time. The second condition on which my approval depends would be if I were mistaken in my belief that, provided all external pressures were removed, J. with her to my mind almost magical personality would content herself, either temporarily or permanently, with fidelity and love outside of marriage, or what now passes for marriage, without sacrificing too much personal happiness. These are the two conditions on which I would give my approval. If they are met, I would be prepared, indeed I would be only too eager, to sign or otherwise confirm and to publicize any statement establishing our separation, no matter what it contained, i.e., even if it made me appear infamous, ridiculous, or despicable. Whatever this statement was like, it would always be a true statement insofar as I have been the cause of so much suffering for J., who is the most blameless and kindly creature imaginable, that by comparison any purely social act of reparation must appear quite paltry.

But if, as I believe, these two conditions do not obtain, then please let us stay together, since despite all my frailties we feel that we belong together. In February I intend to go to Munich for a period of perhaps three months, and I am quite hopeful about this visit. Perhaps J., who has always wanted to get away from Prague, could come to Munich too. We would see another part of the world, certain things might perhaps change slightly, certain frailties, certain fears might at least change their form, their direction.

I will say no more, for it seems to me that recently I have said far too many harsh and bitter things. Please be patient; I am not asking you to be indulgent, just patient and attentive, so as to ensure that as far as is humanly possible you overlook nothing in, and read nothing into, my letter.   [Kafka-Symposion, 52 f.]

F.K.'s father strongly objected to his son's plan to marry Julie Wohryzek. In November F.K. wrote the Letter to His Father, *parts of which were used in the initial chapter of this volume.*

From F.K.'s Letter to His Father, *written in Schelesen; his mother was supposed to hand it to his father, but, knowing that the letter would not improve the relationship between father and son, refused to do so and returned the letter to F.K.*

Dearest Father,

You asked me recently why I maintain that I am afraid of you. As usual, I was unable to think of any answer to your question, partly for the very reason that I am afraid of you, and partly because an explanation of the grounds for this fear would mean going into far more details than I could even approximately keep in mind while talking. And if I now try to give you an answer in writing, it will still be very incomplete, because, even in writing, this fear and its consequences hamper me in relation to you and because the magnitude of the subject goes far beyond the scope of my memory and power of reasoning.

Compare the two of us: I, to put it in a very much abbreviated form, a Löwy with a certain amount of Kafka at the bottom, which, however, is not set in motion by the Kafka will to life, to do business, to conquer, but by a Löwyish spur that impels more secretly, more diffidently, and in another direction, and which often fails to work entirely. You, on the other hand, a true Kafka in strength, health, appetite, loudness of voice, eloquence, self-satisfaction, worldly dominance, endurance, presence of mind, knowledge of human nature, a certain way of doing things on a grand scale, of course also with all the defects and weaknesses that go with these advantages and into which your temperament and sometimes your temper drive you.

My sisters were only partly on my side. The one who was happiest in her relation to you was Valli. Being closest to Mother, she fell in with your wishes in a similar way, without much effort and without suffering much harm. And because she reminded you of Mother, you did accept her in a more friendly spirit, although there was little Kafka material in her. But perhaps that was precisely what you wanted; where there was nothing of the Kafkas, even you could not demand anything of the sort; nor had you the feeling, as with the rest of us, that something was getting lost which had to be saved by force. Besides, it may be that you were never particularly fond of the Kafka element as it manifested itself in women. Valli's relationship to you would perhaps have become even friendlier if the rest of us had not disturbed it somewhat.

Elli is the only example of the almost complete success of a breaking-away from your orbit. When she was a child she was the last person I should have expected it of. For she was such a clumsy, tired, timid, bad-tempered, guilt-ridden, overmeek, malicious, lazy, greedy, miserly child, I could hardly bring myself to look at her, certainly not to speak to her, so much did she remind me of myself, in so very much the same way was she under the same spell of our upbringing. Her miserliness was especially abhorrent to me, since I had it to an, if possible, even greater extent.

I scarcely dare write of Ottla; I know that by doing so I jeopardize the whole effect I hope for from this letter. In ordinary circumstances, that is, so long as she is not in particular need or danger, all you feel is only hatred for her; you yourself have confessed to me that in your opinion she is always intentionally causing you suffering and annoyance, and while you are suffering on her account she is satisfied and pleased. In other words, a sort of fiend. What an immense estrangement, greater still than that between you and me, must have come about between you and her, for such an immense misunderstanding to be possible. She is so remote from you that you scarcely see her any more; instead, you put a specter in the place where you suppose her to be. I grant you that you have had a particularly difficult time with her. I don't, of course, quite see to the bottom of this very complicated case, but at any rate here was something like a kind of Löwy, equipped with the best Kafka weapons. Between us there was no real struggle; I was soon finished off; what remained was flight, embitterment, melancholy, and inner struggle. But you two were always in a fighting position, always fresh, always energetic. A sight as magnificent as it was desperate. At the very beginning you were, I am sure, very close to each other, because of the four of us Ottla is even today perhaps the purest representation of the marriage between you and Mother and of the forces it combined. I don't know what it was that deprived you both of the happiness of the harmony between father and child, but I can't help believing that the development in this case was similar to that in mine. On your side there was the tyranny of your own nature, on her side the Löwy defiance, touchiness, sense of justice, restlessness, and all that backed by the consciousness of the Kafka vigor. Doubtless I too influenced her, but scarcely of my own doing, simply through the fact of my existence. [. . .] Ottla has no contact with her father and has to seek her way alone, like me, and the degree of confidence, self-confidence, health, and ruthlessness by which she surpasses me makes her in your eyes more wicked and treacherous than I seem to you. I understand that. From your point of view she can't be different. Indeed, she herself is capable of regarding herself with your eyes, of feeling what you suffer, and of being—not desperate (despair is my business) but very sad.

You struck nearer home with your aversion to my writing and to everything that, unknown to you, was connected with it. Here I had, in fact, got some distance away from you by my own efforts, even if it was slightly reminiscent of the worm that, when a foot treads on its tail end, breaks loose with its front part and drags itself aside. To a certain extent I was in safety; there was a chance to breathe freely. The aversion you naturally and immediately took to my writing was, for once, welcome to me. My vanity, my ambition did suffer under your soon proverbial way of hailing the arrival of my books: "Put it on my bedside table!" (usually you were playing cards when a book came), but I was really quite glad of it, not only out of rebellious malice, not only out of delight at a new confirmation of my view of our relationship, but quite spontaneously, because to me that formula sounded something like: "Now you are free!" Of course it was a delusion; I was not, or, to put it most optimistically, was not yet, free. My writing was all about you; all I did there, after all, was to bemoan what I could not bemoan upon your breast. It was an intentionally long-drawn-out farewell from you, yet, although it was enforced by you, it did take its course in the direction determined by me.

But I showed no foresight at all concerning the significance and possibility of a marriage for me; this up-to-now greatest terror of my life has come upon me almost completely unexpectedly. The child had developed so slowly, these things were outwardly all too remote; now and then the necessity of thinking of them did arise; but that here a permanent, decisive, and indeed the most grimly bitter ordeal loomed was impossible to recognize. In reality, however, the marriage plans turned out to be the most grandiose and hopeful attempts at escape, and, consequently, their failure was correspondingly grandiose.

I am referring to a brief discussion on one of those few tumultuous days that followed the announcement of my latest marriage plan [to Julie Wohryzek]. You said to me something like this: "She probably put on a fancy blouse, something these Prague Jewesses are good at, and right away, of course, you decided to marry her. And that as fast as possible, in a week, tomorrow, today. I can't understand you: after all, you're a grown man, you live in the city, and you don't know what to do but marry the next-best girl. Isn't there anything else you can do? If you're frightened, I'll go with you [to the brothel] to see her." You put it in more detail and more plainly, but I can no longer recall the details, perhaps too things became a little vague before my eyes, I paid almost more attention to Mother who, though in complete agreement with you, took something from the table and left the room with it.

Now, regarding my attempts at marriage there is much you can say in reply, and you have indeed done so: you could not have much respect for my decision since I had twice broken the engagement with F. and had twice renewed it; since I had needlessly dragged you and Mother to Berlin to celebrate the engagement, and the like. All this is true—but how did it come about? [. . .]

Although both girls were chosen by chance, they were extraordinarily well chosen. Again a sign of your complete misunderstanding, that you can believe that I—timid, hesitant, suspicious—can decide to marry in a flash, out of delight over a blouse. Both marriages would rather have been commonsense marriages, insofar as that means that day and night, the first time for years, the second time for months, all my power of thought was concentrated on the plan.

Neither of the girls disappointed me, only I disappointed both of them. My opinion of them is today exactly the same as when I wanted to marry them.

It is not true either that in my second marriage attempt I disregarded the experiences gained from the first attempt, that I was rash and careless. The cases were quite different; precisely the earlier expe-

rience held out a hope for the second case, which was altogether much
more promising. I do not want to go into details here.

Why then did I not marry? There were certainly obstacles, as there
always are, but then, life consists in facing such obstacles. Then essential obstacle, however, which is, unfortunately, independent of the
individual case, is that obviously I am mentally incapable of marrying.
This manifests itself in the fact that from the moment I make up my
mind to marry I can no longer sleep, my head burns day and night, life
can no longer be called life, I stagger about in despair. It is not actually
worries that bring this about; true, in keeping with my sluggishness and
pedantry countless worries are involved in all this, but they are not
decisive; they do, like worms, complete the work on the corpse, but the
decisive blow has come from elsewhere. It is the general pressure of
anxiety, of weakness, of self-contempt.   [LF, 7–113]

*Winter: Schelesen. Meets Minze E., a patient recuperating there.
Exchange of friendly letters.*

December 8. Spent Monday, a holiday, in the park, the restaurant and
the Gallerie. Sorrow and joy, guilt and innocence, like two hands
indissolubly clasped together; one would have to cut through flesh,
blood, and bones to part them.   [DII, 191]

December 9. A lot of Eleseus.[1] But wherever I turn, the black wave
rushes down on me.   [DII, 191]

December 11. Thursday. Cold. With J. in Rieger Park, said not a word.
Seduction on the Graben. All this is too difficult. I am not sufficiently
prepared. It is the same thing, in a certain sense, as twenty-six years ago
my teacher [Moritz] Beck saying, of course without realizing the prophetic joke he was making: "Let him continue in the fifth grade for a
while, he still isn't strong enough; rushing him in this way will have its
consequences later on." And in fact such has been my growth, like a
shoot forced too soon and forgotten; there is a certain hothouse delicacy in the way in which I shrink from a puff of wind, if you like, even
something affecting in it, but that is all.   [DII, 192]

From "The Test"

"Why do you want to run away? Sit down and have a drink! I'll pay." So I sat down. He asked me several things, but I couldn't answer, indeed I didn't even understand his questions. So I said: "Perhaps you are sorry now that you invited me, so I'd better go," and I was about to get up. But he stretched his hand out over the table and pressed me down. "Stay," he said, "that was only a test. He who does not answer the questions has passed the test."

Description of a Struggle, pp. 208 f.

January: Promotion to Secretary of the Insurance Institute.

January 9. It is no disproof of one's presentiment of an ultimate liberation if the next day one's imprisonment continues on unchanged, or is even made straiter, or if it is even expressly stated that it will never end. All this can rather be the necessary preliminary to an ultimate liberation.

[DII, 193]

Here follows a gap in F.K.'s diary; the next entry is for October 15, 1921; the notebooks or pages of that time span are missing and were probably removed by F.K.

In January–February F.K. writes a series of aphorisms where the "I" of F.K. hides behind the figure of "He":

He has the feeling that merely by being alive he is blocking his own way. From this sense of hindrance, in turn, he deduces the proof that he is alive.

[GW, 154]

This is the problem: Many years ago I sat one day, in a sad enough mood, on the slopes of the Laurenziberg. I went over the wishes that I wanted to realize in life. I found that the most important or the most delightful was the wish to attain a view of life (and—this was necessarily bound up with it—to convince others of it in writing) in which life, while still retaining its natural full-bodied rise and fall, would simultaneously be recognized no less clearly as a nothing, a dream, a dim hovering. A beautiful wish, perhaps, if I had wished it rightly. Considered as a wish, somewhat as if one were to hammer together a table with painful and methodical technical efficiency, and simultaneously do nothing at all, and not in such a way that people could say: "Hammering a table together is nothing to him," but rather: "Hammering a table together is really hammering a table together to him, but at the same time it is nothing," whereby certainly the hammering would have become still bolder, still surer, still more real, and, if you will, still more senseless.

But he could not wish in this fashion, for his wish was not a wish, but only a vindication of nothingness, a justification of nonentity, a touch of animation which he wanted to lend to nonentity, in which at that time he had scarcely taken his first few conscious steps, but which he already felt as his element. It was a sort of farewell that he took from the illusive world of youth; although youth had never directly deceived him, but only caused him to be deceived by the utterances of all the authorities he had around him. So is explained the necessity of his "wish." [GW, 156 f.]

He proves nothing but himself, his sole proof is himself, all his opponents overcome him at once, but not by refuting him (he is irrefutable) but by proving themselves. [GW, 156]

The original sin, the ancient wrong committed by man, consists in the complaint, which man makes and never ceases making, that a wrong has been done to him, that the original sin was once committed upon him. [GW, 157]

The reason why posterity's judgment of individuals is juster than the contemporary one lies in their being dead. One develops in one's own style only after death, only when one is alone. Death is to the individual like Saturday evening to the chimney sweep; it washes the dirt from his body. Then it can be seen whether his contemporaries harmed him more, or whether he did the more harm to his contemporaries; in the latter case he was a great man. [GW, 159]

He is thirsty, and is cut off from a spring by a mere clump of bushes. But he is divided against himself: one part overlooks the whole, sees that he is standing here and that the spring is just beside him; but another part notices nothing, has at most a divination that the first part sees all. But as he notices nothing he cannot drink. [GW, 160]

Brod, recording a conversation with F.K., February 28, 1920:
He: *"We are nihilistic thoughts that came into God's head."* I quoted in
support the doctrine of the Gnostics concerning the Demiurge, the evil
creator of the world, the doctrine of the world as a sin of God's. *"No,"*
said Kafka, *"I believe we are not such a radical relapse of God's, only
one of His bad moods. He had a bad day." "So there would be hope
outside our world?"* He smiled, *"Plenty of hope—for God—no end of
hope—only not for us."*   [B, 75]

To Minze E., from Prague, February:
Youth is, of course, always beautiful; one dreams of the future and
incites others to dream, or rather one is oneself a dream, so how could it
be anything but beautiful. But this is a kind of beauty that is common to
all young people and which no one has the right to appropriate for himself.   [Br, 262]

*End of March: Meets Gustav Janouch, a young man of seventeen
who sought the acquaintance of F.K. and kept a diary of their
talks (*Conversations with Kafka: Notes and Reminiscences. With
an Introduction by Max Brod. New York, 1953). *Early April: A
three-month sick leave from the Workers' Accident Insurance
Institute, spent at Meran (Tyrol, Italy), Pension Ottoburg.
Here he writes the first letters to Milena Jesenská-Polak, a Czech
writer whom he had met in Prague. She was now living in Vienna, unhappily married to Ernst Polak.*

To Brod, from Meran, beginning of May:
She [Milena] is a living fire, the like of which I have never seen before, a
fire which incidentally, despite everything, burns only for him [her
husband]. She is also extremely delicate, courageous, and intelligent,
and throws everything into her sacrifice, or rather has acquired everything as a result of her sacrifice. But, of course, he must also be a very
special kind of man to have inspired all this.   [Br, 275]

To Brod, from Meran, June:
But there is a difference between us. Surely you see, Max, that our
situations are not the same at all. You have an enormous fortress, the
outer ring has been overrun by distress, but you are in the citadel or
anywhere you choose to be, and you work; you have to contend with
disruptions and with restlessness, but you still work, whereas I myself
am burning, suddenly I find that I have nothing, save a few beams
which I have to support with my head to prevent them from collapsing,
and now my whole impoverished being is burning. Was I complaining?

I am not complaining. My persona is complaining. And I am aware of the honor that has been conferred on me. [. . .]

Your letter is marred by just one passage. The one where you talk about recovery. No, for the past month there has been no question of recovery.   [Br, 276]

From Letters to Milena:

I live here pretty well, more care the mortal body could hardly stand, the balcony of my room is lowered into a garden, surrounded, overgrown by flowering shrubs (the vegetation here is strange, in a weather which in Prague practically freezes the puddles, the flowers open slowly in front of my balcony), at the same time fully exposed to the sun (or rather to the deeply clouded sky, as it has been for nearly a week). Lizards and birds, ill-assorted couples, visit me: I so much wish you could be in Meran, recently you wrote about not being able to breathe, in this word image and meaning are very close and in Meran both might become a little easier.   [M, 21]

I have never lived among German people, German is my mother-tongue and therefore natural to me, but Czech feels to me far more intimate, which is why your letter dispels many an uncertainty, I see you clearer, the movements of your body, your hands, so quick, so determined, it's almost a meeting, although when I try to raise my eyes to your face, then in the flow of the letter—what a story!—fire breaks out and I see nothing but fire.   [M, 30]

You must also consider, Milena, the kind of person who comes to you, the 38-year journey lying behind me (and since I'm a Jew an even much longer one), and if at an apparently accidental turning of the road I see you, whom I've never expected to see and least of all so late, then, Milena, I cannot shout, nor does anything shout within me, nor do I say a thousand foolish things, they are not in me (I'm omitting the other foolishness of which I have more than enough), and the fact that I'm kneeling I discover perhaps only through seeing your feet quite close before my eyes, and by caressing them.   [M, 47]

I don't want to (Milena, do help me! Do understand more than I say!) I don't want to (this isn't stammering) come to Vienna, because I couldn't stand the mental strain. I'm mentally ill, the disease of the lung is nothing but an overflowing of my mental disease. I've been ill like this since the 4, 5 years of my first two engagements (at first I couldn't explain to myself the cheerfulness of your last letter, only later did the explanation occur to me, I keep forgetting it: You're so young, after all, perhaps not yet 25, possibly only 23. I'm 37, almost 38, almost a short generation older, almost white-haired from the past nights and head-aches). I won't spread out before you the long story with its veritable forests of details of which I'm still afraid, like a child, only without the child's power of forgetting. What the three engagements had in com-mon was that everything was all my fault, quite undoubtedly my fault. Both girls I made unhappy and—I'm talking here only about the first, about the second I cannot speak, she's sensitive, and any word, even the kindest, would be the most appalling offense to her, something I understand—and actually only because through her (who, had I in-sisted, would perhaps have sacrificed herself) I couldn't become last-ingly happy, calm, determined, capable of marriage, although I had re-peatedly and quite voluntarily assured her of it, although I sometimes loved her desperately, although I know nothing more desirable than marriage in itself. Almost five years I battered at her (or, if you prefer, at myself)—well, fortunately, she was unbreakable, Prussian-Jewish mixture, a strong invincible mixture. I wasn't all that robust, after all she only had to suffer, whereas I battered *and* suffered.   [M. 53 f.]

Milena asked F.K. to take his trip home from Meran via Vienna and to visit her.

Whether you still wish to see me after my Wednesday, Thursday letters I cannot judge. My relationship to you I know *(you belong to me* even if I were never to see you again)—I know it insofar as it doesn't belong to the unfathomable realm of fear, but your relationship to me I don't know at all, it belongs entirely to fear. Neither do you know me, Milena, I repeat that.

For me, you see, what's happening is something prodigious. My world is tumbling down, my world is building itself up, watch out how you (this is me) survive it. The tumbling I don't deplore, it was in the process of tumbling, but what I do deplore is the building up of it. I deplore my lack of strength, deplore the being born, deplore the light of the sun.

How shall we continue to live? If you say "Yes" to my letters, then you must not continue to live in Vienna, that's impossible.

Milena, for me you are not a woman, you are a girl, as girl a one as I ever saw, I don't think I'll dare to offer you my hand, girl, this dirty, twitching, clawlike, unsteady, uncertain, hot-cold hand.   [M. 71]

Tomorrow I'll send the Father-letter [*Letter to His Father*] to your apartment, please take good care of it, one day perhaps I might want to give it to my father. If possible let no one else read it. And in reading try to understand all the lawyer's tricks, it's a lawyer's letter. [M, 79]

And in spite of everything I sometimes believe: If one can perish from happiness, then this must happen to me. And if a person designated to die can stay alive through happiness, then I will stay alive. [M, 85]

I somehow can no longer write of anything but what concerns us, us in the turmoil of the world, just us. Everything else is remote. Wrong! Wrong! But the lips are mumbling and my face lies in your lap. [M, 86]

I won't tell you anything but just seat you in the armchair (you said you hadn't been kind enough to me, but could there be more love and honor conferred on me than for you to sit there and let me sit in front of you and be with you). So now I'm seating you in the armchair and don't know how to grasp this happiness with words, eyes, hands, and the poor heart, the happiness that you are here and that you belong to me. And perhaps it isn't you at all I really love, but the existence presented to me by you. [M, 96]

If only you were already here! As it is, I have no one, no one here but the Fear, locked together we toss through the nights. There is really something very serious about this Fear (which strangely enough used to be directed only toward the future, no, that isn't true), which in a certain sense can be explained by the fact that it shows me continuously the necessity for the great admission: Milena, too, is only a human being. What you say about it is indeed so beautiful and true that one would like to hear nothing more after hearing it, but the assertion that what's at stake here is not of ultimate value is still very debatable, this Fear is after all not my private Fear—this is only part of it, and terribly so—but it is as much the Fear of all faith since the beginning of time. [M, 100]

How things will develop later is not the question, all that's certain is that *away from you I can't live otherwise than by giving in completely to fear, giving in more than it asks, and I do so without compulsion, with rapture, I pour myself into it.* [M, 106]

In the evening I talked again to a Palestinian Jew. I believe it's impossible in a letter to make you understand his importance for me—a small, almost tiny, weak, bearded, one-eyed man. But the memory of him has cost me half the night. More about this soon. [M, 121]

And actually we both write the same things all the time. Now I ask you if you're ill, then you write about it, now I want to die, then you, now I want to cry in front of you like a little boy, and then you in front of me like a little girl. And once and ten times and a thousand times and all the time I want to be with you and you say the same. Enough, enough.

[M, 135]

The most beautiful of your letters (and that means a lot, for as a whole they are, almost in every line, the most beautiful thing that ever happened to me in my life) are those in which you agree with my "fear" and at the same time try to explain that I don't need to have it. For I too, even though I may sometimes look like a bribed defender of my "fear," probably agree with it deep down in myself, indeed it is part of me and perhaps the best part. And as it is my best, it is also perhaps this alone that you love. For what else worthy of love could be found in me? But this is worthy of love.

And when you once asked me how I could have called that Saturday "good" with that fear in my heart, it's not difficult to explain. Since I love you (and I do love you, you stupid one, as the sea loves a pebble in its depths, this is just how my love engulfs you—and may I in turn be the pebble with you, if heaven permits), I love the whole world and this includes your left shoulder, no, it was first the right one, so I kiss it if I feel like it (and if you are nice enough to pull the blouse away from it) and this also includes your left shoulder and your face above me in the forest and my resting on your almost bare breast. And that's why you're right in saying that we were already one and I'm not afraid of it, rather it is my only happiness and my only pride and I don't confine it at all only to the forest.

But just between this day-world and that "half-hour in bed" of which you once spoke contemptuously as "men's business," there lies for me an abyss which I cannot bridge, probably because I don't want to. That over there is a concern of the night, thoroughly and in every sense a concern of the night: this here is the world and I possess it and now I'm supposed to leap across into the night in order to take possession of it once more. Can one take possession of anything twice? Does that not mean: to lose it? Here is the world which I possess, and I'm supposed to leap across for the sake of a sinister black magic, of a hocus-pocus, a philosopher's stone, an alchemy, a wish-ring. Away with it, I'm terribly afraid of it.   [M, 136 f.]

I won't meddle in the fight between you and Max [Brod]. I stand aside, see each one's point of view, and am safe. You are undoubtedly right in what you say, but now we are changing places. You have your homeland and can also renounce it and that's perhaps the best one can do with one's homeland, especially since those things that are unrenounceable in it one doesn't renounce anyhow. But he has no homeland, and therefore nothing to renounce, and has to think all the time of seeking or building it, all the time, whether he is taking his hat off a peg or lying in the sun in the swimming bath or writing the book you're to translate (here he is perhaps the least tense—but you, poor dear, how much work you burden yourself with from a sense of guilt, I see you bent over your work, your neck is bare, I stand behind you, you aren't aware of it—please don't be frightened if you feel my lips on the back of your neck, I didn't mean to kiss, it's only helpless love)—yes, Max, he has to think about it all the time, even when he's writing you a letter.   [M, 157]

Do you know, by the way, that you were given to me as a present for my confirmation (there's also something like a Jewish confirmation)? I was born in '83, so was 13 when you were born. The 13th birthday is a special occasion. Up near the altar in the temple I had to recite a piece learned by heart with great difficulty, then at home I had to make a brief speech (also learned by heart). I also received many presents. But I imagine that I was not entirely satisfied, one particular present I missed, I demanded it from heaven; it hesitated until August 10.   [M, 171]

So beautiful, so beautiful, Milena, so beautiful. Nothing in the letter (of Tuesday) is so beautiful as the calm, the trust, the clarity, from which it comes.   [M, 189]

If I'd been given the choice to be what I wanted, then I'd have chosen to be a small East European Jewish boy in the corner of the room, without a trace of worry, the father in the center discussing with other men, the mother, heavily wrapped, is rummaging in the traveling bundles, the sister chatters with the girls, scratching in her beautiful hair—and in a few weeks one will be in America. It isn't as simple as that, of course, there have been cases of dysentery, there are people standing in the street, shouting threats through the windows, there's even quarreling among the Jews themselves, two have already attacked one another with knives. But if one is small, if one takes in and judges everything quickly, what can happen to one? And there were enough boys like this running around, clambering over the mattresses, creeping under chairs, and lying in wait for the bread which someone—they are one people—was spreading—with something—everything is edible.   [M, 196]

So the thought of death frightens you? I'm terribly afraid only of pains. This is a bad sign. To want death but not the pains is a bad sign. But otherwise one can risk death. One has just been sent out as a biblical dove, has found nothing green, and slips back into the darkness of the ark.   [M, 208]

I've spent all afternoon in the streets, wallowing in the Jew-baiting. "Prašivé plemeno"—"filthy rabble"—I heard someone call the Jews the other day. Isn't it the natural thing to leave the place where one is hated so much? (For this, Zionism or national feeling is not needed.) The heroism that consists of staying on in spite of it all is that of cockroaches which also can't be exterminated from the bathroom.

Just now I looked out of the window: Mounted police, *gendarmerie* ready for a bayonet charge, a screaming crowd dispersing, and up here in the window the loathsome disgrace of living all the time under protection.   [M, 213]

We both know, after all, enough typical examples of West European Jews, I am as far as I know the most typical West European Jew among them. This means, expressed with exaggeration, that not one calm second is granted me, nothing is granted me, everything has to be earned, not only the present and the future, but the past too—something after all which perhaps every human being has inherited, this too must be earned, it is perhaps the hardest work. When the earth turns to the right—I'm not sure that it does—I would have to turn to the left to make up for the past. But as it is I haven't the least particle of strength for these obligations, I can't carry the world on my shoulders, can barely stand my winter overcoat on them. This lack of strength, incidentally, is not necessarily something to be deplored; what strength would be sufficient for these tasks! Any attempt to get through this on my own strength is madness and is rewarded with madness. For this reason it's impossible to "keep up" as you suggest. On my own I can't go the way I want to go, in fact I can't even want to go it, I can only be quiet, I cannot want anything else, neither do I want anything else.   [M, 219]

I won't say goodbye. It is no goodbye, unless it be that the gravity lying in wait pulls me down completely. But how could it do this so long as you are alive?   [M, 225]

> On the way home from Meran, F.K. had visited Milena in Vienna; four happy days with her.
> Early summer: Breaking-off of the engagement with Julie Wohryzek. July: Ottla's wedding to Josef David. Summer and fall: Prague. Writing several stories.

To Minze E., from Prague, summer:
Things are just about bearable, Meran did not improve my health. It is this "internal enemy" that consumes me and prevents any real recovery. If only one could take it on one's lap like a living piglet, but then who could induce it to leave its deep lair. Not that I am complaining; to complain about this would be to complain about life, and that would be very foolish.   [Br. 278]

Brod was working on a study, Paganism, Christianity, and Judaism, *which appeared in 1921. To Brod, from Prague, August 7:* I do not believe in "paganism" as you understand it. The Greeks, for example, were well acquainted with a kind of dualism, how else are we to explain *Moira* and so many other mythological figures. But then—where religion was concerned—the Greeks were tremendously humble. The truly divine was something they had to keep at bay at all costs, the whole Olympian world was conceived as a means of keeping this true divinity well away from their earthly bodies, of creating an atmosphere in which human beings could hope to live. It was a great educational system which provided a focal point of interest for the whole Greek nation; although less profound than the Jewish law, it may well have been more democratic (there were scarcely any leaders or religious innovators), more liberal (it commanded allegiance, but I do not know how), and more humble (for when they reflected on the Olympian world their attitude was quite prosaic: so we are not even gods; and if we were gods, would that be so very much?). I suppose the closest approximation to your view would be to say: In theory it is possible to achieve complete happiness in this world, namely, by believing in the truly divine but refusing to strive toward it. Such a possibility is both blasphemous and unattainable; but the Greeks may well have come closer to this idea than most. However, this still does not constitute paganism as you understand the term. Nor have you proved that the Greek soul was in a state of despair, but merely that you would despair if you had to be a Greek. Granted, this attitude is valid for you and me, although not entirely so.

There are three principal motifs in this chapter: your positive qualities which remain unimpaired and which I have not touched upon in this letter, then your concentric and exhilarating attack on the ancient Greeks, and finally their silent defense of their attitude, to which, in the final analysis, you too contribute.   [Br. 279 f.]

Gustav Janouch quoted Léon Bloy, who wrote that the tragic guilt of the Jews is that they did not recognize the Messiah. F.K.: Perhaps that is really so. Perhaps they really did not recognize him. But what a cruel God it is who makes it possible for His creatures not to recognize Him. After all, a father always makes himself known to his children, when they cannot think or speak properly. But this is not a subject for a conversation on the street. Besides, I've reached home.

[J, 70]

September 16. Sometimes it seems like this: You have the task, have the resources adequate to carry it out (not too much, not too little of them, you do have to keep them together, but you don't need to be nervous about it), there is sufficient time put at your disposal, and besides, you have the good will to do the work. Where·is the obstacle to success in the tremendous task? Do not spend time in search of the obstacle; perhaps there is none.

[DF, 270 f.]

September 17. There is only a goal, no way. What we call the way is hesitation.

I have never been under the pressure of any responsibility but that imposed on me by the existence, the gaze, the judgment of other people.

[DF, 271]

F.K. prepared for his December trip to the Tatra Mountains sanatorium (Matliary) and Janouch said: "Go as quickly as possible—if it is possible." F.K. smiled sadly:

That is precisely what is irritating and difficult. Life has so many possibilities, and each one only mirrors the inescapable impossibility of one's own existence.

Kafka's voice broke into a cough; Janouch comforted him: "Everything will soon be all right." F.K.:

It is already all right. I have said yes to everything. In that way suffering becomes an enchantment, and death—it is only an ingredient in the sweetness of life.

[J, 100 f.]

Janouch asked F.K. to reflect on a quarrel he had with an older friend. F.K.:

Now you would like to have some advice from me. But I am not a good advisor. All advice [Rat] seems to me to be at bottom a betrayal [Verrat]. It is a cowardly retreat in face of the future, which is the touchstone of our present. But only those fear to be put to the proof who have a bad conscience. They are the ones who do not fulfill the tasks of the present. Yet who knows precisely what his task is? No one. So that every one of us has a bad conscience, which he tries to escape by going to sleep as quickly as possible.

[Janouch] remarked that "Johannes R. Becher in one of his poems
describes sleep as a friendly visitation by death."
Kafka nodded.
That is true. Perhaps my insomnia is only a kind of fear of the visitor
whom I must pay for my life.   [J, 50]

> To Brod who was in Berlin to give a lecture, from Matliary,
> December 31:
Confidentially, to have been in Berlin without seeing F. [Felice] does
not seem right to me, although I would, of course, find myself in exactly
the same position. The love I bear F. is the love of a disconsolate
general for the town he failed to conquer but which has "nonetheless"
become something great, namely, the happy mother of two children.
You had no news of the first child?

As for myself, I have found a good place here; good, that is, if you
want something that has the appearance of a sanatorium without really
being one. It is not one because it takes in tourists, hunters, in fact
anyone at all, provides no unnecessary luxury, and only charges people
for what they actually eat; and yet it is a sanatorium because it has a
doctor, facilities for open-air bed rest, food à la carte, good milk and
cream. [. . .] A good doctor? Yes, a specialist. If only I had become a
specialist. Life would have been so simple! As far as he is concerned,
my weak stomach, my insomnia, my restlessness, in fact everything I
am and have is due to my tuberculosis; and until it became manifest, it
simply used my weak stomach and my nerves as a mask. Apparently
—and in this I agree with him—many tuberculosis cases never throw off
this mask. And since he sees the sorrows of the world so clearly, the
doctor always carries with him in a small leather case, no bigger than a
[Jewish] National Fund box, the world's salvation, which he will inject
into its veins, if asked to do so, for twelve kronen. [. . .]

In general, it would be true to say that if I can endure this regime,
physically and mentally, for a few months (the principal difficulty is
that I am tied to the one place) I will come very near to being healthy.
                                                              [Br, 285]

From "First Sorrow"

A trapeze artist—this art, practiced high in the vaulted domes of the great variety theaters, is admittedly one of the most difficult humanity can achieve—had so arranged his life that, as long as he kept working in the same building, he never came down from his trapeze by night or day, at first only from a desire to perfect his skill, but later because custom was too strong for him. [. . .]

Besides, it was quite healthful up there, and when in the warmer seasons of the year the side windows all around the dome of the theater were thrown open and sun and fresh air came pouring irresistibly into the dusky vault, it was even beautiful. True, his social life was somewhat limited, only sometimes a fellow acrobat swarmed up the ladder to him, and then they both sat on the trapeze, leaning left and right against the supporting ropes, and chatted, or builders' workmen repairing the roof exchanged a few words with him through an open window, or the fireman, inspecting the emergency lighting in the top gallery, called over to him something that sounded respectful but could hardly be made out. Otherwise nothing disturbed his seclusion.   *The Penal Colony*, pp. 231 f.

January to August: Matliary.

To Brod, January 13:
I do not believe there is any essential difference between us in this major respect, as you have suggested. I would put it this way: you want the impossible while for me the possible is impossible. I may be just one step behind you, but we are standing on the same staircase. You are able to achieve the possible; you have married; and although you have had no children, this was not because it was impossible but because you did not want to; you have loved and been loved, and not only within your marriage; but this was not enough for you because you wanted the impossible. Perhaps I was unable to achieve the possible for the same reason; it was simply that the lightning struck me one step

earlier than you, before I was able to achieve the possible; and although there is a big difference between us, it is hardly an essential difference.   [Br, 289]

To Brod, from Matliary, end of January:
I have hardly slept, but I had two comforters. In the first place, severe
headaches, which reminded me of another torturer, but one who is
much gentler because he is much quicker. And then I had this dream,
the last of a whole welter: on my left sat a child dressed only in a vest (I
was not quite sure, or rather I could not remember, whether it was my
child, but that did not bother me) and on my right sat Milena; both of
them snuggled up close to me, and I told them a story about my wallet,
which I had lost and then found again, but which I had not yet opened
and so did not know whether my money was still in it. But even if it was
lost, it did not matter, as long as I had the two of them by my side. Now,
of course, I no longer feel the happiness that was mine toward morning.

That was the dream, but the reality is that three weeks ago (after
many similar letters, albeit not as definitive as this one, which reflects
the dire necessity that has now signaled, and will continue to signal, the
end for me) I made just one request: that she [Milena] should not write
to me any more, and should take steps to ensure that we do not see one
another again.

I have to return to this question. You ask: "Why be more afraid of
love than of other things in life?" and just before that you write: "In
love I experienced the divine most readily and most frequently." Taking these two statements together, it is as if you were saying: "Why be
more afraid of the burning bush than of any other bush?"   [Br, 294 f., 297]

To Milena, when her friendship with F.K. began to disintegrate:
What you are to me, Milena, are to me beyond all the world in which
we live, cannot be found in the daily scraps of paper that I have been
writing to you. These letters, as they are, are good for nothing but to
torment, and if they don't torment it's even worse. They can't do
anything but produce a day in Gmünd, produce misunderstandings,
humiliation, almost perpetual humiliation. I want to see you as clearly
as I saw you the first time in the street, but the letters distract more than
the whole L.–strasse with its noise.

This, however, is not even decisive, what is decisive is my power-
lessness, increased by the letters, to reach beyond the letters, power-
lessness toward you as well as toward myself—a thousand letters on
your part and a thousand desires on mine cannot disprove this to
me—and what is more decisive is the (perhaps caused by this power-

lessness, but here all reasons are in the dark) *irresistibly strong voice,
as it were your voice,* which begs me to be silent.   [M, 223]

I wanted to tear up this letter, not send it, not answer the telegram,
telegrams are so ambiguous, but now the card and letter have arrived,
this card, this letter. But even toward them, Milena, even if the tongue
longing to speak would have to be bitten to shreds—how can I believe
that you need letters now, when you need nothing but quiet, as half-
unconsciously you have said so often. And these letters after all are
nothing but torture, *born of torture, incurable torture, create only
torture, incurable torture,* what's the good of it—and it's getting even
worse—during this winter? To be silent, this is the only way to live, here
and there. In sadness, all right, what does it matter? It renders sleep
more childlike and deeper. But torture, this means driving a plow
through the sleep—and through the day—this is unbearable.   [M, 224]

The easy possibility of letter-writing must—seen merely theoretically—have brought into the world a terrible disintegration of souls. It
is, in fact, an intercourse with ghosts, and not only with the ghost of the
recipient but also with one's own ghost which develops between the
lines of the letter one is writing and even more so in a series of letters
where one letter corroborates the other and can refer to it as a witness.
How on earth did anyone get the idea that people can communicate
with one another by letter! Of a distant person one can think, and of a
person who is near one can catch hold—all else goes beyond human
strength. Writing letters, however, means to denude oneself before the
ghosts, something for which they greedily wait. Written kisses don't
reach their destination, rather they are drunk on the way by the ghosts.
It is on this ample nourishment that they multiply so enormously.
Humanity senses this and fights against it and in order to eliminate as
far as possible the ghostly element between people and to create a
natural communication, the peace of souls, it has invented the railway,
the motor car, the airplane. But it's no longer any good, these are
evidently inventions being made at the moment of crashing. The opposing side is so much calmer and stronger; after the postal service it
has invented the telegraph, the telephone, the radiograph. The ghosts
won't starve, but we will perish.   [M, 229]

It's strange nowadays with my writing: you must—when didn't
you?—have patience with me. For years I've not written to anyone, in
this respect I've been as good as dead, a lack of any desire to
communicate, I was as though not of this world but of no other, either.
It was as though, through all these years, I had done everything de-

manded of me mechanically, and in reality only waited for a voice to
call me, until finally the illness called me from the adjoining room and I
ran toward it and gave myself to it more and more. But it's dark in that
room and one isn't quite sure if it is the illness.   [M, 231]

But at the moment the worst thing is—not even I would have expected
it—that I can't go on writing these letters, not even these important
letters. The evil sorcerer of letter-writing begins to destroy my
nights—which anyhow destroy themselves on their own—more than
ever. I must stop, I can no longer write. Oh, your sleeplessness is a
different one from mine. Please let's not write any more.   [M, 234]

To Brod, from Matliary, February:
If you should come, could you not bring one of the kabbalistic works,
which I assume is in Hebrew, with you?   [Br, 303]

To Brod, from Matliary, early March:
I recline in my deckchair for hours on end in the kind of stupor that so
amazed me in my grandparents when I was a child. I do not feel well;
although the doctor insists that my lung is not half as bad as it was, to
my mind it is at least a hundred per cent worse; I have never had such a
cough, I was never so short of breath, or so weak. I do not deny that it
would have been worse still in Prague; but when I consider that, apart
from a few disturbing incidents, my external circumstances have been
tolerably good, I simply cannot see how matters are to improve.
    But it is foolish and idle to talk like this, and to take things so
seriously. When one is seized by a minor paroxysm of coughing, the
only possible reaction is to take it extremely seriously. But once it has
abated, one can, and should, react differently. When it grows dark, one
lights a candle, and when the candle has burned out, one sits quietly in
the darkness. It is precisely because there are so many mansions in Our
Father's house that we should keep our peace.   [Br, 303 f.]

To Oskar Baum, from Matliary, spring:
So you haven't forgotten me. I almost feel like reproaching *you* with the
fact that *I* haven't written to you. But in this great inactivity of mine
writing is almost an act for me, almost a fresh experience of birth, a
fresh burrowing around in the world, which inevitably has to be followed by the deckchair—and so one shrinks back. But that's not meant
to give you the impression that I think I'm right to do so, no, not at all.
                                                                      [Br, 320]

To Brod, from Matliary, mid-April, referring to a book by Brod on his friend Adolf Schreiber, a musician who had committed suicide:
It is not so much an obituary as a wedding between the two of you, lively and sad and a source of despair for those who marry, and a source of astonishment and anxiety for those who look on; and who could look on—even from the loneliest of rooms—without participating in the marriage ceremony. And this liveliness is enhanced still further by the fact that you alone, the strong survivor, are writing about it, and do so so tenderly that, far from being overshadowed, your dead partner is able to join in, and to make himself heard with his toneless voice, and even to lay his hand on your mouth so as to tone down your voice when he feels this to be necessary. That is quite wonderful. And yet, one could say—since, despite its great inner strength, the book none-theless surrenders itself up to the reader's will, nonetheless allows him to exercise his will with complete freedom—that only the living partner, only the speaker, exists, and exists with all the stupendous attributes that life has for the living in the face of death; it stands there like a monument to the dead, and like a pillar of life, and the passages that affect me most immediately you probably find inconsequential. This one, for example: "Was I mad, or was he?" Here stands the man, faithful, unchanging, constantly alert, the spring that never dries up, the man who—and this may sound paradoxical but I mean it quite literally—cannot understand what is readily understandable.   [Br, 315 f.]

To Brod, from Matliary, mid-April, on Milena:
But none of these things would have prompted me to write to you about this, what really matters is, of course, my own involvement. What matters is that you should tell me when M. [Milena] intends to visit Prague (for you will presumably be told about her visit) and how long she intends to stay, and also that you should tell me in case M. should decide to go to the Tatra so that I can get away from here in time. For if we were to meet I would not only be tearing my hair out in despair but raising great weals in my skull and my brain as well. [. . .]
It would seem that because of my sense of dignity, because of my arrogance (however humble he may look, this devious West European Jew!), I can only love things that I am able to place so high above myself that they become unattainable.   [Br, 316 f.]

To Brod, from Matliary, early May:
You will speak to M. [Milena], a happiness I will never know again. If you should speak to her of me, speak as if I were dead, I mean as far as my "external life" is concerned, my "exterritoriality." When [Albert]

Ehrenstein visited me recently he suggested that life was holding out its hand to me through M., and said that I had a choice between life and death; although his statement was rather too grandiose (not in respect of M. but in respect of myself), basically it was true, the only stupid thing being that he seemed to think I had the possibility of a choice. If we still had a Delphic oracle I would have questioned it, and it would have answered: "A choice between life and death? How can you hesitate?"

You write about girls, no girl is keeping me here (certainly not the girls in the picture, they also left months ago), and no girl will ever keep me anywhere. It is surprising how unobservant women are, they want to know if they are attractive, if one feels sympathy for them, and above all if one is seeking compassion from them, but no more than that, although by and large that is, of course, enough.   [Br, 322 f.]

F.K. to Janouch:
What is love? After all, it is quite simple. Love is everything that enhances, widens, and enriches our life. In its heights and in its depths. Love has as few problems as a motor car. The only problems are the driver, the passengers, and the road.   [J, 102]

I love her and cannot talk to her. I lie in wait for her in order not to meet her.   [DF, 224]

February: At Matliary, F.K. meets Robert Klopstock, a medical student, later a doctor (from Hungary); they become close friends.

To Klopstock, from Matliary, June with regard to Kierkegaard's interpretation of the Abraham story (Fear and Trembling):
I could imagine another Abraham who—although he could never hope to become a patriarch or even an old-clothes dealer—would be prepared to perform the sacrifice without hesitation, like an attentive waiter, but who would nonetheless fail to do so because he could never get away from home; at home he is indispensable, he is needed there, his house is not finished, and until it is finished, until he has this security behind him, he cannot leave; this is acknowledged in the Bible, which tells us that "he put his house in order," and it must be said that Abraham already had everything in abundance beforehand; if he had not had a house, where would he have reared his son, in which beam would the sacrificial knife have been stuck?

But there is yet another Abraham. One who really does want to perform the sacrifice properly, and who has the right feeling for the whole affair, but who cannot believe that he has been chosen, the repulsive old man and his dirty son. He does not lack the true faith, he would sacrifice in the proper frame of mind if he could only believe that he has been chosen. He fears that he will ride out as Abraham with his son but be transformed into Don Quixote en route. The world would have been horrified if it had seen what Abraham was doing, but he was afraid that the world would laugh itself silly. But although he was afraid of being laughed at, and even more afraid of joining in the laughter, his greatest fear was that, if he were laughed at, he would look even older and even more repulsive, and his son even dirtier. An Abraham who comes uncalled! It is as if, when the best pupil is waiting to receive his prize at the end of the school year, the worst pupil, mistakenly thinking that the teacher has called his name, breaks the expectant silence by rising from his dirty desk at the back of the room, whereupon the whole class roars with laughter. And perhaps he was not mistaken, he really did hear his name called, the teacher felt that if the best pupil was to be rewarded, the worst should be punished.

[Br, 333 f.]

To his sister Ottla, from Matliary, August 8 (the reference is to Ottla's baby, Věra):
Věra I recognized instantly; you were more difficult, it was only your pride that I recognized instantly; mine would be even greater, it would not even fit on the card. She seems to have an open, honest face, and to my mind there is nothing better in the whole world than openness, honesty, and reliability.   [Br, 338]

To Ottla, from Matliary (1921?):
I haven't written to you for a long time, for when I'm feeling good, in the forest, in complete stillness, with birds, the stream, and the wind, one grows silent, and when I'm despairing, in the villa, on the veranda, in the forest when it's destroyed by noise, then I can't write, because my parents will read the letter too.

The amount of peace and quiet I need doesn't exist in the whole world, which means that one oughtn't to need as much peace and quiet as that.

From September on: Prague.

To Robert Klopstock, mid-September, on Gustav Janouch:
Janouch was here recently, he came in from the country just for the

day, having first written to announce his arrival; he is not at all angry, and was particularly pleased over your letter. He came to the office, weeping and laughing and shouting, he produced a pile of books for me to read, then apples, and finally his sweetheart, a small, friendly forester's daughter; he lives out in the country with her parents. He says he is happy, but there are times when he seems frightfully confused, he also looks unwell; he wants to prepare himself for matriculation and then study medicine ("because it is a quiet, humble task") or law ("because it leads on to politics"). What devil is stoking this fire? [Br, 352]

Two days after Janouch introduced his friend Helene Slaviček to F.K.:
Women are snares, which lie in wait for men on all sides in order to drag them into the merely finite. They lose their dangers if one voluntarily falls into one of the snares. But if, as a result of habit, one overcomes it, then all the jaws of the female trap open again.   [J, 101 f.]

Talking about young writers, F.K. said, "I envy the young," to which Janouch remarked, "You are not so old yourself." F.K. smiled:
I am as old as Jewry, as the wandering Jew.

Now you are shocked. That was only a miserable effort to make a joke. But I really do envy youth. The older one grows, the larger one's horizon. But the possibilities of life grow smaller and smaller. In the end, one can give only one look upwards, give one breath outwards. At that moment a man probably surveys his whole life. For the first time—and the last time.   [J, 90 f.]

Actual reality is always unrealistic. Look at the clarity, purity, and veracity of a Chinese colored woodcut. To speak like that—that would be something!   [J, 87]

Reacting to photographs of constructivist pictures:
They are merely dreams of a marvelous America, of a wonderland of unlimited possibilities. That is perfectly understandable, because Europe is becoming more and more a land of impossible limitations.

[J, 85]

To preserve calm; to remain extremely aloof from whatever that passion wants; to know the way the current flows and for that reason to swim against it; to swim against the current out of a liking for being buoyed up.   [DF, 256]

The manifold things that resolve, in manifold ways, in the manifoldness of the one moment in which we live. And still the moment is not over, just see!
   Far, far away world history takes its course, the world history of your soul.   [DF, 243]

Fresh abundance. Gushing water. Tempestuous, peaceful, high, spreading growth. Blissful oasis. Morning after riotous night. Breast to breast with heaven. Peace, reconciliation. Submerging.   [DF, 268]

   To Robert Klopstock, from Prague, September–October:
Yesterday I was at a gathering [. . .], and afterward felt so weak that I went into a coffeehouse, then returned home with quivering nerves (nowadays I cannot even endure the way people look at me; not because I hate people, but simply because their presence, the way they sit there and look across the room, is too much for me), lay coughing for hours on end until I drifted off to sleep toward morning, and would dearly have liked to have drifted right out of this life, a simple matter, I thought, considering how short my journey would seem to be.   [Br, 357]

   To Robert Klopstock, from Prague, October:
Although this mysterious fever is wretched enough in itself, the worst thing as far as you are concerned is not the actual illness but the fact that it coincides with the bouts of depression that sometimes overcome you, and which also have their roots in chaos, in youth, in Judaism, and in the general sorrows of the world. The only comfort in normal everyday life comes from the realization that, incredible though it may seem, one does in fact reemerge from the bottomless abyss into which one so often sinks.   [Br, 362]

For healthy people, life is only an unconscious and unavowed flight from the consciousness that one day one must die. Illness is always a warning and a trial of strength. And so illness, pain, suffering are the most important sources of religious feeling.
   "In what sense?" Janouch asked.
   In a Jewish sense. I am bound to my family and my race. They outlive the individual. But that also is only an attempted flight from the knowledge of death. It is only a wish. And by such means one gains no

knowledge. On the contrary—by such a wish the little, terribly egoistic "I" prefers itself to the truth-seeking soul.   [J, 61]

Referring to Arnold Böcklin's picture War, *and V. V. Verescha-gin's* The Pyramid of Skulls:
The terrible thing about war is the dissolution of all existing certainties and conventions. The animal and physical grow rank and stifle everything spiritual. It is like a cancer. Man no longer lives for years, months, days, hours, but only for moments. And even the moment is not really lived. Man is only conscious of it. He merely exists.
"That is because he is near to death," Janouch said.
It is because of the knowledge and the fear of death.
"Isn't that the same thing?"
No, it is not the same. Anyone who grasps life completely has no fear of dying. The fear of death is merely the result of an unfulfilled life. It is a symptom of betrayal.   [J, 74]

Milena came to visit F.K. in Prague.

October 15. About a week ago gave M. [Milena] all the diaries. A little freer? No. Am I still able to keep a diary? It will in any case be a different kind of diary, or rather it will hide itself away, there won't be any diary at all. [. . .] I could probably write about M., but would not willingly do it, and moreover it would be aimed too directly at myself; I no longer need to make myself so minutely conscious of such things, I am not so forgetful as I used to be in this respect, I am a memory come alive, hence my insomnia.   [DII, 193]

October 16. Among the young women up in the park. No envy. Enough imagination to share their happiness, enough judgment to know I am too weak to have such happiness, foolish enough to think I see to the bottom of my own and their situation. Not foolish enough; there is a tiny crack there, the wind whistles through it and spoils the full effect.
    Should I greatly yearn to be an athlete, it would probably be the same thing as my yearning to go to heaven and to be permitted to be as despairing there as I am here.   [DII, 194]

October 17. I do not envy particular married couples, I simply envy all married couples together; and even when I do envy one couple only, it is the happiness of married life in general, in all its infinite variety, that I envy—the happiness to be found in any one marriage, even in the likeliest case, would probably plunge me into despair.

I don't believe people exist whose inner plight resembles mine; still, it is possible for me to imagine such people—but that the secret raven forever flaps about their heads as it does about mine, even to imagine that is impossible.

It is astounding how I have systematically destroyed myself in the course of the years, it was like a slowly widening breach in a dam, a purposeful action. The spirit that brought it about must now be celebrating triumphs; why doesn't it let me take part in them? But perhaps it hasn't yet achieved its purpose and can therefore think of nothing else.   [DII, 194 f.]

October 18. Eternal childhood. Life calls again.

It is entirely conceivable that life's splendor forever lies in wait about each one of us in all its fullness, but veiled from view, deep down, invisible, far off. It *is* there, though, not hostile, not reluctant, not deaf. If you summon it by the right word, by its right name, it will come. This is the essence of magic, which does not create but summons.

[DII, 195]

October 19. The essence of the Wandering in the Wilderness. A man who leads his people along this way with a shred (more is unthinkable) of consciousness of what is happening. He is on the track of Canaan all his life; it is incredible that he should see the land only when on the verge of death. This dying vision of it can only be intended to illustrate how incomplete a moment is human life, incomplete because a life like this could last forever and still be nothing but a moment. Moses fails to enter Canaan not because his life is too short but because it is a human life. This ending of the Pentateuch bears a resemblance to the final scene of [Flaubert's] *Education sentimentale.*   [DII, 195 f.]

In any case we Jews are not painters. We cannot depict things statically. We see them always in transition, in movement, as change. We are story-tellers. [. . .] A story-teller cannot talk about story-telling. He tells stories or is silent. That is all. His world begins to vibrate within him, or it sinks into silence. My world is dying away. I am burned out.

[J, 86 f.]

October 19. Anyone who cannot come to terms with his life while he is alive needs one hand to ward off a little his despair over his fate—he has little success in this—but with his other hand he can note down what he sees among the ruins, for he sees different (and more) things than do the others; after all, dead as he is in his own lifetime, he is the real survivor.

This assumes that he does not need both hands, or more hands than he has, in his struggle against despair.
[DII, 196]

October 21. All is imaginary—family, office, friends, the street, all imaginary, far away or close at hand, the woman; the truth that lies closest, however, is only this, that you are pressing your head against the wall of a windowless and doorless cell.
[DII, 197]

October 29. I have seldom, very seldom crossed this borderland between loneliness and fellowship, I have even been settled there longer than in loneliness itself. What a fine bustling place was Robinson Crusoe's island in comparison!
[DII, 198]

October 30. Feeling of complete helplessness.

What is it that binds you more intimately to these impenetrable, talking, eye-blinking bodies than to any other thing, the penholder in your hand, for example? Because you belong to the same species? But you don't belong to the same species, that's the very reason why you raised this question.

The impenetrable outline of human bodies is horrible.

The wonder, the riddle of my not having perished already, of the silent power guiding me. It forces one to this absurdity: "Left to my own resources, I should have long ago been lost." My own resources.
[DII, 199]

November 1. Free command of the world while disregarding its laws. Imposition of the law. The happiness in obeying the law.

But the law cannot merely be imposed upon the world, and then everything left to go on as before except that the new lawgiver be free to do as he pleases. Such would be not law, but arbitrariness, revolt against law, self-defeat.
[DII, 199]

November 2. Vague hope, vague confidence.
[DII, 199]

November 7. I envy the ease with which all those who fall out with me, or grow indifferent, or find me a nuisance, can shake me off—provided, probably, that it is not a life-and-death matter for me; once, with F. [Felice], when it seemed to be a matter of life and death, it was not easy to shake me off, though of course I was young then, and strong, with strong desires.
[DII, 200]

December 1. After visiting me four times, M. [Milena?] left; she goes away tomorrow. Four calmer days in the midst of tormented ones. I feel no sadness at her departure, no real sadness; it is a long way from this unconcern to the point where her departure would cause me endless sadness. Sadness, I confess it, is not the worst thing.   [DII, 200]

Milena to Brod, on F.K. (the original letter is in Czech):
I would have to spend many days and nights replying to your letter. You ask how it is that Frank [Franz] is afraid of love and not afraid of life. But it seems to me that the matter is otherwise. For him life is something entirely different from what it is to everyone else. Above all, for him money, the stock market, foreign exchange, a typewriter, are utterly mystical things (and they are that in fact, only not for the rest of us). To him they are the strangest enigmas, toward which he has an attitude altogether different from ours. Is his work as an official, say, anything like an ordinary job? For him the entire office—including his own part in it—is something as mysterious and remarkable as a loco-motive is to a small child. He does not understand the simplest thing in the world. Have you ever gone to a post office with him? After he has filed away at a telegram and then, shaking his head, picked out the window he likes best, and after he has tramped from one window to the next, without in the least understanding why and wherefore until he finally stumbles on the right one, and after he has paid and received his change—he counts up what he has received, finds that he has been given a krone too much, and returns the krone to the girl at the window. Then he walks slowly away, counts his change again, and on the last step down to the street he sees that the returned krone did belong to him after all. Now you stand helplessly beside him—he shifts his weight from one foot to the other and ponders what he ought to do. To go back is hard; there is a crowd at the window upstairs, "Then let it be," I say. He looks at me in utter horror. How can you let it be? Not that he cares about the krone. But it's wrong. There is a krone too little. How can a thing like that be ignored? He talked for a long time about the matter; was very dissatisfied with me. And variations of that incident would be repeated in every shop, in every restaurant, in front of every beggar. Once he gave a beggar a two-krone piece and wanted to have one krone back. She said she had no change. We stood there a good two minutes thinking how to regulate the matter. Then it oc-curred to him that he could let her have two kronen. But no sooner had he taken a few steps than he became very annoyed. And this same person would unhesitatingly, with enthusiasm, filled with happiness, at once give me twenty thousand kronen. But if I were to ask him for twenty thousand and one kronen, and we had to change money somewhere and did not know where, he would seriously consider what he should do about the extra krone which I was not supposed to

receive. His constraint with regard to money is almost the same as his constraint toward women. Likewise his fear of his job. I once telegraphed, telephoned, wrote, implored him in God's name to come to me for a day. At the time it was very necessary for me. I cursed him and railed against him. He did not sleep for nights on end, tormented himself, wrote letters full of self-abasement—but he did not come. Why? He had been unable to ask for some days off. He had not been able to bring himself to say to the director that he wanted to come to me—this same director whom he admires from the bottom of his heart (seriously!) because he can type so fast. And to invent some pretext or other—another horrified letter. What did I mean? Was he supposed to lie? Tell the director a lie? Impossible. When you ask him why he loved his first fiancée, he answers: "She was so good at business." And his face begins to shine with sheer respect.

Ah no, this whole world is and remains mysterious to him. A mystical enigma. Something that he cannot afford and that, with a pure, touching naïveté, he esteems because it is "efficient." When I told him about my husband, who is unfaithful to me a hundred times a year, who holds me and many other women in a kind of spell, his face lit up with the same reverence it had held that time he spoke of his director who types so fast and is therefore such an excellent person, and as it did the time he spoke of his fiancée as "good at business." All such things are alien to him. A person who types fast and a man who has four mistresses are just as incomprehensible to him as the krone piece at the post office and the beggar's krone piece, incomprehensible because these things are alive. But Frank cannot live. Frank does not have the capacity for living. Frank will never get well. Frank will die soon.

For, obviously, we are capable of living because at some time or other we took refuge in lies, in blindness, in enthusiasm, in optimism, in some conviction or others, in pessimism or something of that sort. But he has never escaped to any such sheltering refuge, none at all. He is absolutely incapable of living, just as he is incapable of getting drunk. He possesses not the slightest refuge. For that reason he is exposed to all those things against which we are protected. He is like a naked man among a multitude who are dressed. Everything that he says, that he is, and in which he lives cannot even be called truth. Rather, it is such a predetermined state of being in and for itself, stripped of all trimmings that could help him by distorting life—distorting it in the direction of beauty or of misery, no matter. And his asceticism is altogether unheroic—and by that very fact all the greater and more sublime. All "heroism" is lie and cowardice. One who conceives his asceticism as a means to an end is no true human being; the true human being is one who is compelled to asceticism by his terrible clarity of vision, purity, and incapacity for compromise.

There are very intelligent people who also do not wish to make any compromises. But these put on rose-colored glasses and see everything in a different light. For that reason they do not need to make compromises. For that reason they can type rapidly and have women. He stands beside them and looks at them in astonishment, looks at everything, including the typewriter and the women, in equal amazement. He will never understand it.

His books are amazing. He himself is far more amazing.   [B, 227 ff.]

Another letter by Milena to Brod, on F.K.:
Thank you for your kindness. In the meantime I have to some degree come to my senses. I can think again. Not that that makes me feel any better. You may be absolutely sure that I will not write to Frank. How could I! If it is true that people have a task to fulfill on this earth, I have fulfilled this task at his side very badly. How could I be so immodest and harm him when I have not been able to help him?

What his terror is, I know down to the last nerve. It existed before he met me, too, all the while he did not know me. I knew his terror before I knew him. I armored myself against it by understanding it. In the four days that Frank was with me, he lost it. We laughed at it. I know for certain that no sanatorium will succeed in curing him. He will never become well, Max, as long as he has this terror. And no psychic strengthening can overcome this terror, because the terror prevents the strengthening. This terror does not refer to me alone, but to everything that lives shamelessly, also to the flesh, for example. The flesh is too exposed; he cannot bear to see it. That was the thing I was able to dispel, that time. When he felt this terror, he looked into my eyes, and we waited awhile, just as though we could not catch our breath, or as though our feet hurt, and after a while it passed. Not the slightest exertion was necessary; everything was simple and clear; for example, I dragged him over the hills on the outskirts of Vienna, I running ahead, since he walked slowly—he tramped along behind me, and when I close my eyes I can still see his white shirt and tanned throat, and the effort he was making. He tramped all day, up and down, walked in the sun, and not once did he cough; he ate a fearful amount and slept like a log; he was simply healthy, and during those days his illness seemed to us something like a minor cold. If I had gone to Prague with him that time, I would have remained what I was to him. But I had sunk both feet so firmly, so infinitely firmly into the ground here; I was not able to leave my husband, and perhaps I was too feminine, too weak, to want to subject myself to this life, which I knew

would mean strictest asceticism for life. But there is in me an insup-
pressible longing, a raging desire for an altogether different kind of life
from the one I lead and probably will always lead, for a life with a
child, for a life that would be very close to the soil. And probably that
weakness won out in me over everything else, over love, over the desire
to take flight, over my admiration, and again over my life. You know,
whatever one tries to say about that, only a lie comes out. This one is
perhaps the least of the lies. And then it was already too late. Then this
struggle in me came too plainly to the surface, and that frightened him
off. For that is the very thing he fought against all his life, from the
other side. With me he would have been able to find peace. But then it
began to pursue him even with me. Against my will. I knew very well
that something had happened which could no longer be thrust aside. I
was too weak to do the one and only thing that I knew would have
helped him. That is my fault. And you too know that it is my fault. The
thing that you all call Frank's non-normality—just that is his greatest
trait. The women who were with him in the past were ordinary women
and did not know how to live except as women. I rather think that all
of us, each and every one of us, is sick and that he is the only well
person, the only one who sees rightly and feels rightly, the only pure
person. I know that he does not resist life, but only this kind of life: that
is what he resists. If I had been capable of going with him, he could
have lived happily with me. But only now do I know all that. At the
time I was an ordinary woman, like all women on the face of the earth,
a little instinct-ridden female. Hence his terror. It was perfectly right.
Can this man feel anything that is not perfectly right? He knows ten
thousand times more about the world than all other people in the
world. That terror of his was right. And you are mistaken; Frank will
not write to me of his own accord. There is nothing he could write to
me. In fact there is not a single word that he could say to me in this
terror of his. I know that he loves me. He is too good and chaste to stop
loving me. He would feel guilty if he did. He always thinks himself the
guilty and weak one. And yet there is not another person in the whole
world who has his tremendous strength: that absolute, irrevocable,
necessary drive toward perfection, purity, truth. That is how it is. I
know down to the last drop of my blood that that is how it is. Only I
cannot bring this knowledge fully into my consciousness. When that
does come about, it will be frightful. I dash through the streets, sit at the
window whole nights through; often my thoughts skip like little sparks
when a knife is honed and my heart hangs inside me as if it were stuck
on a fish hook, you know, a very thin little hook, and it pierces me so
and gives a very thin, terribly sharp pain.

  As far as my health is concerned, I've reached the end, and if anything is sustaining me, it's happening against my will; probably it is the same thing that has kept me going so far, something extremely unconscious, an involuntary love of life. Recently, somewhere at the other end of Vienna, I suddenly came across an array of tracks—imagine streets stretching on for miles, like a great oblong pit—and down below tracks, red lights, locomotives, viaducts, freight cars—it was such a horrible black organism; I sat nearby and it was as though something were breathing. I thought I should go mad for sheer grief, longing, and terrible love of life. I am as lonely as the mute are lonely, and if I speak to you of myself as I do, it is because I am vomiting out the words; they rush forth entirely against my will, because I can no longer keep silent. Forgive me.

I shall not write to Frank, not a line, and I do not know what is going to come of it all. In the spring I am coming to Prague and will call on you. And if you write to me how he is from time to time—I cannot cure myself of the habit of going to the post office daily—I should be very glad.   [B, 233 ff.]

December 20. Suffered much in my thoughts.   [DII, 201]

> In 1921 Grete Bloch's son died in Munich at the age of seven. On April 21, 1940, she wrote to a friend, the musician Wolfgang Schocken, that "he [F.K.] was the father of my boy. I have never spoken of all this. I believe this is the first time I have told anyone the story."[1]

1922

The Village and the Castle

It was late in the evening when K. arrived. The village was deep in snow. The Castle hill was hidden, veiled in mist and darkness, nor was there even a glimmer of light to show that a castle was there. On the wooden bridge leading from the main road to the village K. stood for a long time gazing into the illusory emptiness above him.   *The Castle, p. 3*

January–September: The Castle *written. January–February: In Spindelmühle, then back in Prague.*

January 16. This past week I suffered something very like a breakdown; the only one to match it was on that night two years ago; apart from then I have never experienced its like. Everything seemed over with, even today there is no great improvement to be noticed. One can put two interpretations on the breakdown, both of which are probably correct.

First: Breakdown, impossible to sleep, impossible to stay awake, impossible to endure life, or, more exactly, the course of life. The clocks are not in unison; the inner one runs crazily on at a devilish or demoniac or in any case inhuman pace, the outer one limps along at its usual speed. What else can happen but that the two worlds split apart, and they do split apart, or at least clash in a fearful manner. There are doubtless several reasons for the wild tempo of the inner process; the most obvious one is introspection, which will suffer no idea to sink tranquilly to rest but must pursue each one into consciousness, only itself to become an idea, in turn to be pursued by renewed introspection.

Second: This pursuit, originating in the midst of men, carries one in a direction away from them. The solitude that for the most part has been forced on me, in part voluntarily sought by me—but what was this if not compulsion too?—is now losing all its ambiguity and approaches its denouement. Where is it leading? The strongest likelihood is that it may lead to madness; there is nothing more to say, the pursuit goes

right through me and rends me asunder. Or I can—can I?—manage to
keep my feet somewhat and be carried along in the wild pursuit.
Where, then, shall I be brought? "Pursuit," indeed, is only a metaphor.
I can also say, "assault on the last earthly frontier," an assault, moreover, launched from below, from mankind, and since this too is a
metaphor, I can replace it by the metaphor of an assault from above,
aimed at me from above.

All such writing is an assault on the frontiers; if Zionism had not
intervened, it might easily have developed into a new secret doctrine, a
Kabbalah. There are intimations of this. Though of course it would
require genius of an unimaginable kind to strike root again in the old
centuries, or create the old centuries anew and not spend itself withal,
but only then begin to flower forth.   [DII, 201 ff.]

January 18. A moment of thought: Resign yourself, learn (learn, forty-
year-old) to rest content in the moment (yes, once you could do it). Yes,
in the moment, the terrible moment. It is not terrible, only your fear of
the future makes it so. And also looking back on it in retrospect. What
have you done with your gift of sex? It was a failure, in the end that is
all that they will say. But it might easily have succeeded. A mere trifle,
indeed so small as not to be perceived, decided between its failure and
success. Why are you surprised? So it was with the greatest battles in
the history of the world. Trifles decide trifles.

M. [Milena] is right: fear means unhappiness but it does not follow
from this that courage means happiness; not courage, which possibly
aims at more than our strength can achieve (there were perhaps only
two Jews in my class possessed of courage, and both shot themselves
while still at school or shortly after); not courage, then, but fearlessness
with its calm, open eye and stoical resolution. Don't force yourself to
do anything, yet don't feel unhappy that you force yourself, or that if
you were to do anything, you would have to force yourself. And if you
don't force yourself, don't hanker after the possibilities of being forced.
Of course, it is never as clear as all that, or rather, it is; it is always as
clear as all that; for instance: sex keeps gnawing at me, hounds me day
and night, I should have to conquer fear and shame and probably
sorrow too to satisfy it; yet on the other hand I am certain that I should
at once take advantage, with no feeling of fear or sorrow or shame, of
the first opportunity to present itself quickly, close at hand, and
willingly; according to the above, then, I am left with the law that fear,
etc., should not be conquered (but also that one should not continually
dally with the idea of conquest), but rather take advantage of opportunities as they come (and not complain if none should come). It is true
that there is a middle ground between "doing" and the "opportunity to

do," namely this, to make, to tempt one's "opportunities" to one, a practice I have unfortunately followed not only in this but everything. As far as the "law" is concerned, there is hardly anything to be said against this, though this "tempting" of opportunities, especially when it uses ineffectual expedients, bears a considerable resemblance to "dallying with the idea of conquest," and there is no trace in it of calm, open-eyed fearlessness. Despite the fact that it satisfies the "letter" of the "law," there is something detestable in it which must be unconditionally shunned. To be sure, one would have to force oneself to shun it—and so I shall never have done with the matter.   [DII, 203 f.]

January 19. The infinite, deep, warm, saving happiness of sitting beside the cradle of one's child opposite its mother.

There is in it also something of this feeling: matters no longer rest with you, unless you wish it so. In contrast, this feeling of those who have no children: it perpetually rests with you, whether you will or no, every moment to the end, every nerve-racking moment, it perpetually rests with you, and without result. Sisyphus was a bachelor.

Evil does not exist; once you have crossed the threshold, all is good. It is another world and you must not talk.

The two questions [addressed to Milena]:
Because of several piddling signs I am ashamed to mention, it was my impression that your recent visits were indeed kind and noble as ever but somewhat tiresome to you nevertheless, somewhat forced, too, like the visits one pays an invalid. Is my impression correct?

Did you find in the diaries some final proof against me?   [DII, 204 f.]

January 21. No one's task was as difficult, so far as I know. One might say that it is not a task at all, not even an impossible one, it is not even impossibility itself, it is nothing, it is not even as much of a child as the hope of a barren woman. But nevertheless it is the air I breathe, so long as I shall breathe at all.

Without forebears, without marriage, without heirs, with a fierce longing for forebears, marriage, and heirs. They all of them stretch out their hands to me: forebears, marriage, and heirs, but too far away for me.

There is an artificial, miserable substitute for everything, for forebears, marriage, and heirs. Feverishly you contrive these substitutes, and if the fever has not already destroyed you, the hopelessness of the substitutes will.   [DII, 206 f.]

To Robert Klopstock, from Prague, end of January:
Letters are able to give me pleasure, to stir my emotions, to arouse my admiration, but previously they meant much more to me, too much for them to be an essential *modus vivendi* for me today. It is not that I was deceived by letters, simply that I deceived myself with letters, for years on end I warmed myself in advance in the heat generated when my whole pile of letters was consigned to the flames.   [Br, 369]

January 23. I have not shown the faintest firmness of resolve in the conduct of my life. It was as if I, like everyone else, had been given a point from which to prolong the radius of a circle, and had then, like everyone else, to describe my perfect circle around this point. Instead, I was forever starting my radius only constantly to be forced at once to break it off. (Examples: piano, violin, languages, Germanics, anti-Zionism, Zionism, Hebrew, gardening, carpentering, writing, marriage attempts, an apartment of my own.) The center of my imaginary circle bristles with the beginnings of radii, there is no room left for a new attempt; no room means old age and weak nerves, and never to make another attempt means the end. If I sometimes prolonged the radius a little farther than usual, in the case of my law studies, say, or engagements, everything was made worse rather than better just because of this little extra distance.

Told M. [Milena] about the night, unsatisfactory. Accept your symptoms, don't complain of them; immerse yourself in your suffering.
                                                                      [DII, 209]

You say I should go down farther still, but I am already very deep down, and yet, if it must be so, I will stay here. What a place! It is probably the deepest place there is. But I will stay here, only do not force me to climb down any deeper.   [DF, 295]

January 24. How happy are the married men, young and old both, in the office. Beyond my reach, though if it were within my reach I should find it intolerable, and yet it is the only thing with which I have any inclination to appease my longing.

Hesitation before birth. If there is a transmigration of souls then I am not yet on the bottom rung. My life is a hesitation before birth.

My development was a simple one. While I was still contented I wanted to be discontented, and with all the means that my time and tradition gave me, plunged into discontent—and then wanted to turn back again. Thus I have always been discontented, even with my contentment. Strange how make-believe, if engaged in systematically enough, can change into reality. Childish games (though I was well aware that they were so) marked the beginning of my intellectual decline. I deliberately cultivated a facial tic, for instance, or would walk across the Graben with arms crossed behind my head. A repulsively childish but successful game. (My writing began in the same way; only later on its development came to a halt, unfortunately.) If it is possible so to force misfortune upon oneself, it is possible to force anything upon oneself. Much as my development seems to contradict me, and much as it contradicts my nature to think it, I cannot grant that the first beginnings of my unhappiness were inwardly necessitated; they may have indeed had a necessity, but not an inward one—they swarmed down on me like flies and could have been as easily driven off.

My unhappiness on the other shore would have been as great, greater probably (thanks to my weakness); after all, I have had some experience of it, the lever is still trembling somewhat from the time when I last tried to shift it—why then do I add to the unhappiness that this shore causes me by longing to cross over to the other?

Sad, and with reason. My sadness depends on this reason. Always in danger. No way out. How easy it was the first time, how difficult now! How helplessly the tyrant looks at me: "Is that where you are taking me!" And yet no peace in spite of everything; the hopes of the morning are buried in the afternoon. It is impossible amicably to come to terms with such a life; surely there has never been anyone who could have done so. When other people approached this boundary—even to have approached it is pitiful enough—they turned back; I cannot. It even seems to me as if I had not come by myself but had been pushed here as a child and then chained to this spot; the consciousness of my misfortune only gradually dawned on me, my misfortune itself was already complete; it needed not a prophetic but merely a penetrating eye to see it.

In the morning I thought: "Perhaps I could go on living in this fashion, only guard such a way of life against women." Guard it against women—why, they are already lurking in the "in-this-fashion."

[DII, 210 ff.]

January 27. The strange, mysterious, perhaps dangerous, perhaps redeeming comfort that there is in writing: it is a leap out of murderers' row; it is a seeing of what is really taking place. This occurs by a higher type of observation, a higher, not a keener type, and the higher it is and the less within reach of the "row," the more independent it becomes, the more obedient to its own laws of motion, the more incalculable, the more joyful, the more ascendant its course.   [DII, 212]

January 28. A little dizzy, tired from the tobogganing; weapons still exist for me, however seldom I may employ them; it is so hard for me to lay hold of them because I am ignorant of the joys of their use, never learned how when I was a child. It is not only "Father's fault" that I never learned their use, but also my wanting to disturb the "peace," to upset the balance, and for this reason I could not allow a new person to be born elsewhere while I was bending every effort to bury him here. Of course, in this too there is a question of "fault," for why did I want to quit the world? Because "he" would not let me live in it, his world. Though indeed I should not judge the matter so precisely, for I am now a citizen of this other world, whose relationship to the ordinary one is the relationship of the wilderness to cultivated land (I have been forty years wandering from Canaan); I look back at it like a foreigner, though in this other world as well—it is the paternal heritage I carry with me—I am the most insignificant and timid of all creatures and am able to keep alive thanks only to the special nature of its arrangements; in this world it is possible even for the humblest to be raised to the heights as if with lightning speed, though they can also be crushed forever as if by the weight of the seas. Should I not be thankful despite everything? Was it certain that I should find my way to this world? Could not "banishment" from one side, coming together with rejection from this, have crushed me at the border? Is not Father's power such that nothing (not I, certainly) could have resisted his decree? It is indeed a kind of Wandering in the Wilderness in reverse that I am undergoing: I think that I am continually skirting the wilderness and am full of childish hopes (particularly as regards women) that "perhaps I shall keep in Canaan after all"—when all the while I have been decades in the wilderness and these hopes are merely mirages born of despair, especially at those times when I am the wretchedest of creatures in the desert too, and Canaan is perforce my only Promised Land, for no third place exists for mankind.   [DII, 213 f.]

January 30. Waiting for pneumonia. Afraid, not so much of the illness, as for and of my mother, my father, the director, and all the others. Here it would seem clear that the two worlds do exist and that I am as ignorant in face of the illness, as detached, as fearful, as, say, in face of a headwaiter. And moreover the division seems to me to be much too definite, dangerous in its definiteness, sad, and too tyrannical. Do I live in the other world, then? Dare I say that?

Someone makes the remark: "What do I care about life? It is only on my family's account that I don't want to die." But it is just the family that is representative of life, and so it is on life's account that he wants to stay alive. Well, so far as my mother is concerned, this would seem to be the case with me as well, though only lately. But is it not gratitude and compassion that have brought this change about in me? Yes, gratitude and compassion, because I see how, with what at her age is inexhaustible strength, she bends every effort to compensate me for my isolation from life. But gratitude too is life.   [DII, 216]

January 31. This would mean that it is on my mother's account that I am alive. But it cannot be true, for even if I were much more important than I am, I should still be only an emissary of Life, and, if by nothing else, joined to it by this commission.

The Negative alone, however strong it may be, cannot suffice, as in my unhappiest moments I believe it can. For if I have gone the tiniest step upward, won any, be it the most dubious kind of security for myself, I then stretch out on my step and wait for the Negative, not to climb up to me, indeed, but to drag me down from it. Hence it is a defensive instinct in me that won't tolerate my having the slightest degree of lasting ease and smashes the marriage bed, for example, even before it has been set up.   [DII, 217]

February 1. Nothing, merely tired. The happiness of the truck driver, whose every evening is as mine has been today, and even finer. An evening, for example, stretched out on the stove. A man is purer than in the morning; the period before falling wearily asleep is really the time when no ghosts haunt one; they are all dispersed; only as the night advances do they return, in the morning they have all assembled again, even if one cannot recognize them; and now, in a healthy person, the daily dispersal of them begins anew.

Looked at with a primitive eye, the real, incontestable truth, a truth marred by no external circumstance (martyrdom, sacrifice of oneself for the sake of another), is only physical pain. Strange that the god of pain was not the chief god of the earliest religions (but first became so in the later ones, perhaps). For each invalid his household god, for the tubercular the god of suffocation. How can one bear his approach if one does not partake of him in advance of the terrible union?   [DII, 217 f.]

Perhaps my insomnia only conceals a great fear of death. Perhaps I am afraid that the soul—which in sleep leaves me—will never return. Perhaps insomnia is only an all too vivid sense of sin, which is afraid of the possibility of a sudden judgment. Perhaps insomnia is itself a sin. Perhaps it is a rejection of the natural.

Replying to Janouch's remark that insomnia is an illness:
Sin is the root of all illness. That is the reason for mortality.   [J, 85]

February 2. The Negative having been in all probability greatly strengthened by the "struggle," a decision between insanity and security is imminent.

The happiness of being with people.   [DII, 218]

February 3. Almost impossible to sleep; plagued by dreams, as if they were being scratched on me, on a stubborn material.

There is a certain failing, a lack in me, that is clear and distinct enough but difficult to describe: it is a compound of timidity, reserve, talkativeness, and halfheartedness; by this I intend to characterize something specific, a group of failings that under a certain aspect constitute one single clearly defined failing (which has nothing to do with such grave vices as mendacity, vanity, etc.). This failing keeps me from going mad, but also from making any headway. Because it keeps me from going mad, I cultivate it; out of fear of madness I sacrifice whatever headway I might make and shall certainly be the loser in the bargain, for no bargains are possible at this level. Provided that drowsiness does not intervene and with its nocturnal-diurnal labor break down every obstacle and clear the road. But in that event I shall be snapped up by madness—for to make headway one must want to, and I did not.   [DII, 218 f.]

February 12. The gesture of rejection with which I was forever met did not mean: "I do not love you," but: "You cannot love me, much as you would like; you are unhappily in love with your love for me, but your love for me is not in love with you." It is consequently incorrect to say that I have known the words "I love you"; I have known only the expectant stillness that should have been broken by my "I love you," that is all that I have known, nothing more.   [DII, 221]

February 19. Hopes?

February 20. Unnoticeable life. Noticeable failure.

February 27. Slept badly in the afternoon; everything is changed; my misery pressing me hard again.

March 7. Yesterday the worst night I have had; as if everything were at an end.

March 9. But that was only weariness; today a fresh attack, wringing the sweat from my brow. How would it be if one were to choke to death on oneself? If the pressure of introspection were to diminish, or close off entirely, the opening through which one flows forth into the world. I am not far from it at times. A river flowing upstream. For a long time now, that is what for the most part has been going on.   [DII, 223]

March 9. In the past, when I had a pain and it passed away, I was happy; now I am merely relieved, while there is this bitter feeling in me: "Only to be well again, nothing more."

Somewhere help is waiting and the beaters are driving me there.

[DII, 224]

Whoever has faith cannot define it, and whoever has none can only give a definition that lies under the shadow of grace withheld. The man of faith cannot speak and the man of no faith ought not to speak. And in fact the prophets always talk of the levers of faith and never of faith alone. [. . .]

God can only be comprehended personally. Each man has his own life and his own God. His protector and judge. Priests and rituals are only crutches for the crippled life of the soul.   [J, 92 f.]

March 13. This pure feeling I have and my certainty of what has caused it: the sight of the children, one girl especially (erect carriage, short black hair), and another (blonde; indefinite features, indefinite smile); the rousing music, the marching feet. A feeling of one in distress who sees help coming but does not rejoice at his rescue—nor is he res-cued—but rejoices, rather, at the arrival of fresh young people imbued with confidence and ready to take up the fight; ignorant, indeed, of what awaits them, but an ignorance that inspires not hopelessness but admiration and joy in the onlooker and brings tears to his eyes. Hatred too of him whom the fight is against is mingled in it (but little Jewish feeling, or so I think).   [DII, 224]

April 6. Yesterday an outbreak I had been afraid of for two days; further pursuit; the enemy's great strength. One of the causes: the talk with my mother, the jokes about the future.—Planned letter to Milena.

The three Erinyes. Flight into the grove. Milena.   [DII, 226]

April 10. The five guiding principles on the road to hell (in genetic succession):

1. "The worst lies outside the window." All else is conceded to be angelic either openly or (more often) by silently ignoring it.

2. "You must possess every girl!" not in Don Juan fashion, but according to the devil's expression, "sexual etiquette."

3. "This girl you are not permitted to possess!" and for this very reason cannot. A heavenly fata morgana in hell.

4. "All comes back to mere needs." Since you have needs, resign yourself to the fact.

5. "Needs are all." But how could you have all? Consequently you have not even needs.   [DII, 226 f.]

Spring: "A Hunger Artist" written.

To Robert Klopstock, spring:
Now your third letter has arrived, so many letters unanswered, and I have nothing to write, and am just tired. All I can say is, come, leave the Matlar [Matliary], which are sapping your strength, and come among people, among people whom you are so wonderfully able—far more than you yourself know—to handle, to animate, to lead, and you will soon realize that this phantom, which has only taken shape in your letters, in your letters and under your guiding hand, which did not exist in the Matlar, which is supposed to be me, and which I find so fearful that I am sorely tempted to turn my back on it, never to mention it again (not because it is fearful in itself, but fearful in relationship to me), you will realize without regret that this phantom does not exist, that I am in fact quite simply a difficult, introspective person, a person who has been forced to withdraw into himself by external pressures but who still has eyes to see with and who will derive great pleasure from every positive step you take and from your great struggle with the incursive world. Otherwise? I began to write a little some time ago in order to save myself from so-called nerves, I sit at the table from about seven o'clock in the evening, but it is futile, a defensive position in the war cut from the earth with my bare hands, and next month even this will come to an end and the office will start again.   [Br, 373 f.]

May: Last meeting with Milena. The friendship with Milena had lasted a little more than two years.

May 8. M. was here, won't come again; probably wise and right in this, yet there is perhaps still a possibility whose locked door we both are

guarding lest it open, or rather lest we open it, for it will not open of
itself.   [DII, 228 f.]

May 19. He feels more deserted with a second person than when alone.
If he is together with someone, this second person reaches out for him
and he is helplessly delivered into his hand. If he is alone, all mankind
reaches out for him—but the innumerable outstretched arms become
entangled with one another and no one reaches to him.   [DII, 229]

> To Robert Klopstock, from Prague, May–June:
I have just written a letter to a young lady, the first for a long time,
although I have to confess that this letter is no more than a humble
request about her piano playing, which is driving me mad. The amount
of peace that I need is not to be found above the ground. I wanted to
hide myself away with my notebook and talk to nobody for at least a
year. The most trivial things shake me to the core.   [Br, 374]

> End of June to mid-September: In Planá on the Luschnitz
> (southeastern Bohemia) at his sister Ottla's.

> To Robert Klopstock, from Planá, June 26:
I have been very well received here; Ottla, who sends her love, looks
after me as well as she looks after [her daughter] Věra, which is very
well indeed, but since there are live people and animals in Planá, it is
also noisy here, and this noise rouses me from my sleep and devastates
my mind, but in all other respects Planá is extraordinarily beautiful
with its forest, river, and gardens. And also with its Ohropax, the
possession of which brings me some respite and which, when I had
inserted it in my ears this morning, although it failed to obliterate the
sound of a hunting horn being blown in the forest by a farm laborer on
his day of rest, eventually prompted him to desist. Why does one
person's pleasure always have to disturb another person's pleasure?
The fact that I need to sit at a table has also forced Ottla, together with
her child and servant girl, to move from their big, warm, two-win-
dowed room to a small, cold room, while I sit enthroned in the big room
and suffer from the happiness of a large family which is turning hay
almost directly beneath my window with shouts of innocent glee.
  How is your life?   [Br, 376]

> To Brod, from Planá, end of June, with reference to the assas-
> sination (June 24) of German Foreign Minister Walther Rathe-
> nau by German reactionaries:
The terror reports? Had you anything else in mind besides Rathenau's

assassination? I am astonished that they let him live for as long as this, in Prague people were talking about his assassination months ago, the rumor was put about by Professor Münzer, it was so very credible, and so very much in keeping with the fate of the Jewish and German peoples, and had also been described in precise detail in your book. But I am not competent to pass an opinion, this affair far transcends my view of the world, even the view of the little world outside my window is too big for me. [. . .]

Incidentally, the problematical nature of "philosophy" seems to me to be a decidedly Jewish phenomenon which has its roots in the confusion caused by the fact that we wrongly regard the natives as too alien and our fellow Jews as too related, and so are unable to maintain a just balance between them. This problem is, of course, aggravated in the country, where even complete strangers, although not all complete strangers, greet one another, and where it is quite impossible, however hard we may try, to respond quickly enough to the greeting of some venerable old man who strides past us on a country road with an axe on his shoulder.   [Br, 378 f.]

To Oskar Baum, who apparently invited F.K. to visit him in Georgental, from Planá, July 4:
To tell the truth, I have a terrible fear of the journey, not just this journey of course, and not just any journey, but any change; the greater the change, the greater the fear, although in the final analysis the question of size is purely relative; if I were to restrict myself to the most minute changes—not that life allows me to do so—the rearrangement of a table in my room would become just as fearful as the journey to Georgental. Incidentally, it is not only my journey to Georgental that is fearful but also my departure from Georgental. Ultimately, or penultimately, it is simply a fear of death. But there is also the fear that I might make the gods take notice of me; if I just go on living here in my room, following a regular routine from day to day, I will naturally have to be taken care of, but the course will already have been determined, the gods will have only a mechanical grip on the reins, it is so pleasant, so very pleasant, to pass unnoticed, and if a good fairy stood by my cradle, it was surely the good fairy of boarding houses. And now to abandon this pleasant course, to go out alone beneath the heavens and walk to the station with my luggage, to set the world in a turmoil while noticing only the turmoil in one's own breast, that is fearful. And yet it has to be, otherwise—and it would not take very long at all—I would lose touch with life completely.   [Br, 382]

Summer: "Investigations of a Dog" written.

To Brod, from Planá, July 5:
When I was turning everything over between my throbbing temples in
this last sleepless night I realized once again what I had almost completely forgotten in the relatively peaceful period that has just passed,
namely, that I live my life on extremely shaky or nonexistent ground,
above a dark void, from which the dark power emerges at will and,
paying no heed to my stuttering, disrupts my life. My writing preserves
me, or would it perhaps be more accurate to say that it preserves this
kind of life. Of course, I am not suggesting that my life is better when I
do not write. On the contrary, it is far worse, quite intolerable in fact,
and must end in madness. But, of course, only if—as is, in fact, the
case—I continue to be a writer even when I am not writing, for a writer
who does not write is a monster who positively invokes madness. But
what are the advantages of being a writer? Writing is a sweet and
wonderful reward, but a reward for what? Last night it was as clear to
me as the catechism learned in childhood that it is a reward for devil
worship. This descent to the powers of darkness, this unleashing of
spiritual forces normally kept under restraint, the dubious embraces,
and all the other things that doubtless occur down below and which we
know nothing about up here when we write our stories in the sunshine.
Perhaps there are other kinds of writing, this is the only one I know; at
night, when fear prevents me from sleeping, this is the only one I know.
The diabolical nature of this process seems to me to be perfectly
obvious. It is the vanity and the hedonism, which flutter around and
around either one's own or another's form in a ceaseless search for
pleasure until in the end, by this constant repetition, a whole planetary
system of vanity is created. The wish-dream sometimes conceived by
naïve people—"I would like to die just to see how sorry people would
be"—is constantly realized by this kind of writer: he dies (or does not
live) and always feels sorry for himself. This produces a terrible fear of
death, which does not have to appear as a fear of death but can, on the
contrary, manifest itself simply as a fear of change, as fear of
Georgental.[1] The reasons for this fear of death may be divided into
two principal categories. In the first place, he has a terrible fear of dying
because he has not yet lived. By this I do not mean to say that in order to
live a man needs a wife and child, a field and a cow. All he needs in order
to live is to abjure his narcissism; to move into the house instead of
admiring and adorning it. It could of course be argued that this is all a
matter of fate and beyond anybody's control. But if that is so, why do we
repent, why does our repentance never cease? To make ourselves more

attractive and more delectable? That too. But then again, why, after
such a night, do we always say to ourselves: I could live, and I do not live.
The second principal reason—perhaps there is only one, for now I find it
difficult to distinguish between them—is the thought: "What I have acted
out will actually happen. I have not bought my freedom by writing. I
have died all my life and now I really will die. My life was sweeter than
the lives of others, my death will be all the more fearful. The writer in
me will, of course, die at once, for such a figure has no ground beneath its
feet, has no substance, is not even made of dust; such a figure is only
remotely conceivable in the most fantastic earthly existence, it is only
an artificial construction of a hedonistic attitude. So much for the
writer. As for myself, I cannot go on living because I have never lived; I
have remained clay, I have not fanned the spark of life to a flame but
simply used it to illuminate my corpse." It will be a strange funeral; the
writer, who is nonexistent, will yield up the old corpse, the lifelong
corpse, to the grave. Although it will never happen now, I am writer
enough to enjoy or—and this amounts to the same thing—to tell this
story, using every one of my senses in the process and completely
forgetting my self, for in the final analysis writing depends not on
vigilance but on the ability to forget one's self. But why am I talking only
about real dying? Living produces exactly the same dilemma. I sit here
with the complacent attitude of the writer, intent on the creation of
beauty in all its forms, and am obliged to witness without attempting to
intervene—since all I can do is write—how my real self, this poor,
defenseless thing I call my self (the existence of the writer is an argument
against the existence of the soul, for in his case the soul has quite
evidently left the real self, and yet has only become a writer, has failed to
become anything better; can the soul really be so undermined by its
separation from the self?) is tormented, beaten, and all but demolished
by the devil on every conceivable account, on account of a short journey
to Georgental [a few words illegible]. Why should I take fright, since I
am no longer at home, because the house suddenly collapses; do I know
what led up to the collapse, did I not move out and relinquish the house
to the powers of evil?

I wrote to Oskar [Baum] yesterday, and although I mentioned my
anxiety, I nonetheless confirmed my arrival, but I have not yet mailed
the letter, and meanwhile there is last night to consider. Perhaps I will
wait for one more night; if I am unable to endure it I suppose I will have
to write and say that I will not be coming. This would mean that I could
no longer leave Bohemia, soon I would be confined to Prague, then to
my room, then to my bed, then to a particular position in bed, then to
nothing at all. Perhaps I would then be able to renounce voluntarily the
happiness that comes from writing—for if it is to be done at all, it must

be done voluntarily and joyously. [. . .] A writer's life actually does depend on his desk; if he is to avoid going mad, really he should never leave his desk, he must cling to it like grim death.

If I were to define the writer, such a writer, and explain his function, if he has a function, I would say: he is a scapegoat for humanity, he enables people to enjoy sin without—or almost without—a sense of guilt.   [Br, 384 ff.]

To Robert Klopstock, from Planá, July 24:
You must not despair over this apparent failure, which I am admittedly unable to understand but with which I am well able to sympathize. If we were on the right path, such a failure would be truly desperate, but since we are only on one path, which leads to a second, which then leads to a third, and so on, and since it will be a long time before the right path is found, if it is ever found, and we are, therefore, utterly exposed to the uncertainty and to the incredibly beautiful multiplicity of life, the fulfillment of our hopes, especially hopes of this kind, will be something of a miracle which, although always unexpected, is none-theless always possible.   [Br, 398]

Janouch: "Without any certainty, what is life itself?" F.K.:
It is a fall. Perhaps it is the fall into sin.

What is sin? . . . We know the word and the practice, but the sense and the knowledge of sin have been lost. Perhaps that is itself damna-tion, God-forsakenness, meaninglessness.   [J, 73]

Sin is turning away from one's own vocation, misunderstanding, im-patience, and sloth—that is sin. The poet has the task of leading the isolated and mortal into eternal life, the accidental into conformity to law. He has a prophetic task.   [J, 97]

July: Retires from the Workers' Accident Insurance Institute.

To Brod, who had informed F.K. of Mr. Weltsch's (father of Felix Weltsch) remark that F.K.'s father had spoken proudly of F.K., from Planá, end of July:
The letter from Herr Weltsch, on the other hand, is not particularly cogent, he is quite convinced that one should praise one's own son and lavish affection on him at all times. But in this case, what is there to bring a gleam to a father's eye? A son who can never marry and will never produce children to carry on the family name; pensioned off at 39 years of age; completely preoccupied with eccentric writing that is concerned only with the salvation or damnation of his own soul; love-

less; alienated from faith, he will not even pray for salvation; tubercular; and, what is more, he contracted this illness—according to his father, whose opinion is entirely sound in all external respects—when, having left his nursery for the very first time and being quite incapable of leading an independent existence, he found that unhealthy room for himself in Schönborn. That is a son to enthuse over!   [Br, 401]

To Brod, from Planá, mid-September:
What is this due to? As far as I have been able to fathom it out, it is due to one thing only. [. . .] You say, I should try to test myself in a larger milieu. In one sense you are quite right, but in the final analysis size is not the crucial factor, I could also test myself in my mousehole. And the one thing is: fear of complete loneliness. If I were to remain here alone, I would be utterly lonely. I cannot speak to the people here, and if I were to do so, it would simply make me more lonely. And I have some idea of the terrors of loneliness, not so much the loneliness of isolation, but loneliness among people, such as I experienced when I first went to Matliary, and on certain days in Spindelmühle, although I would rather not talk about that. But then just what does loneliness mean to me? Ultimately, loneliness is my only goal, my greatest attraction, my opportunity, and if I may speak of having "arranged" my life, then I always did so in such a way as to ensure that loneliness would feel at home in it. And yet this fear of the thing I love so much! Far more understandable is the fear I feel over the preservation of my loneliness, which is just as great. [. . .] Between them, these two fears are grinding me to a pulp—the third fear makes its presence felt only when it becomes apparent that I am trying to run away—and to cap it all some huge miller will come chasing after me, complaining because, for all my work, I have produced nothing capable of sustaining life. On the other hand, the sort of life led by my Christian uncle [Rudolf Löwy] I would find quite fearful, even though it is very much in my line of country, albeit not as a goal in itself; but then he did not regard it as a goal either, save in his declining years. Incidentally, it is significant that I should feel so well in empty apartments, although not in completely empty apartments, but rather in the kind that are full of memories of people and have been made ready for further living, apartments with conjugal bedrooms, children's rooms, and kitchens, apartments where mail arrives for others, to which newspapers are delivered for others, at the start of each day. Only the real occupant must never appear, as happened recently, for then I am deeply perturbed.   [Br, 415 f.]

To Minze E., from Prague, fall:
The confession. To be chosen to hear it is in itself an inescapable and a

serious obligation, only please do not expect to profit from it. What sort of a man would you need to be for somebody to profit from confessing to you? To confess to somebody, or to shout one's confession to the wind, is usually much the same thing, no matter how good one's weak intentions may be. When one is caught up in the confusion of one's own life and hears about the confusions of another's, what can one say except: "Yes, of course, that is the way it is, that is the way things go," which may be a comfort, but not a great comfort. Please write though, my dear Minze, if you feel the need. Your confession will receive all the respect and sympathy of which I am capable.   [Br, 420 f.]

In answer to Janouch's question of why he allows his stories to be published if, as he put it, "publication of some scribble of mine always upsets me":

That's just it! Max Brod, Felix Weltsch, all my friends always take possession of something I have written and then take me by surprise with a completed contract with the publisher. I do not want to cause them any unpleasantness, and so it all ends in the publication of things which are entirely personal notes or diversions. Personal proofs of my human weakness are printed, and even sold, because my friends, with Max Brod at their head, have conceived the idea of making literature out of them, and because I have not the strength to destroy this evidence of solitude.

After a short pause he said in a different voice:

What I have just said is, of course, an exaggeration, and a piece of malice against my friends. In fact, I am so corrupt and shameless that I myself cooperate in publishing these things. As an excuse for my own weakness, I make circumstances stronger than they really are. That, of course, is a piece of deceit. But after all, I am a lawyer. So I can never get away from evil.   [J, 32]

September 26. No entries for two months. With some exceptions, a good period thanks to Ottla. For the past few days collapse again. On one of the first days made a kind of discovery in the woods.   [DII, 232]

December 18. All this time in bed. Yesterday [Kierkegaard's] *Either-Or*.
                                                                      [DII, 232]

Fall and winter: Prague.

1923

On Parables

Many complain that the words of the wise are always merely parables and of no use in daily life, which is the only life we have. When the sage says: "Go over," he does not mean that we should cross to some actual place, which we could do anyhow if the labor were worth it; he means some fabulous yonder, something unknown to us, something that he cannot designate more precisely either, and therefore cannot help us here in the very least. All these parables really set out to say merely that the incomprehensible is incomprehensible, and we know that already. But the cares we have to struggle with every day: that is a different matter.

Concerning this a man once said: Why such reluctance? If you only followed the parables you yourselves would become parables and with that rid of all your daily cares.

Another said: I bet that is also a parable.

The first said: You have won.

The second said: But unfortunately only in parable.

The first said: No, in reality: in parable you have lost.

The Great Wall of China, p. 150

Hugo Bergmann relates:
In March 1923, I journeyed from Jerusalem, where I had been living since 1920, to Prague, at the invitation of the Keren Hayesod [Land of Israel Foundation Fund] to speak about my Palestinian experiences in support of Keren Hayesod fund-raising. A large gathering was organized in the hall of the Produktenbörse in Prague, at which Arthur Hantke, the Keren Hayesod director, and I spoke. Kafka was present, and when I was resting in a side room after my address he came to me enthusiastically, pressed my hand, and said: "This speech you gave for me alone."

[Orot (September 1969), 79]

To Robert Klopstock, from Prague, end of March:
Meanwhile, after being lashed through periods of madness, I have

started to write, and although the way in which I write is extremely (not to mention diabolically) cruel for those around me, this writing is the most important thing in the world for me, as important as madness to a madman (without it he would go "mad") or pregnancy to a woman. It has, I repeat, nothing at all to do with the value of the writing, I recognize its intrinsic value with absolute precision, but I also recognize the value it has for me with the same precision. . . . And that is why in my agitation I hold my writing in a tight embrace to protect it from every disturbance, and not only my writing, but also the privacy that goes with it. And when I told you, I think it was yesterday, that you should not come on Sunday evening but only on Monday, and you asked me twice: "Not in the evening, then?" and when, because you had repeated the question, I was forced to reply, and said: "It would be better if you were to take a proper rest for once," I was in fact telling a downright lie, for what really concerned me was my being alone.

[Br, 431]

June 12. The horrible spells lately, innumerable, almost without interruption. Walks, nights, days, incapable of anything but pain.

More and more fearful as I write. It is understandable. Every word, twisted in the hands of the spirits—this twist of the hand is their characteristic gesture—becomes a spear turned against the speaker. Most especially a remark like this. And so ad infinitum. The only consolation would be: It happens whether you like or no. And what you like is of infinitesimally little help. More than consolation is: You too have weapons.   [DII, 232 f.]

The diary ends at this point.

Beginning of July: With his sister Elli and her children in Müritz, a Baltic seaside resort. Notices a vacation camp of the Berlin Jewish People's Home. (In the summer of 1916, F.K. encouraged Felice to do volunteer work at that Home.) At the camp he met Dora Dymant [Diamant], a nineteen-year-old East European Jewess of hasidic background, who became his companion.

To Brod, July 10:
A colony from the Jewish People's Home—healthy, cheerful, blue-eyed children—gives me pleasure.   [Br, 435]

F.K. had a vague plan to visit Palestine in October. To Hugo Bergmann, from Müritz, July:
Thank you for your greeting and your wish. This was the first Hebrew

writing that I have received from Palestine. The wish it contains may
prove very powerful. In order to test my transportability [for a journey
to Palestine], after so many years of bed rest and headaches, I have
made a short journey to the Baltic. And this journey has been fortunate
in one respect at least. Fifty paces from my balcony there is a vacation
home run by the Jewish People's Home in Berlin. Through the trees I
can see the children playing. Cheerful, healthy, high-spirited children.
East European Jews who have been saved from the threat to which
they were exposed in Berlin by West European Jews. Half the day and
half the night, the house, the forest, and the beach are full of singing.
When I am with them, although I am not happy, I am on the threshold
of happiness.   [Br, 436]

> To Else Bergmann, Hugo Bergmann's first wife, from Müritz, July
> 13:

I derive [. . .] pleasure from the vacation colony from the Berlin Jewish
People's Home—healthy children, whose cheerfulness warms me. Today, I shall celebrate Friday evening with them, I believe for the first
time in my life.   [Br, 437]

> To Else Bergmann, from Müritz, July, on the plan to go to Pales-
> tine:

I know that I will not now be making the journey—how could I—but the
fact that when I read your letter I could actually see the ship coming
alongside my threshold, and could see you standing there asking me,
and asking me in such a manner, that is no small recompense. Incidentally, you yourself—strangely close to me in your concern for the
darker side of life—have given a partial answer to your question. Always assuming that I would be capable of undertaking such a journey,
it would not have been a genuine Palestine journey, far from it—what it
would have been I am afraid I cannot say at present. [. . .]

I repeat: I would have had no right to make the journey even if I had
been able to do so; to which you add: "All the berths have been taken."
And then the temptation begins again and is answered by the absolute
impossibility of the undertaking, and, sad though it may be, in the final
analysis this is as it should be. And hope remains for the future, and
you will have the goodness not to disturb this hope.   [Br, 437 f.]

> To Tile Rössler, from Müritz, August 3:

Perhaps I should not stay too long in one place; there are people who
can only acquire a sense of belonging when they travel. Outwardly,
everything is the same as it was, I am very fond of all the people in the

Home, far more than I am able to show them, and Dora [Dymant] especially, with whom I spend most of my time, is a marvelous creature, but the Home itself seems to be less clear than it was, one small tangible detail has rather spoiled it for me while other small intangible details are contriving to spoil it still further; as a guest, an outsider, a tired guest at that, I have no opportunity of speaking my mind, of clarifying the situation, and so I am falling away; up to now I was there every evening, but today, even though it is Friday evening, I fear I shall not be going. [Br, 439]

To Robert Klopstock, from Müritz, early August:
The colony, which helped me to sleep at first, is now preventing me from doing so, but perhaps it will help me again later, for ours is a vital relationship.

On Monday morning we shall be leaving here; I could stay on alone, if only I were capable of being alone. But as things are, I could not live from the colony alone, for I am only a guest there. And I am not even a normal guest, which I find painful; no, not normal, for my general relationship to the colony has been complicated by a personal relationship.

But although it may contain disturbing features, and although it may not be enough to sustain life, to me the colony is more important than anything in Müritz, or anywhere else. [Br, 441]

Dora Dymant relates:
I first met Kafka on the Baltic in the summer of 1923. I was very young at the time, just nineteen, and was working as a voluntary helper in a holiday camp run by a Berlin Jewish People's Home at Müritz, near Stettin. One day I saw a family playing on the beach, a father and mother and their two children. The man made such a powerful impression on me that I could not get him out of my mind. I even followed these people into the town, and later I met them again. One day it was announced in the Home that Dr. Franz Kafka was coming to dinner. I was busy in the kitchen at the time, and when I looked up from my work I found that the room had turned quite dark; but I saw somebody standing outside the window, and recognized the gentleman from the beach. Then he came in. I did not know that it was Kafka, or that the woman I had seen him with on the beach was his sister. He spoke softly: "Such delicate hands, and they have to perform such bloody work!" (At that time Kafka was a vegetarian.) In the evening we all sat on benches at long tables. A little boy rose to leave the room, but was so embarrassed that he fell over. Kafka, his eyes shining with admiration, said to him: "How skillfully you fell, and how

skillfully you got up again!" When I thought about these words later, it seemed to me that what he had really been saying was that everything could be redeemed—except Kafka. Kafka was beyond redemption.

He was tall and slim, he had a dark complexion and took long strides, so that at first I thought he must be a Red Indian, and not a European. He swayed a little, but always held himself very erect, although he did allow his head to incline slightly to one side; he had the posture of a lonely man who is always trying to relate to something outside of himself. He listened attentively; there was something very lovable about the way he stood there; I would say that this posture was an outward symbol of a need for relationships, as if he were trying to say: "Alone I am nothing, I only become something when I make contact with the external world."

Why did Kafka make such a powerful impression on me? I came from the East, a dark creature full of dreams and premonitions, like a character from a Dostoevski novel. I had heard so much of the West, of its knowledge, its clarity, and its life style, and so I came to Germany with a receptive soul, and Germany has given me a great deal. But time and again I had the feeling that the people in the West were searching for something that I could give them. After the catastrophe of the war everybody was looking to the East for salvation, while I had fled from the East because for me the West was the source of light. Later, my dreams became less demanding. Europe had failed to live up to my expectations, its people were essentially restless. There was something they lacked. In the East we knew about the human person; we may have been less at our ease in society, and we may have expressed ourselves less elegantly, but we knew about the essential unity of man and creation. The very first time I saw Kafka I realized that he embodied my conception of what a human being should be. But Kafka also turned to me, as if he expected something from me.   [Der Monat I, No. 8–9 (1949), 91]

Janouch mentioned his mother's visit to a Jewish town in Galicia. F.K.:
And I should like to run to those poor Jews of the ghetto, kiss the hem of their coats, and say not a word. I should be completely happy if only they would endure my presence in silence.   [J, 43]

Mid-August: First Prague, then, for more than a month's stay, with his sister Ottla in Schelesen.

To Milena, on Müritz, the Jewish People's Home, and Dora Dymant:
Then in Müritz the Berlin possibility unexpectedly developed. I had

actually meant to go to Palestine in October, I think we talked about it, of course it would never have come off, it was a fantasy, the kind of fantasy someone has who is convinced he will never again leave his bed. If I'm never going to leave my bed again, why shouldn't I travel as far as Palestine? But in Müritz I came into contact with a summer colony of a Jewish People's Home from Berlin, most of them East European Jews. It attracted me very much, it lay on my way. I began considering the possibility of moving to Berlin. At the time this possibility was not much more real than the Palestine plan, but then it grew stronger. To live alone in Berlin was of course impossible, in every respect, not only in Berlin but for that matter anywhere. For this, too, a solution [Dora Dymant]—surprising in its special way—offered itself in Müritz.   [M, 236]

To Brod, from Schelesen, August 29:
There is not much to tell you about myself, I am trying desperately to put on a bit of weight—when I came here I weighed 54½ kilos, the lightest I have ever been—but I am making little headway, there is too much opposition; so, it is a struggle. I quite like the district, and up to now the weather has been kind, but the forces opposing my recovery must regard me as a really precious possession, for they are fighting like—or perhaps they are—the devil.   [Br, 443]

To Carl Seelig, editor of a Vienna publishing house, who invited F.K. to participate in a literary venture, from Schelesen, September:
I am in the country for a few days, your letter was sent on to me. Many thanks for your friendly invitation. Unfortunately, I cannot contribute to the series at present. The earlier manuscripts I have are completely unusable, I cannot show them to anybody, while recently I have been diverted from my writing. But perhaps I could get in touch later if the situation improves.

I well remember the letter you wrote me two years ago, please forgive this old debt. At that time I felt so ill that I was quite unable to reply.   [Br, 444]

End of September: Moves with Dora Dymant to Berlin-Steglitz, later to Berlin-Zehlendorf. Writes several stories, most of them destroyed. Attends lectures at the Berlin Academy (Hochschule) for Jewish Studies.

To Felix Weltsch, from Berlin-Steglitz, October 9:
The days are so short, they seem to pass even more quickly than in

Prague and, fortunately, much more unobtrusively. The fact that they are passing so quickly is sad, but then that is the nature of time, once you remove your hand from the wheel, it flashes past you, and you are unable to grasp it again. I scarcely leave the immediate vicinity of the house; this, however, is quite wonderful, my street is the last in the whole town that is even semiurban, behind it the terrain is given over to gardens and villas, old mature gardens. On mild evenings there is a really powerful scent such as I have scarcely known elsewhere. And then there is the large botanical garden, a quarter of an hour's walk from my apartment, and the forest, which I have yet to see, not quite half an hour's walk.   [Br, 451]

To Brod, from Berlin-Steglitz, mid-October:
What is bad, however, is that just recently the ghosts have tracked me down again, but that is no reason for returning either; if I am to succumb to them, then rather here than there, although things have not yet reached such a pitch.   [Br, 451]

To Brod, from Berlin-Steglitz, end of October:
So if I do not write, it is due primarily to "strategic considerations," which have come to govern my whole life of recent years; I no longer trust words and letters, not my words and letters, I want to share my feelings with people, but not with ghosts, who play with words and read letters with total apathy. I mistrust letters especially, and find the commonly held belief—that merely to seal an envelope is enough to ensure that its contents will reach their destination safely—quite re-markable. Incidentally, the censorship set up during the war, a period in which the ghosts were particularly audacious and quite unabashed in their mockery, taught us a great deal in this respect.

But another reason why I write so little (there is something else I forgot to mention re the above: there are times when I feel that the essence of art, the existence of art, can be explained only in terms of such "strategic considerations," which enable human beings to speak truth to one another) is that I am, of course, continuing with my Prague life, my Prague "work," about which there has also been very little to report. You must also bear in mind that I am leading a semirural existence here, and so have been spared not only the cruel, but also the pedagogical, pressure of Berlin proper.   [Br, 452 f.]

October: "A Little Woman" written. Winter: "The Burrow." The Hunger Artist, a collection of stories, sent to the publisher.

To Brod, from Berlin-Steglitz, November 25:
I was not sick, my little lamp flickered a little, otherwise nothing
serious has happened as yet.   [Br. 466]

To his sister Valli, from Berlin-Steglitz, November:
The table is standing by the fire. I have just moved from the fireplace
because it's too warm there, even for my back which is always cold. My
oil lamp burns wonderfully, a masterpiece of lamp-making, and of
shopping—it has been put together out of bought and borrowed little
bits—not of course by me—how could I manage a thing like that! You
can light it without taking the lamp glass and the globe off; really there
is only one thing wrong with it, it won't burn without oil; but after all
the rest of us don't do that—and so I sit down and take out your dear
letter, now so old. The clock is ticking, I have got used even to the
ticking of the clock, I don't hear it very often, besides, and that generally when I am doing something particularly praiseworthy. In fact the
clock has certain personal relations to me, like many things in the
room, save that now, particularly since I gave notice—or, more accurately, since I was given notice, which is a good thing from every angle,
and, moreover, a complicated affair it would take pages to describe
—they seem to be beginning to turn their backs on me, above all the
calendar,[1] about whose mottoes I have already written to Father and
Mother. Lately it is as if it has been metamorphosed. Either it is absolutely uncommunicative—for example, you want its advice, you go up
to it, but the only thing it says is "Feast of the Reformation"—which
probably has a deeper significance, but who can discover it?—or, on the
contrary, it is nastily ironic. Lately, for example, I was reading something and hit upon an idea as I was doing so that seemed to me very good,
or rather full of significance, so much so that I wanted to ask the
calendar's opinion on it—it's only on such accidental occasions that it
answers, in the course of its day, not like, say, by tearing off a page of the
calendar punctually at a fixed time—"Even a blind dog finds something
sometimes," it said. Another time I was horrified at the coal bill, whereupon it told me, "Happiness and contentment are the joy of life," in
which there is admittedly together with the irony an offensive insensi-
tivity: it is impatient, it can't wait any longer for the day I leave; but
perhaps it is only that it wishes to make parting easy for me. Perhaps,
under the page giving the date of the day I leave, there will be a page
which I shall no longer see on which is written, "God has told each
loving heart, the day will come when we must part." No, one should not
write down everything one thinks about one's calendar, "He is only a
man, like yourself, after all."

If I tried to write you about everything I come into contact with in this way, I should of course never come to the end, and it would give the appearance that I am leading a busy social life, but in reality it is very quiet where I am, yet never too quiet. Of the excitements of Berlin, bad and good, I know very little; more of the former, of course. [. . .]

How are things [. . .] in the Jewish school? Have you read the paper by the young teacher in [the Zionist periodical] *Selbstwehr?* Very well intentioned, and zealous. I have again heard that A. is doing very well, and Miss M., they say, has reformed the whole of gymnastics in Palestine. You must not be too annoyed at old A.'s head for business. After all, it was already a tremendous thing to take the whole family on his back and cart them over the sea to Palestine. That so many of his kind do it is no less a miracle of the waters than Moses in the Red Sea.

[B. 199 f.; Br, 461 ff.]

To Robert Klopstock, from Berlin-Steglitz, December 19:
As far as I am concerned, you must not think, Robert, that my life is such that I have either the freedom or the strength to report, or even to write, whenever I wish, for there are chasms into which one sinks quite unwittingly and out of which one is only able to crawl, if at all, after a long period of time. Such situations are not conducive to writing.—Your decision to go to the Ivriah is a very good one, perhaps in addition to the courses in Hebrew you will join the Talmud class (once a week! you will not understand everything, but what does that matter? You will hear it from a distance, and what is the Talmud if not a message from the distance). The Hochschule für Jüdische Wissenschaft provides me with a peaceful oasis in this wild city of Berlin and in the wild districts of my mind. [. . .] A whole house with beautiful lecture rooms, a library, a peaceful atmosphere, well heated, few pupils, and all for nothing. Of course, I am not a regular pupil, I just attend the preparatory department, where I see only one teacher, and him only rarely, so that in the final analysis all this splendor becomes decidedly insubstantial in my particular case; but even if I am not a pupil, the school exists, and is beautiful, and yet it is not so much beautiful as strange, a combination of grotesqueness and incredible tenderness (I mean the scientific and the liberal reform aspect of the whole complex).   [Br, 469 f.]

From Dora Dymant's memoir:
The most striking thing about his face was his eyes, for no matter whether he was talking or listening, they were always alert, and sometimes positively vigilant. But they did not stare at you in fear, as some have claimed; on the contrary, they seemed to express astonish-

ment. He had shy, brown eyes, which shone when he spoke. Occasionally a glint of humor would appear in them, which was more roguish than ironical, as if he knew things that other people do not know about. There was nothing solemn about him at all. As a rule, he was a very lively talker, and he liked to talk. His conversational style was as rich in imagery as his writings. When he succeeded in describing his ideas especially well, he seemed to obtain the same kind of satisfaction as a craftsman feels when he produces a successful piece of work. His wrists were very slender, and his fingers long and sensitive. Those fingers came to life when he told a story, providing an accompaniment to his words that was virtually another form of speech. Where others speak with their hands, he spoke with his fingers. We often amused ourselves by making silhouettes on the wall, a thing he did extremely well. Kafka was always cheerful. He liked to play; in fact, he was a born playmate and was always ready for some prank or other. I do not believe that his depressions were the dominant feature of his personality. They were not recurring, and most of them had a direct cause, which could be clearly identified. For example, when he came home from the town, there were times when he was more than depressed, times when his whole being was in revolt. It was during the inflation. Life was very hard, and Kafka suffered greatly, but refused to spare himself. He considered that he had no right to withdraw from what was happening all around him. As a result, the journey into town became a sort of Golgotha, which reduced him almost to a state of physical collapse. He would queue for hours on end, not just to buy something, but because he felt that if the blood of martyrs was to be shed, then his must be shed as well. And so he shared the experiences of an unhappy people at an unhappy time. To my mind, this attitude is clearly manifested in the underlying theme of The Trial, where Kafka condemns K. for refusing to submit to lifelong crucifixion. For there is no life save in the "crucifixion," and before the supreme court nobody is acquitted. That is my interpretation. "How can things ever be any different," he once wrote to me. "We have Helfferich, Hilferding, and Rathenau—but no Hilfe [help] and no Rat [counsel]." It seemed to him that people were trying to cover up the whole tragedy with glib phrases because they lacked the courage to describe things as they really were.

We lived in Steglitz, then in Zehlendorf; first in one room, and later in two. We moved from the first apartment on account of the landlady. Kafka described her in "A Little Woman": "It is only disgust, persistent and active disgust, that drives her to be preoccupied with me."

Kafka had to write because writing was the very air he breathed. He breathed it in the rhythm of the days on which he wrote. When people say that he wrote for a period of fourteen days, what this really means is that he wrote for fourteen consecutive evenings and fourteen consecutive nights. Before starting to write, he usually wandered around in a lethargic and gloomy frame of mind. At such times he spoke very little, had no appetite for food, took no interest in the world around him, and was very depressed; he just wanted to be alone. At first, I did not understand these moods, but later I was always able to respond when he began to write. As a rule, he took a lively interest in even the most trivial matters, but on working days nothing could hold his attention. I can only distinguish between the different degrees of tension which marked those days in terms of color. Thus, some appeared purple, others dark green or blue. Later, he liked me to remain in the room while he wrote. On one occasion, he began to write after supper, and continued for a long time, so that despite the glare of the electric light I fell asleep on the sofa. Suddenly, I awoke to find him sitting by my side. I looked at him. His face was quite different; the signs of mental exertion were so distinct that they completely transformed his appearance.

One of his last short stories, "The Burrow," was written in a single night. It was winter; he began to write early in the evening, and finished toward morning, then worked on the story again. He told me about it, half jokingly and half in earnest. It was an autobiographical work, and it may also have been a premonition of his return to his parents' house, a prospect that always filled him with panic because it meant he would lose his freedom. He told me that I was the "citadel" in this building. He often read out the things he had written, but he never analyzed or explained them. Some of his writing struck me as full of humor, and it also contained an element of self-irony. From time to time he used to say: "I would dearly like to know if I have escaped from the ghosts!" Under the heading of "ghosts" he included everything that had tormented him prior to his arrival in Berlin. He seemed obsessed by this idea, which frequently assumed the form of a protest. Thus, there were times when he wanted to burn everything he had written in order to free his soul from these "ghosts." I respected this wish, and once, when he lay ill in bed, burned some of his works in his presence. What he really wanted to write would emerge later, after he had gained his "freedom." For him literature was something sacred, absolute and inviolable, something pure and great; it had nothing to do with journalism. Since he was not quite sure of most things in life, he normally expressed himself very cautiously. But when it came to literature he would brook no argument, and refused to make any kind of compromise, for literature impinged on his whole being. It was not that he wanted to get to the bottom of things; he did not have to, for he himself had already struck rock bottom. When it came to solving complex human problems, he was not content with half-measures. He had experienced life as a labyrinth, from which he could find no way out; he never advanced beyond despair; and for him everything was linked with cosmic causes, even the most mundane matters. This kind of attitude, this insistence on the totality of life, is found in the East. There are certain spiritual requirements in the East that have to be met if people are to live fruitful lives. Kafka sensed that. The West has forgotten it. That is why God has forsaken the West. That is why the things we have experienced were able to happen. And that seems to me to be one of the reasons why people are so interested in Kafka today: because he knew that God has forsaken us.

I have been reproached for having burned some of Kafka's works. I was so young at the time, and although young people may dream of the future, they live in the present. In the final analysis, Kafka regarded everything as a means of freeing himself, and in Berlin he believed that he really had freed himself from the tyranny of the past. But the problems of his early years were part and parcel of his whole existence. As soon as one chord was struck, all the others chimed in. His inner life was infinitely profound, and quite intolerable. It was not that he hated Prague, but he spoke of his native city in the way that a European might speak of Europe. Most of all, he was tormented by the fear of again becoming dependent on his parents, for such dependence would have endangered his "burrow." That is why he was so frugal, why he sought to inure himself to a Spartan existence. For a while, in Berlin, he thought he had found a personal solution to his internal and external problems, which he hoped would save his life. He wanted to feel that he was a perfectly ordinary person, an average man, with no special needs or desires. We made many plans. At one time we thought of opening a small restaurant, in which he proposed to work as a waiter. In that way he could have observed everything without being seen himself, he could have stood in the midst of life. He did that in any case, but in his own way.

Kafka was very particular about his clothes. He regarded it as a mark of disrespect to go anywhere with a badly tied tie. He had his suits made by a first-class tailor, and he always took a long time to dress, although not from vanity. He studied himself critically in the mirror, without a hint of self-conceit, simply to ensure that he did not give offense.

He loved to go shopping, for he loved to meet ordinary people. With his basket or his milk can in his hand, he was a familiar figure in our district. In the mornings he often went walking alone. His day was carefully organized to suit his work. He took his notebook with him on his walks, and if he ever forgot it, he bought a new one when he was out. He loved nature, although I never actually heard him say so.

One of the things he held especially dear was his pocket watch. And when we quarreled with our landlady over the electric light—for he often wrote all night long—I bought a kerosene lamp, whose gentle, glowing light pleased him greatly. He always insisted on filling the lamp himself, he used to play with the wick, and was constantly discovering new virtues in that lamp of his. But he disliked the telephone, and could not bear the sound of the bell. I had to take all the calls. I believe machines, and mechanical things in general, made him nervous. Another thing he loved was my calendar, which had a different motto for every day of the year. Later, we both had one, and whenever anything special happened Kafka would "consult the calendar." Once, when a glass bowl in which I was washing grapes (he was particularly fond of grapes and pineapple) broke in my hands, he came into the kitchen carrying the calendar and with glaring eyes declaimed: "Destruction is the work of a moment!" Then he handed me the page. The maxim sounded so banal. He smiled.

Although Kafka did not like to be disturbed, we had many visitors. I still remember Willy Haas, the editor of the Literarische Welt, and Rudolf Kayser of the Neue Rundschau. Once Werfel came to read to Kafka from his latest book. After they had been together for a long time, I saw Werfel walk out in tears. When I entered the room Kafka was sitting in his chair, completely shattered, and he murmured to himself several times in succession: "To think that something so terrible can exist!" He too was crying. He had allowed Werfel to leave without saying a single word to him about his book. Those who exposed themselves to Kafka's judgment either received the strongest possible confirmation or were driven to despair—there was nothing in between. He criticized his own works with the same inexorable severity. But although he considered that he had never fully realized his intentions, I am sure he never thought of himself as a dilettante.

Nobody felt ill at ease with Kafka. On the contrary, everybody was drawn to him, although his visitors invariably displayed an air of solemnity; it was as if they were walking on tiptoe or gliding over soft carpets. But for the most part we were alone, and Kafka often read to me, from Grimm's and Anderson's fairy tales, from E. T. A. Hoffmann's Kater Murr or from Hebel's Schatzkästlein. One of the things he read to me was the story of the miner's sweetheart, who accompanied her lover to the mine one day, little thinking that she would never see him alive again. The years passed by, and she grew old and gray. Then, one day, his body was discovered in an abandoned shaft, where it had been preserved by the action of the coal gas, and so looked exactly the same as it had looked in life. The old lady came, and kissed her lover;

she had waited for him for years, and now they were married, and
buried, at one and the same time. Kafka loved this story because it was
"all of a piece," because it was so natural, like all great things. And, of
course, he loved Kleist. He was quite capable of reading the Marquise
of O to me five or six times in succession. He also read to me on many
occasions from Goethe's Hermann and Dorothea, to which he was
attracted above all by its tender portrayal of ordinary life. In the hope
that it would enable him to lead the kind of life he wanted, Kafka
established a concrete—but by no means bourgeois—relationship to his
home, to his family, and to money. I mention this because I remember
how quietly and objectively he spoke to me about his former fiancée
[Felice]. She was a splendid girl, but completely bourgeois in outlook.
Kafka felt that by marrying her he would have been marrying the
whole deceitful world in which she moved; and he also feared that he
would have had no time for writing. Initially, of course, Kafka had
tried to come to terms with middle-class life. That was one of the
principal reasons for his engagement. The other was curiosity. He
wanted to get to know everything, and to get to know it in personal
terms. Eventually a hemorrhage, which was brought on by his tuber-
culosis, freed him from all his doubts.   [Der Monat I, No. 8-9 (1949), 91-94]

From "Josephine the Singer, or the Mouse Folk"

Yet there is something else behind it which is not so easy to explain by this relationship between the people and Josephine. Josephine, that is to say, thinks just the opposite, she believes it is she who protects the people. When we are in a bad way politically or economically, her singing is supposed to save us, nothing less than that, and if it does not drive away the evil, at least gives us the strength to bear it. She does not put it in these words or in any other, she says very little anyhow, she is silent among the chatterers, but it flashes from her eyes, on her closed lips—few among us can keep their lips closed, but she can—it is plainly legible. Whenever we get bad news—and on many days bad news comes thick and fast at once, lies and half-truths included—she rises up at once, whereas usually she sits listlessly on the ground, she rises up and stretches her neck and tries to see over the heads of her flock like a shepherd before a thunderstorm. [. . .] True, she does not save us and she gives us no strength; it is easy to stage oneself as a savior of our people, inured as they are to suffering, not sparing themselves, swift in decision, well acquainted with death, timorous only to the eye in the atmosphere of reckless daring which they constantly breathe, and as prolific besides as they are bold—it is easy, I say, to stage oneself after the event as the savior of our people, who have always somehow managed to save themselves, although at the cost of sacrifices which make historians—generally speaking we ignore historical research entirely—quite horror-struck. And yet it is true that just in emergencies we hearken better than at other times to Josephine's voice.   The Penal Colony, pp. 263 f.

To Robert Klopstock, from Berlin-Steglitz, January 26:
There is little to tell about myself, a somewhat shadowy life, those who do not actually see it would not even notice it.   [Br, 474]

To Robert Klopstock, from Berlin-Zehlendorf, early March:
No, no journey, no such wild act, we will come together without that, in

a quieter way more in keeping with our weak bones. Perhaps we will-
visit Prague soon—in fact, we are seriously thinking of doing so—and if
a sanatorium in the Wiener Wald were to be considered, we will
certainly do so. I resist the idea of a sanatorium, and also a convales-
cent guest house, but what is the point, since I am unable to resist the
fever. 38 degrees has become my daily bread, all evening and half the
night. Otherwise, and despite everything, it is very beautiful here, lying
on the veranda and seeing how the sun tackles two quite distinct
problems, one so very much weightier than the other: inspiring natural
life in me and the birch tree at my side (the birch tree seems to have
taken the lead). I am extremely loath to leave here, but I cannot completely dismiss the idea of a sanatorium, for since I have been unable to
leave the house for weeks on account of my fever—although I feel quite
strong when I am lying down, the mere thought of taking a stroll I find
quite overpowering—the idea of burying myself, alive but at peace, in
some sanatorium is not all that unpleasant at times. At other times,
when one considers that one would lose one's freedom during the few
warm months of the year, which are made for freedom, it is, of course,
quite repellent. But then again there is the morning and evening cough,
which racks me for hours on end, and the bottle which is full almost
every day—these are factors that naturally work in favor of the sanatorium. But then, yet again, there is the fear of the terrible dietary
regimen that is imposed there.   [Br, 477 f.]

> Early March: Visit of Uncle Siegfried, the "country doctor." F.K.
> was brought as a patient from Berlin to Prague. "Josephine the
> Singer, or the Mouse Folk" written. Early April: To Sanatorium
> Wiener Wald, then to Professor M. Hajek's clinic in Vienna, and
> from there to the sanatorium of Dr. Hoffmann in Kierling, near
> Klosterneuburg. Tuberculosis of the larynx. With him were Dora
> Dymant and, later, Robert Klopstock, who broke off his medical
> studies in Berlin to devote himself to F.K.

> Dora Dymant relates:
> He left Prague a sick man, yet of an undaunted spirit. I met him
> again in a sanatorium in the Wiener Wald, to which his sister had
> taken him. It was there that tuberculosis of the larynx was first diag-
> nosed. Kafka was not allowed to speak, and so he wrote everything
> down for me, including his impressions of Prague, which had had a
> devastating effect on him. After three weeks in the sanatorium his
> condition had deteriorated, and he was transferred to a hospital in
> Vienna, where he could receive specialist care, and where he shared a
> ward with several other patients, all of them seriously ill. Every night
> one of those patients died. The next day Kafka would inform me of the

fact by pointing silently to an empty bed. There was one patient in the ward, a cheerful fellow, who was very active and enjoyed his food enormously despite the pipe that had been inserted in his throat. He had sparkling eyes and sported a mustache. Kafka, who took great pleasure in his hearty appetite, pointed him out to me one day. The next day he pointed to his empty bed. But Kafka was not so much shaken by this incident as angry; it was as if he simply could not understand why this man, who had always been so cheerful, should have to die. I will never forget his faintly malicious, ironical smile.

[Der Monat I, No. 8–9 (1949), 95]

To Robert Klopstock, from Sanatorium Wiener Wald, April 7:
I suppose the big thing is the larynx. One is told nothing definite, of course, because when people talk about laryngal tuberculosis they become embarrassed, their eyes grow glazed, and they give evasive answers. But if one is told that "infiltration" has occurred, that there is a "swelling at the back," albeit a "nonmalignant" swelling, but that it is "not possible to say anything definite as yet," then this, combined with some decidedly malignant pains, is enough. [Br. 480]

To Robert Klopstock, from Sanatorium Wiener Wald, April 13:
My larynx is so swollen that I cannot eat, alcohol will have to be injected into the nerve (I am told), and I will probably have to have a resection. So I will stay in Vienna for a few weeks. [Br. 480]

To Robert Klopstock, April 18:
Robert, my dear Robert, no acts of violence, no sudden journey to Vienna, you know how I fear acts of violence, and yet you always involve me in them. Since I left that lavish, oppressive, and yet helpless (albeit beautifully situated) sanatorium, I feel better, the regime in the clinic (apart from minor details) has done me good, the swallowing pains and the burning sensation are less troublesome, no injections have been given as yet, just oil of peppermint sprayed onto the larynx. On Saturday, unless some special misfortune prevents me from doing so, I will enter Dr. Hoffmann's sanatorium in Kierling near Kloster-neuburg, Lower Austria. [Br. 481]

To Brod, from Kierling, April 28:
The two parcels you sent, especially the second, gave me great plea-sure, and I could not have wished for anything better than the Reclam books. It is not that I actually read (although I have at long last started to read Werfel's novel, slowly but regularly), I am too tired to do so, the natural condition for my eyes is closed, but playing with books and booklets makes me happy.

Farewell, my dear good Max.   [Br, 482]

Dr. Oskar Beck, who was consulted on F.K.'s state, to Felix Weltsch, May 3:
Yesterday I was called to Kierling by Miss Diamant [Dymant]. Dr. Kafka was having very sharp pains in the larynx, particularly when he coughed. When he tries to take some nourishment the pains increase to such an extent that swallowing becomes almost impossible. I was able to confirm that there is a decaying tubercular action which includes also a part of the epiglottis. In such a case an operation cannot even be thought of, and I have given the patient alcohol injections in the nervus laryngeus superior. Today Miss Diamant rang me up again to tell me that the success of this treatment was only temporary and the pains had come back again with all their former intensity. I advised Miss Diamant to take Dr. Kafka to Prague, since Professor Neumann, too, estimated his expectation of life at about three months. Miss Diamant rejected this advice, as she thinks that through this the patient would come to realize the seriousness of his illness.
    It is your duty to give his relations a full account of the seriousness of the situation. Psychologically I can quite understand that Miss Diamant, who is looking after the patient's interests in a self-sacrificing and touching fashion, feels she ought to call a number of specialists to Kierling for a consultation. I had, therefore, to make it clear to her that Dr. Kafka was in such a state, both with regard to his lungs and with regard to his larynx, that no specialist could help him any more, and the only thing one can do is to relieve pain by administering morphine or Pantopon.   [B, 205]

Brod came to visit his friend. To Brod, from Kierling, May 20:
If only I had been given an alcohol injection so as to make me a little more like a human being during your visit, which I had looked forward to so much and which proved so dismal in the event. Not that it was an especially bad day, I would not like you to think that, it was just that it was worse than the day before, but that is how time and the fever run their course. (Now Robert is trying to sell me on Pyramidon.) Apart from these, and other, causes for complaint, there are, of course, a few tiny joys, but these cannot be communicated, save perhaps during a visit like the one I have so regrettably ruined.
    Farewell, thank you for everything.   [Br, 483]

Brod relates:
The first thing Dora told me, and Franz bore her out—he was not allowed to speak a lot—was the remarkable story of his wooing. He

wanted to marry Dora, and had sent her pious father a letter in which he had explained that, although he was not a practicing Jew in her father's sense, he was nevertheless a "repentant one, seeking 'to return,' " and therefore might perhaps hope to be accepted into the family of such a pious man. The father set off with the letter to consult the man he honored most, whose authority counted more than anything else for him, to the "Gerer Rebbe." The rabbi read the letter, put it on one side, and said nothing more than the single syllable, "No." Gave no further explanation. He never used to give explanations. The wonder-rabbi's "No" was justified by Franz's death, which followed very soon afterward, and Franz, too, took his letter from Dora's father, which had arrived just before I did, and more or less formed the topic of the day for the "little family," as a bad omen. He smiled, and yet he was affected by it; we made efforts to put other thoughts into his head. But shortly afterward Dora took me to one side and whispered to me that that night an owl had appeared at Franz's window. The bird of death. [. . .] Dora told me how Franz cried for joy when Professor Tschiassny—when he was in the last stage already—told him things looked a little better with his throat. He embraced her again and again, and said he had never wished for life and health so much as now.

[B, 208 f.]

In the last few weeks of F.K.'s life, the doctor asked him to speak as little as possible. He used slips of paper to communicate.

To Klopstock, when he refused to give him a morphine injection: Kill me, or else you are a murderer.   [B, 76]

Other notes:
Often offer the nurse wine.

Here it is nice to give people a drop of wine, because everyone is a little bit of a connoisseur, after all.

That is a pleasure, to give someone something that gives him pleasure certainly and honestly at the moment you give it to him.

One must take care that the lowest flowers over there, where they have been crushed into the vases, don't suffer. How can one do that? Perhaps bowls are really the best.   [B, 207]

Somewhere in today's newspapers there is an excellent little article on the treatment of cut flowers, they are so terribly thirsty, another such newspaper . . .

But it is just a stupid observation. When I started to eat, something in my larynx dropped down, whereupon I felt wonderfully free and began to imagine all sorts of miracles, but it passed immediately.

Above all, I would like to tend the peonies because they are so fragile.

And place lilac in the sun.

Have you a moment to spare? If so, would you please lightly spray the peonies?

Please make sure that the peonies are not touching the bottom of the vase. That is why they should be kept in bowls.

The way I torment you, it is quite mad.

Naturally, it causes me more pain, because you are so good to me, in that respect the hospital is, of course, very good.

I should write it here and now, using the strength still left to me. And they have only just sent me the materials [proofs of *The Hunger Artist*].

The trouble is that I am unable to drink a single glass of water, although the craving for water satisfies one's thirst to some extent.

If it is true—and it is probable—that my present diet is not enough to effect a cure, then, barring miracles, my situation is quite hopeless.

Look at the lilac, fresher than the morning.

Where is the eternal spring?

How marvelous it is, do you not think so? The lilac—even though it is dying, it still drinks, still sucks in water.

There is no such thing that a dying creature drinks.

Lay your hand on my brow for a moment, to give me courage.

[Br, 484 ff.; 490 f.]

Klopstock informed Brod of the final stage of F.K.'s illness:
Monday evening, Franz was feeling very well; he was jolly, showed great pleasure in everything that Klopstock had brought back from the city with him, ate strawberries and cherries, smelled them for a very long time, enjoyed their fragrance with the double intensity with which he enjoyed everything those last days. He wanted people to take long drinks of water and beer in front of him, because it was impossible for him to do so; he enjoyed the others' pleasure. In the last few days he talked a lot about drinks and fruit. [B, 209]

To his parents, June 2:
Dearest Father and Mother,

Well, these visits you write to me about sometimes. I think it over every day, because for me it's something very important. It would be so lovely, we haven't been together for such a long time, I don't count being together in Prague, that was just upsetting the household, but being together a few days in peace in some beautiful district, only I can't remember when that was, really, a few hours once in Franzensbad. And then to drink a "good glass of beer" together, as you write, from which I see that Father doesn't think much of this year's wine, in which, as far as the beer is concerned, I agree with him. Apart from that, a thing I often look back on now during the heat, there was a time once when we often used to be beer-drinkers together, many years ago, when Father used to take me with him to the public baths.

That and much more speaks for your coming, but there's a lot that speaks against it. Now, first of all, Father would probably not be able to come because of the difficulty with passports. That, of course, robs your visit of a lot of its sense; but above all Mother, whomever else she may be accompanied by, will be far too much thrown on me, dependent on me, and I am still not very beautiful, not worth looking at. The difficulties I met with in the beginning here in and around Vienna, you know; they got me down a little; they kept my temperature from subsiding quickly again, which all helped toward my getting weaker later; the shock of the larynx business weakened me at first more than it deserved to in reality.

Now for the first time I am working myself out of all these weaknesses with the help of Dora and Robert, and how great that help is you cannot imagine so far away—where should I be without them! There are still troubles, as for example a cold on the stomach which I caught in the last few days, and which has not yet quite gone. All that works together, so that in spite of wonderful helpers, in spite of good air and food, and a bath of fresh air almost every day, I am not yet quite better, in fact, on the whole, am not even in such a fit state as I was the last time I was in Prague. On top of that, take into account that I may only talk in whispers, and that not too much, and you will be glad to put off your visit. Everything is beginning to go well. Lately a professor found a real improvement in my larynx, and if I can't altogether believe this extremely kind and unselfish man—he comes out once a week in his own car and charges almost nothing for it, so his words were after all a great comfort to me—everything is, as I said, beginning to go well. But the best of beginnings is nothing if I can't show visitors—and especially such visitors as you would be—great, undeniable progress, progress that can be recognized even by the lay eye, it's better to leave it. Well, then, shall we not leave it for the moment, dear Father and Mother?

[B, 210 f.]

The final hours as related to Brod by Klopstock:
At four o'clock in the morning Klopstock was called into the room by Dora, because Franz "is breathing badly." Klopstock recognized the danger, and woke the doctor, who gave him a camphor injection.

Then began the fight for morphine. Franz said to Klopstock: "You have always been promising it to me for four years. You are torturing me; you have always been torturing me. I am not talking to you any more. I shall die like that." He was given two injections. After the second he said, "Don't cheat me, you are giving me an antidote." They gave him Pantopon; he was very happy about that. "That's good, but more, more, it isn't helping me." Then he went slowly to sleep. His last words were about his sister Elli. Klopstock was holding his head. Kafka, who was always terribly afraid he might infect someone, said—imagining it was his sister he saw instead of his doctor friend—"Go away, Elli, not so near, not so near," and as Klopstock moved away a little, he was satisfied, and said, "Yes, like that—it's all right like that."

Before this last scene he made a brusque gesture of dismissal to the nurse. "So brusque as he never was ordinarily," Klopstock told me. Then with all his strength he tore off his icepack and threw it on the floor. "Don't torture me any more, why prolong the agony." As Klopstock moved away from the bed to clean some part of the syringe, Franz said, "Don't leave me." His friend answered, "But I am not leaving you." Franz answered in a deep voice, "But I am leaving you."

[B, 211 f.]

The evening before his death he read proofs of his last book, A Hunger Artist. Death came on Tuesday, June 3, 1924, about noontime. He was buried in the Jewish cemetery of Strašnice, on the outskirts of Prague, on June 11.

From a letter by Klopstock to F.K.'s sister Elli, June 4:
Poor Dora, oh, we are all poor, who is so utterly poor in the world as we—she is whispering without stopping; one can only make out, "My love, my love, my good one"—I promised her that we should go and see Franz again this afternoon if she would lie down. So she lay down. See him, "who is so alone, so quite alone, we have nothing to do, and sit here and leave him there [in the mortuary] alone in the dark, uncov-

ered—O my good one! My love" ... *and so it goes on. What is hap-pening here with us—I say always "us," we called ourselves, you see, "Franz's little family," is indescribable, and should not be described. Who knows Dora, only he can know what love means. So few under-stand it, and that increases pain and suffering. But you, won't you, you will understand it!* ... *We don't yet know at all what has happened to us, but slowly, slowly it will get clearer and clearer, and more pain-fully dark at the same time. Particularly we don't know it, who have him still with us. Now we are going there again to Franz. So stiff, so severe, so unapproachable is his face, as his soul was pure and severe. Severe—a king's face from the oldest and noblest stock. The gentleness of his human existence has gone, only his immortal soul still forms his stiff, dear face. So beautiful is it as an old marble bust.*   [B, 212 f.]

After F.K.'s death, a slip of paper was found in his writing desk, addressed to Brod.
Dearest Max, my last request: Everything I leave behind me (in my bookcase, linen cupboard, and my desk both at home and in the office, or anywhere else where anything may have got to and meets your eye), in the way of diaries, manuscripts, letters (my own and others'), sketches, and so on, to be burned unread; also all writings and sketches which you or others may possess; and ask those others for them in my name. Letters which they do not want to hand over to you, they should at least promise faithfully to burn themselves.   The Trial, 265 f.

Later, an apparently older version of this request was found:
Dear Max, perhaps this time I shan't recover after all. Pneumonia after a whole month's pulmonary fever is all too likely; and not even writing this down can avert it, although there is a certain power in that.

For this eventuality, therefore, here is my last will concerning every-thing I have written:

Of all my writings the only books that can stand are these: The Judgment, The Stoker, Metamorphosis, Penal Colony, Country Doctor and the short story: "Hunger Artist." (The few copies of Meditation can remain. I do not want to give anyone the trouble of pulping them; but nothing in that volume must be printed again.) When I say that those five books and the short story can stand, I do not mean that I wish them to be reprinted and handed down to posterity. On the contrary, should they disappear altogether that would please me best. Only, since they do exist, I do not wish to hinder anyone who may want to, from keeping them.

But everything else of mine which is extant (whether in journals, in manuscript, or letters), everything without exception in so far as it is discoverable or obtainable from the addressees by request (you know most of them yourself; it is chiefly — and whatever happens don't forget the couple of notebooks in —'s possession)—all these things, without exception and preferably unread (I won't absolutely forbid you to look at them, though I'd far rather you didn't and in any case no one else is to do so)—all these things without exception are to be burned, and I beg you to do this as soon as possible.   The Trial, 266 f.

> Brod has told F.K. in 1921, when F.K.first mentioned the matter,
> that he refused to destroy any of the writings. Brod therefore felt
> justified in not carrying out his friend's request.

Milena's Obituary of Kafka

FRANZ KAFKA. *The day before yesterday Dr. Franz Kafka, a German writer who used to live in Prague, died in the Kierling Sanatorium at Klosterneuburg, near Vienna. Here in Prague very few people knew him, for he was a hermit, a man of insight who was frightened by life. He had suffered for years from consumption, and although he accepted treatment for it, he also consciously fostered it and spiritually encouraged it. "When soul and heart cannot bear the burden any longer, the lung takes over one half of it, so that the weight is, to some extent at least, evenly distributed," he once wrote in a letter, and such was the case with his illness too. It endowed him with a refinement of feeling that bordered on the miraculous and a spiritual honesty that was almost horrifyingly uncompromising; conversely it was he, the human being, who loaded onto his illness the entire burden of his spiritual anguish of life. He was shy, timid, gentle, and kind, but the books he wrote were cruel and painful. He saw the world as being full of invisible demons which assail and destroy defenseless man. He was too clear-sighted, too wise, to be able to live; he was too weak to struggle. But his weakness was that of noble and beautiful men, who are not capable of taking up the struggle against fear, against misunderstandings, against unkindnesses and spiritual untruths, who are aware from the outset of their incapacity, who submit and, in submitting, put the victor to shame. He had that knowledge of human beings which comes only to those who lead solitary lives, whose highly sensitive nerves and clairvoyant eye can interpret a whole person merely from his facial expressions. His knowledge of the world was extraordinary and profound. He was, in himself, an extraordinary and profound world. He wrote the most significant books of recent German literature. They contain, in unpolemical form, the present-day struggle between the generations. They possess a truthfulness and nakedness* which make them appear naturalistic even when they speak in symbols. They have the dry irony and sensitive vision of a man who observed the world with such distinctness and clarity that he could not bear it and had to die; for he did not want to make any concessions or take refuge, as others did, in intellectual errors, however noble. Dr. Franz Kafka wrote the fragment "The Stoker," which forms the first chapter of a beautiful and as yet unpublished novel. "The Judgment," in which he expresses the conflict between two generations. The Metamorphosis, the most powerful book in modern German literature. "In the Penal Colony," and the sketches in Meditation and A Country Doctor. The last piece, "Before the Law," has for some years existed in manuscript form, ready for publication; it is one of those books that leaves the reader with such an all-embracing impression that any comment is superfluous. All his works describe the terror of mysterious misconceptions and guiltless guilt in human beings. He was a man and an artist of so scrupulous a conscience that he remained on the alert even when others, less keen of hearing, regarded themselves as being already in safety.   Milena Jesenská

[Forum IX (1962), 28 f.]

NOTES

1910

1. Franz Blei (1871-1943), novelist and satirist.

1911

1. Founded in the thirteenth century and still standing.
2. "All Vows": introductory prayer on the eve of the Day of Atonement.
3. Founded in the fifteenth century.
4. See entry of November 19, 1911.
5. An asbestos factory that belonged to F.K.'s brother-in-law Karl Hermann and the Kafka family. F.K. was made an active partner and expected to take part in its management—a matter that caused him much aggravation. See also entry of December 28, 1911, and letter to Brod, October 8, 1912.
6. Franz Werfel (1890-1945), poet and novelist.
7. Moule: properly mohel, circumcisor.

1912

1. Paris, 1911.
2. Der babylonische Talmud zur Herstellung einer Realkonkordanz vokalisiert, übersetzt und signiert. 1. Einleitung: Der Organismus des Judentums. Berlin, 1909.
3. A Jewish student organization in Prague.
4. A Prague Jewish literary society that offered lectures attended by about one hundred persons (Professor S. H. Bergman, written communication).

1913

1. "Mythos der Juden" ["Myth in Judaism"], English translation in Martin Buber, On Judaism (New York: Schocken Books, 1967).
2. Frankfurt a.M., 1911.
3. See the editorial note on entry of September 25, 1912.

1914

1. Musil invited F.K. to collaborate in the publication of a literary journal.
2. Elli's husband joined the army.
3. The manuscript is defective at this point.
4. This story cannot be identified.

1915

1. A Miss F.R., a young refugee woman whom F.K. met at a lecture course by Brod in a school for refugee Jewish children.
2. See under September 1913 and letter to Brod, mid-July 1916 (*Br*, p. 139).
3. Not identical with "The Investigations of a Dog" written in 1922.
4. George Mordecai Langer of Prague, who had attached himself to one of the religious communities of the Hasidim.
5. "All Vows": See 1911, note 2.

1916

1. See also *Diaries* II, 159.
2. See letter to Felice, July 30, 1916.
3. Oskar Weber, *Der Zuckerbaron*, Cologne, 1914.
4. Children's books by Heinrich Hoffmann, author of *Der Struwwelpeter* (1847).

1917

1. However, see diary, August 21, 1913, on Kierkegaard's *Buch des Richters* and the remark: "He bears me out like a friend."
2. Apparently referring to the Babylonian Talmud, Tractate Sukkah 52a: "In the messianic age the Holy One, blessed be He, will slay the Evil Urge in the presence of the righteous and the wicked. To the righteous it will seem to be like a towering hill, and to the wicked like a hair thread. Both will weep. The righteous will weep, saying, 'How were we able to overcome such a towering hill!' The wicked will weep, saying, 'How is it that we were unable to conquer this hair thread!' "

1918

1. Erich Reiss Verlag, Berlin.
2. Art dealer and publisher, Berlin.

1919

1. A character in Knut Hamsun's *Growth of the Soil*.

1921

1. See Max Brod, *Franz Kafka: A Biography*, p. 241.

1922

1. See letter to Oskar Baum, July 4, 1922.

1923

1. The reference is to the maxims and proverbs for each day of the year. F.K. liked such calendars.

INDEX

The frequent references to Max Brod, Prague, insomnia, headache, have not been included in the Index.